CARING
FOR OUR
GENERATIONS

CARING FOR OUR GENERATIONS

JOHN PATTON &
BRIAN H. CHILDS

Wipf & Stock
PUBLISHERS
Eugene, Oregon

Wipf and Stock Publishers
199 W 8th Ave, Suite 3
Eugene, OR 97401

Caring For Our Generations
By Patton, John H. and Childs, Brian H.
Copyright©2007 by Patton, John H.
ISBN 13: 978-1-55635-625-4
ISBN 10: 1-55635-625-0
Publication date 9/18/2007
Previously published by Abingdon Press, 2007

All scripture quotations designated KJV are from the King James Version of the Bible.

Those designated NEB are from *The New English Bible*. © The Delegates of the Oxford University Press and The Syndics of the Cambridge University Press 1961, 1970. Reprinted by permission.

Those designated NJB are from THE NEW JERUSALEM BIBLE, copyright © 1985 by Darton, Longman & Todd, Ltd. and Doubleday & Company, Inc. Reprinted by permission of the publisher.

Those designated RSV are from the Revised Standard Version of the Bible, copyrighted 1946, 1952, © 1971, 1973 by the Division of Christian Education of the National Council of the Churches of Christ in the U.S.A., and are used by permission.

To the memory of

SEWARD HILTNER

CONTENTS

ACKNOWLEDGMENTS — 9

INTRODUCTION — 11

CHAPTER ONE — Creatures Who Care — 19

CHAPTER TWO — Caring for Our Generations as an Individual — 45

CHAPTER THREE — Generational Care Prior to Marriage and Remarriage — 73

CHAPTER FOUR — Generational Caring for Marriage — 99

CHAPTER FIVE — Generational Caring in the Nuclear Family — 127

CHAPTER SIX — Caring Through Separation and Loss — 159

CHAPTER SEVEN — Care in the Blended Family — 189

CHAPTER EIGHT — Personal and Pastoral Caring for Our Generations — 213

INDEX — 233

ACKNOWLEDGMENTS

The original impetus for this book came from the fact that both of us teach courses on the pastoral care of the family at Columbia Theological Seminary. One course is primarily for M.Div. students and the other for students in the Th.M., D.Min., and S.T.D. programs. We found ourselves comparing notes on what we were doing in our respective classes and occasionally visiting the other's class and engaging in discussion with the students and with each other. Our original assumption was that because our training in marriage and family work had been significantly different, we were presenting quite different points of view. This turned out not to be the case. Certainly, there are differences in the way we approach persons in families and in the way we think about it afterward, but apparently our theological assumptions about the family proved to be more influential. We decided to write this book to clarify just what these theological commonalities were and how they affected our practice as pastoral counselors.

The book was written faster than we thought it could be, and there is more of a "still stirring" than a finished quality about it. We came to the end with a number of things not worked out in relation to our basic premise. One of the most important of these is the place of elderly family members in the family system. We touch on this at several points, but not in a way that gives the topic the systematic development it deserves. What we like most about the book—remembering that question teachers used to ask in elementary school book reports—is the thesis that Christian family living may be described as the care of our generations. It does not require any particular family form but is relevant for single and divorced persons as well as those whom we usually honor during Christian family week—the traditional family of mother, father, and two or more children.

A number of people have been helpful to us in preparing the book for publication. We are grateful, first of all, to our classes at Columbia Theological Seminary, who listened to and discussed with us a number of the book's main ideas. Dean Oscar Hussel was supportive of our writing enterprise as well as were a number of other faculty members with whom we discussed what we were trying to do: Chris Wenderoth, Walter Brueggemann, Charles Cousar, Shirley Guthrie, Ben Kline, David Gunn, and Jap Keith. Colleagues in other places were also helpful: Janet Briscoe, Bradley Binau, Herbert Anderson, Ken Mitchell, P. C. Ennis, William Everett, Richard Bondi, Phyllis Roe, Kathryn Sandifer, an informal Atlanta group of the American Family Therapy Association, and a seminary student, Mark Linker, who shared a pastoral event from his ministry.

There were also a number of groups who listened, asked questions, and responded in a number of stimulating ways: members of adult Sunday school classes at Peachtree Road and Glenn Memorial United Methodist Churches in Atlanta; lecture audiences at Carraway Methodist Medical Center in Birmingham, Alabama; the Duke University Medical Center in Durham, North Carolina; the Northern European Seminar on Pastoral Counseling at Bad Segeberg, West Germany; the Rall Lectureship at Garrett Evangelical Theological Seminary in Evanston, Illinois; and the Australian and New Zealand Association of Theological Schools Conference in Melbourne, Australia.

More personally, our own families are very much involved in the preparation of this book. Brian's special appreciation goes to Sandy for allowing his absence, even though he was physically present. She would see his eyes glaze over as he lost himself in thought and say something like, "You are thinking about the book again, aren't you?" Also to Brian's three-and-a-half-year-old daughter Caitlin, who would ask him, sometimes patiently, "Daddy, when are you going to finish the God book?" For John, Helen again helped immeasurably by listening to ideas from the book and reading the manuscript. The book makes a good deal more sense to persons other than ourselves because of her helpful editorial comments. The other members of our generations are involved in the book in a variety of experiential ways, and inevitably the book is most clearly indebted to our marriages and families.

INTRODUCTION

This book is addressed to three somewhat different audiences. For anyone who is caught up in the issues of family life and who wishes to deal with them from the point of view of Christian faith and practice, it offers a way of thinking and some suggestions for being in a family. For pastors who are not specialists in the pastoral counseling of families, it can provide a way of understanding the family and some useful suggestions about the care and counseling of persons struggling with their family relationships. For our colleagues, the specialists in the practice, or teaching, of pastoral counseling, most of what we say about the care of families will be familiar, but we believe that our method for bringing together Christian anthropology and the practice of pastoral counseling provides a useful model for their teaching and practice. Each attempt to bring together pastoral practice, theology, and data from the psychological and social sciences offers a model for others of us who, by an ongoing commitment to ministry, are challenged to do the same kind of thing.

In most of the chapters, we present pastoral encounters with persons troubled over their family living. These concrete human experiences demonstrate the beginning point in pastoral theological method. The pastor who attempts to minister to a family stands between the faith tradition and its theology which he or she represents, and the particular person or family in need. The pastor must listen to what is said by both. To be sure, the faith tradition is, as it should be, in the background, and its voice is less clear than are the voices of those needing ministry. It is there, and it inevitably affects the pastor's perspective on what is being presented to her or him. Each of these persons and families is caught up in a particular human situation. They are also persons understood in a particular way by the Christian tradition.

Another way of saying this is that pastoral care and counseling inevitably involve Christian anthropology. The particular anthropology we develop is one that understands the term *Christian* more in terms of its function than its form. That function, which we describe as the care of one's generations, is possible for all persons, whether they live together in a group of two or more demographically designated as a family or alone. There is no ideal form for the Christian family toward which we should strive. There is, however, a normative function: care.

The book develops from the theological premise that human beings are God's creatures, entrusted with the care of the earth, and we attempt to explore the meaning of that statement in relation to the particular human beings who appear in the chapters of the book. We look to the biblical/theological tradition, attempting to let it speak from within its own context and through interpreters more skilled in that field than we are. As part of our method, however, we also look to other theoretical resources in psychology, sociology, and ethics that can allow the faith tradition to speak more specifically to particular human situations. The central feature of the method, the integrative feature, is the pastor; one who has to minister to particular persons, attempting in each situation to fit all the resources together and offer care to them. The nature of pastoral theology is that it must facilitate and inform practice. It cannot stand apart from this. Moreover, it is always incomplete. The pastor must deal with particular persons and their needs regardless of whether he or she has finished all of the desirable research on their types of problems.

The present form that the family should take or stages through which it should go is not evident to us; neither, in our judgment, is it necessary that it should be. Our concern, therefore, is not to argue for or against any particular form of the family or for who ought to be living together and for how long, but to present a norm for family life in terms of a three-generational caring relationship. Although we make no claim that this way of viewing the family is genuinely cross-cultural, it may help us to guard against assuming that particular cultural forms of family life or stages in that life can adequately describe what a family ought to be.

We describe Christian family life as the *care of our generations* and the pastoral care of persons in families as a ministry that facilitates that care. What is normative, or essential, for human beings is the care of the generations that immediately touch our lives—usually the generation before, one's own generation, and the generation after. Persons may be deeply involved in family living even when, as single, their households include only themselves. The quality of care for the generations that are closest to us by choice or circumstance is more important for Christian family living than the present form or structure of our households.

Generational care is limited only insofar as there are possible combinations of people living with one another and in relationships of choice or kinship. In developing this point of view, we present in the first chapter of the book the rationale for the book's thesis: that an appropriate Christian norm for persons in families is caring for their generations. The development of this point of view involves a discussion of the centrality of caring for Christian ministry and a description of the context for caring as the generations of each person, past, present, and future.

To develop our position, we make use of some of the biblical themes that are central for Christian anthropology: the care of the earth and all that is in it, both in relationship to God's creatures and in useful work; the calling to live as people with generations, symbolized by the commandment to honor our fathers and mothers; the suggestion in the teachings of Jesus that there be limits to family loyalty; and the concern for household and family as expressed in the epistles. These themes undoubtedly suggest other images for family relationships besides that of generational care, but we believe that this particular image has important continuities with Christian tradition as well as being significantly related to the family issues of today.

In chapter 2 and the following chapters, we present circumstances related to the family with which persons must deal, tensions and problems related to those circumstances and means of addressing or helpfully intervening in them. In chapter 2, we address some of the more important issues of singleness and individuality as they appear in adult life; in chapter 3, preparing for marriage or for remarriage after death or divorce; in chapter 4, living as a couple in a one generational household; in chapter 5, living as a nuclear family in a household of two or more generations; in chapter 6, dealing with the separation and loss of divorce; and in chapter 7, living in a blended family. The final chapter addresses some of the questions that emerge in the earlier chapters about the care of our own families and the pastoral care and counseling of the families of others. In each of the chapters, we make use of events in the lives of persons we have known. The names of persons and details of the events have been changed to respect the privacy of those persons and the confidentiality of the relationships, and sometimes the events as we record them combine elements of the stories of several persons. Because we are all so much alike, however, they will seem familiar to most of those who read about them.

One of the problems, or, perhaps, strengths, of the book may be seen in the difficulty of applying even a functional norm—*caring for our generations*—to the realities of family living. The biblical tradition, as we understand it, tells us to "honor" our fathers and mothers, but to guard against idealizing this or any other human relationship. Jesus' question—"Who are my mother and brothers?"—is symbolic of this critique of human structures, even those of the family. In the norm itself, *caring for our generations*, there is both affirmation and critique. You must care for your parents, your spouse, and your children, but not so much that the care of your other generations and your response to God's care for you are obscured.

Another feature of this book, which may have already been evident but should be specifically acknowledged, is that it views the family not just psychologically or theologically, but clinically—from the perspective of the modern pastoral care tradition. Some of the most important premises of that tradition are: (1) that "I cannot learn to care for the family, or anything else for that matter, apart from learning about myself and my need for care"; (2) that pastoral caring always involves *being* something as well as *doing* something; and (3) that "I can best learn about myself and how to care through relationships analogous to those present in the family"—relationships with authorities, with peers, and with those to whom I am an authority. Although this relational learning has been formalized in clinical pastoral education, it is relevant for all caring persons because the key relationships are those that we first encounter in our families of origin and in which all of us are involved in the rest of our lives.

Although we believe that we have at least partially compensated for some of our biases by the use of consultation from female colleagues, our perspective on the family is limited by the fact that we are both white, middle-class males. We are both married and have children. One of us has been divorced and has remarried. Both of us have one living parent and one who is deceased. One of our spouses has one living parent; the other has two. One of our households is composed of a married couple and a pre-school daughter; the other household includes the married couple only. Two sons and two daughters, most of the time, are living elsewhere.

We are from two different generations of the students of Seward Hiltner. One was his student at the University of Chicago and had a long relationship with him until his death in 1984. The other was Hiltner's student at Princeton Theological Seminary and worked with him in Princeton for three years after graduation until 1984. One of us is a CPE supervisor and past president of the American Association of Pastoral Counselors and, in addition to part-time seminary teaching, has primary responsibility for directing a large pastoral care and counseling center. The other is an associate professor of pastoral theology and counseling in a seminary and has studied with faculty at the Nathan W. Ackerman Family Institute in New York. Both of us are ordained ministers—one United Methodist and one Presbyterian (U.S.A.)—with clinical practices of pastoral counseling.

Thus in our sameness there is diversity. It is our hope that this book not only facilitates our generational care but also offers another perspective on what, in terms of the Christian faith, it is to be human.

Caring For Our Generations

CHAPTER ONE

CREATURES WHO CARE

And God blessed them and God said unto them, Be fruitful and multiply . . . and have dominion over . . . every living thing that moveth upon the earth. (Genesis 1:28 KJV)

In the seventh session of their pastoral counseling, Ann began to cry, and Al looked confused. They had been talking about one of the familiar issues in their relationship: Ann's compulsive working around the house and her inability to get Al to help. The pastor wondered, *Why she is crying now? We've been through all this before.* So he asked:

Pastor: (looking at Al) Do you know what Ann is feeling or where her emotions are coming from?

Al: No, unless it has something to do with her parents coming.

Pastor: Oh, (turning to Ann) then it has to do with more than just painting a room. You're doing something for your parents. I knew you must have been feeling something important. (The pastor and the couple sit for several moments in silence.)

Al: I just wish I could make her stop being sad.

Pastor: I don't think sadness is the main thing Ann is feeling now.

What the pastor thought Ann was feeling then was *care*. As a feeling, care is composed of a number of elements. There is some sadness, but it is not something to be gotten rid of. It is, rather, the sadness of life as it is, in which relationships are so important but can be so imperfect and transitory. Care as feeling includes appreciation, respect, and compassion, when compassion is understood literally to mean "with passion" or "emotional intensity."

But care is not just feeling, positive or negative. It also includes responsibility for someone whether one is aware of one's feelings at the time the responsibility requires action. It includes a good deal more than that, but all that needs to be said here is that in being with Al and Ann, the pastoral counselor attempted to recognize and underscore the importance of what Ann was experiencing. The care the counselor perceived, however, was not just in Ann; it was part of a theoretical understanding of Ann and of all human beings as persons who care. The assumption was that the pastoral care and counseling of persons in families rests on the theological conviction that human beings are God's creatures entrusted with the care of the earth.

Al and Ann did not come for pastoral counseling armed with the same assumption as did their pastoral counselor. They came concerned with communication problems in their six-year-old marriage. Both were in their early forties. Both had been married before. Ann was a social worker in a responsible administrative position. Al was a real estate salesman who, until recently, had worked many years for the state government in a secure, but relatively unrewarding position. At forty, he had entered into a much more rewarding, but considerably more risky, career. Their problem, as presented by Ann, the chief initiator of the counseling, was the familiar "failure to communicate." She felt that Al was holding back from her and seldom let her know what he felt about anything. Al acknowledged that he had trouble expressing himself, but said that the real problem was Ann's "never letting up on me. She's always after me to do something or about something I haven't done. I don't feel like communicating with her; I just want to get away."

Al had grown up in south Alabama, Ann in Pennsylvania. He was the only child in a farming family. His father, as Al remembers him, worked all the time, and Al's time was spent with Mother, who talked a lot and was generally outgoing. He was an average student, who hurt his knee early in high school and became manager for the football team instead of its star player. He fished and hunted often, and was what has come to be called in our section of the country a "good ole boy."

Ann's dad worked for the railroad. Her mother never worked outside the home. Ann had one sister eight years older than she. High school and college came easy to her, so she went on to graduate school—in social work, a profession through which she could help people. Both Al and Ann were first married in their mid-twenties, the marriages lasted about three years. Ann's husband was exciting but undependable, and during the brief marriage her parents' home was a place she could always go to when her husband had abandoned her or "done something crazy." Al was less aware than Ann of what had gone wrong in his first marriage. "It didn't take long," he said, "for both of us to know that we'd made a mistake." Al's family home, however, was less of a resource for him than was Ann's. His father had died while Al was in college, and when he went back home, his mother "kind of drove him crazy talking all the time." Al did what he had learned to do early in life: "I just had to tune her out."

"Tuning out" is what Ann perceives him doing now. "I just can't get through to him," she says tearfully. Not surprisingly, their sexual communication is similar to their verbal communication. When the pastoral counselor asked them about it, Ann responded almost before the sentence was finished, "Seven times last year, four times so far this year!" Al perceives Ann as being demanding and, as he puts it, "It's hard for me to do anything when I'm angry."

Much involved in their sexual experience is the uncertainty, earlier in their marriage, about whether to have children. They apparently struggled with this for several years during their late thirties, and then, as Al sees it, Ann decided that she was too old, and he was to get a vasectomy. Al experienced both of those decisions, which he reluctantly accepted, as injuries to his self-image as a man. His recovery from the vasectomy took longer than he had thought it would, and afterward, when it had stopped hurting, intercourse simply did not feel as good to him as it had before. In his quiet, somewhat passive, way Al was still angry about it.

Al and Ann's story is unique, but at the same time very familiar. As we attempt to show in this and the following chapters, the issues of the marriage are inseparable from the issues of their relationship to their families of origin—the prior generation—and, even as a childless couple, from their relationship to the generation that comes after them. Al and Ann, like their famous forebears, Adam and Eve, have been "given" each other to deal with the loneliness of life and with God's challenge to be fruitful and multiply and have dominion over all the earth. They are to care for the earth and for each other—an impressive challenge indeed, and one that is repeated in Genesis to the post-flood

Adam, Noah, in this later statement of covenant: "And God blessed Noah and his sons, and said to them, 'Be fruitful and multiply, and fill the earth. . . . Behold, I establish my covenant with you and your descendants after you. . . .' These are the generations of the sons of Noah" (Gen. 9:1, 9, 10:1 RSV).

Although an awareness of Old Testament genealogies is not likely to assist Al and Ann with their marital problem, it is important to affirm that the perspective brought by the Christian pastor includes quite a few elements that are not immediately operational. One of the most important of these is a Christian understanding of what a human being *really* is. Although one's Christian anthropology may be far from awareness in the initial concern to be helpful, it is never fully absent. Our understanding of who Al and Ann really are—our normative view of them—clearly affects both the way we respond to our own families and the type of intervention we make with other families within our pastoral care.

As pastoral counselors, we are not likely to remind Al and Ann that humankind was enjoined by God to "be fruitful and multiply and to have dominion over all the earth." Noting that they are a childless couple in their forties, we might assume that the issue of whether to have children had been settled and was not really relevant in their relationship. It was certainly not mentioned in their initial statement of why they had come for help. Without, at this point, going into a discussion of the authority of the creation stories for issues of childbearing and contraception today, we would simply say that what one decides about how to contribute to or participate in the generation that comes afterward is as important and has as much effect on how one lives in one's own generation as is the decision of how one cares for the generation that came before.

As pastoral counselors, we are also not likely to say directly to Al and Ann that we are responding to their creaturehood. In fact, however, both the pastoral counselor's inquiry into Ann's tearfulness and his interpretation of it to Al were doing just that. Important anthropological assumptions were involved in both the pastor's discovery that painting the room had something to do with Ann's relation to her parents and his suggesting to Al that Ann's feelings were not just something unpleasant that should be gotten rid of as quickly as possible. All that was involved in painting the room is still not clear. It may have had to do with an unfinished transaction between Ann and her parents, such as an old need to please them and to care for them as they had cared for her. The striking thing is that her most evident and important feeling is in relation to the parents rather than to the husband. In some way or another, she was attempting to honor her father and mother while there was yet time, recognizing without wanting to say it that their time was limited and that the relationship between them would someday be interrupted by death. The pastor's response was simply an acknowledgment of the importance of that relationship without either a detailed interpretation of its meaning or a suggestion about what should be done. His intervention, perhaps more intuitively than intentionally, was designed to call attention to Ann's concern about her relationship to her parents and the limits imposed upon it by human finitude—being a part of one generation and having at least two other generations to be concerned about.

PASTORAL THEOLOGICAL METHOD

The foregoing discussion of the pastoral experience with Al and Ann illustrates the beginning point in pastoral theological method. The pastor who attempts to minister to a family stands between the faith tradition, which she or he represents, and the particular family in need. The pastor is one who must listen to what is said by both parties. To be sure, the faith tradition is, as it should be, in the background, and its voice is less clear than the voices of Al and Ann. But it is there, and it inevitably affects the pastor's perspective on what is being presented to her or him. The couple is having trouble communicating with each other. They are also understood in a particular way by the Christian tradition.

Pastoral theological method involves the dual exploration of whom Al and Ann are in the light of Christian anthropology and what their particular life as a couple says to a theological understanding of humankind. Stated simply, perhaps too simply, what the experience with Al and Ann appears to be saying is that one cannot work out the relationship to the intimate partner in one's own generation without dealing with the relationship to the generations before and after. How does that affirmation relate to traditional Christian understanding about the human being? The rest of this chapter is intended to address that question. Family living, in the light of Christian anthropology, is more appropriately described in terms of its function than of its form. That function, which we are describing as the care of one's generations, can take place within virtually any form of the family from singleness to a blended or reconstituted family.

From the point of view of Christian anthropology, Al and Ann are not simply a middle-aged couple, both in their second marriage, struggling to communicate with each other. They are generational human beings with responsibilities to care for those related to them in their own generation and in the generations before and after. That theological assumption can be as important to their care by the pastor as is his or her careful listening to their "problem." Because traditional assumptions about human beings have been influenced more by Genesis 1–3 than by any other biblical resource, it is important that we give some attention to that section of the Bible and to some of its more recent interpretations.

CARE IN THE BIBLE

The text with which we began this chapter has been one of the major influences in the Christian tradition's understanding of God's calling to humankind. "And God blessed them, and God said unto them, Be fruitful and multiply . . . and have dominion over . . . every living thing that moveth upon the earth" (Gen. 1:28 KJV). Historically, the church has understood God's calling to rule over the earth in Genesis 1:28 as having been addressed to the male and the task of being fruitful and sustaining those generated through that fruitfulness as having been given to the female. An article entitled "Men, Women, and the Remarriage of Public and Private Spheres," by Celia Allison Hahn, is an example of one of the recent challenges to this view. "Though procreation clearly requires the cooperation of men and women," says Hahn,

> we have tended to view it as the proper role of woman (something shared with the animals) to be carried out in her domain—the private sphere. And the dominion given to male and female has somehow become an exclusively male responsibility (something to be shared with God) exercised in the public sphere, which has come to be regarded as the appropriate arena for the labors of men.

Human beings have not embraced their tasks as partners: men have distanced themselves from their nurturing selves and their bodily lives, and women have tended to distance themselves from their public responsibilities. The earth creature was given what Phyllis Trible has called the paradoxical task of ruling over the earth by serving it, but somehow the ruling and serving have come apart: men have been more likely to rule, and women to serve.[1]

From a different stance, and for a different purpose, Old Testament scholar Claus Westermann sounds a similar note. Although the traditional understanding of the term *dominion*, in Genesis 1:26 and 1:28, involves control over or superiority to, Westermann interprets it as "mastery" in the same sense as a person's mastery of a language. "The second part of v. 26 gives us to understand that it is the attitude of humans toward other living beings that should characterize the human attitude to the world about them; and this means a markedly personal attitude." It is, he suggests, the same attitude as found in John 10:3, the good shepherd passage: "The sheep hear his voice, and he calls his own sheep by name and leads them out."[2]

Similarly, Jurgen Moltmann also addresses the theological misinterpretation of the Genesis text. Placing his anthropology in the context of the ecological crisis, Moltmann speaks of "the crisis of domination," a human being's misuse of power over the earth. He argues that the biblical concept of subduing the earth has nothing to do with ruling over the earth as the theological tradition has taught, but is a "dietary commandment: human beings and animals alike are to live from the fruits which *the earth* brings forth in the form of plants and trees." Moltmann continues: "The *theocentric* biblical world picture gives human being, with his special position in the cosmos, the chance to understand himself as a member of the community of creation." If the world is God's creation, it can only be "accepted as a loan and administered as a trust."[3]

In a number of his writings—for example, *The Ecology of Faith, Essays on Nature and Grace,*—Joseph Sittler,[4] describes what Moltmann calls "a trust," humankind's responsibility for "the care of the earth." In a recently published collection of his "reflections," Sittler comments, "The word *dominion* is a direct English effort to translate the Latin. In English *dominion* suggests *domination*, but that is an incorrect translation." (We think it is less an incorrect translation than the influence of changing understanding of the human situation on a theological, rather than an exegetical, judgment.) "The Hebrew statement," continues Sittler, "is, 'And God said you are to exercise care over the earth and hold it in its proper place.' "[5] Viewed from a different perspective, Sittler's understanding of *dominion* is not unlike the more profound interpretations of the term *empathy*, such as that found in the work of Heinz Kohut: disciplined, informed, and responsive knowledge.[6] For Westermann, Moltmann, and Sittler, then, human beings' dominion over the earth may best be understood as mastery of, or disciplined knowledge about the world and all within it.

Westermann has also addressed another problem in the "Be fruitful and multiply" imperative of Genesis 1:28 by doing what, in discussing family therapy, might be called "reframing." He enlarges the context for the interpretation of the text to include not only Genesis 1–3, but also the first eleven chapters of Genesis. This, he says, broadens the understanding of God's blessing beyond its traditional identification with sexuality and associates it instead with the gift of generations, expressed in the genealogies. God's blessing, he says, "works itself out in the sequence of generations."[7] In chapter 5, it is seen in the generations of Adam, which present God's involvement in the time dimension of human life. In chapter 10, which presents the generations of Noah, God's blessing may be seen in relation to the dimension of space as the generations are identified with particular geographical areas or in "filling the earth," as 1:28 had called them to do.

In viewing Genesis 1–11 as a whole, rather than separating out and focusing on chapters 1–3, Westermann's anthropology is not so much one of prototypical human beings—Adam and Eve—as an "anthropology of generations," of human beings who live and die and whose work and family life is carried on by their descendants. He insists on the inseparability of the creation and the flood stories in presenting God's continuing involvement in the world. The sign of the rainbow is a reminder of God's covenant of care for the world "for all future generations" (9:12). "The creation of humanity includes the living space [the garden], the occupation or work [cultivate and preserve], and the community [man and woman] and, as a medium of community, language." The meaning of creation, according to Westermann, includes "people in all their relationships . . . living space, nourishment, work, and the social realm."[8]

The genealogies, though hardly the most exciting reading of the Bible, are important in demonstrating the foundational fact of God's covenant. Those whom God has chosen to be his live and die, but their descendants continue on, still in God's care. In the genealogies, one sees human beings placed in history, in families, and—through the blessing of God at creation, like Adam and Noah—placed as a part of the orderly sequence of God's creative work.

The Genesis stories strongly suggest that care can be understood as a normative expression of human creaturehood, uniting love and work. In the Hebrew and the Greek scriptures, the noun *care* translates into at least ten words, and the verb forms *care, care for,* and *taking care,* translate into at least thirteen different words.[9] The Old Testament terms for *care* are rather concrete and involve activities that are commonplace. In Genesis 39:22, Joseph takes care of, or receives, prisoners. In Jeremiah 23:2, shepherds care for God's people just as they feed (care for) their flocks 23:4.

New Testament usage of the terms for "care" follow many of the rather practical and concrete uses found in the Old Testament, but the term also carries with it some psychological meanings, along with some powerful theological ones. Rudolph Bultmann, in his *Theology of the New Testament,* connects care with the human's propensity for a self-reliant attitude. *Marimnon* from the verb *marimnao,* "to care," means humanity's will to respond to the world as it sees fit. The human has the ability to see into a future, or at least knows that there is a future. Care is an attempt to forestall the future. "The intention of such 'care' is to insure one's self for the future, or also, to keep what now is for the future." A good example of this aspect of care is to be found in Paul's use of the term in I Corinthians 7:32 ff. The term *care* is translated as "anxiety" (RSV), "devote" and "bother" (NJB), and "care" and "carefulness" (KJV). This notion of care for worldly affairs, which implies the idea that a human can control his or her life, is juxtaposed with the care for the "Lord's affairs," which is to be "care-free" (I Cor. 32) or to be "care-ful for nothing" (Phil. 4:6).[10] It is interesting to note here that this type of care is connected with boasting, as either that of the Jew with the boast of God and Torah or that of the Gentile with the boast of wisdom.

CONTEMPORARY VIEWS OF CARE

Although we have been discussing and describing the concept of care for some time, we have not yet given it formal definition. Over the years, the term has had at least two very distinct meanings. The first notion of care involves the notion of anxiety; the second, the notion of solicitude. The *Oxford English Dictionary* traces these two basic views of care in the development of the English language. To care is to be anxious, troubled, and even to grieve. It also means to be concerned with, to regard, and even to love, in the sense of care for the other rather than for oneself. Both notions are related in what we have experienced as the caring of those who have come to us for counseling.

Care expresses the basic human concerns for control and predictability. It is concerned with either preserving the present or controlling the future. To be careful is to be anxious. It is important to note here the commonly held notion of the difference between anxiety and the fear of the future. Anxiety is objectless; it is the restless waiting for what is not clearly known to be in store. Fear for the future has an object in the sense that the person knows with some predictability what the future has in store. The high school freshman may be anxious for what the future has in store, while the high school senior may fear the prospect of more schooling, work, or military service.

Care also has the meaning of solicitude and concern for the needs of the other. It is based not on the subjective needs of the care giver (though, of course, we all know that no human action is unmixed with a variety of motivations) but on the objective perception of the needs of the other. The still powerful image of the shepherd best illustrates this notion of the term. The shepherd tends to the needs of the flock as a whole but is ever vigilant about the needs of the individual (the one and the ninety-nine).

Most works dealing with the notions of care have tended to deal with the latter notion (concern or solicitude) rather than the former one (anxiety). It is not really difficult to understand why this is the case. From studying Bultmann (and consequently

Heidegger, from whom Bultmann borrowed many basic existential notions) and his handling of care, we see that it is sometimes more than implied by him that human caring is selfish, boastful, and sinful. It is, in Bultmann's language, life devoid of faith in the *kerygma*, or, in Heidegger's language, bad faith and fallen inauthentic existence. It is no wonder then that most writers have chosen to concentrate their energies on a normative, and possibly even idealistic, notion that care is more akin to solicitude.

It seems important to us, however, to hold together the double meaning of the term. To be human is to care, that is, to be both anxious *and* concerned. In fact, to care in the sense of being anxious is not all that bad if we adopt the rather common psychodynamic definition of anxiety: It is the signal to beware of what is now unknown, but can be found with the proper diligent search. The result of the search is the conversion of energy from anxiety to fear, from uncomfortable feeling to fight or flight. It is when anxiety is not converted to a more mobilizing emotion or activity that the mischief comes in and when the normative vision is useful. When the signal is not heeded or is misinterpreted or is mishandled, human fallenness and sinfulness has its way in the human's attempt to control the future or flee from responsibility to and for the other. Our own clinical experience demands that both notions of care be considered, and we believe that making a clear line of distinction between the two may have more heuristic usefulness than experiential accuracy.

Heidegger's understanding of care as the unifying force that makes the psychosomatic unity of human beings vital seems to us to support our view that care always has an element of both anxiety and concern. "In Care," he says, "this entity [*homo*] has the 'source' of its Being . . . the entity is not released from this source but is held fast, dominated by it through and through as long as this entity 'is in the world.' "[11] Family therapist Robert Beavers seems to be saying the same thing in different words when he notes that ambivalence is characteristic of what it is to be human. One sign of health in both the individual and the marital/family system is the ability to tolerate at least a modicum of ambivalence and ambiguity.[12]

Although it necessarily involves care for oneself, human caring operates in the tension of the me and the not me. It is motivated by ideas and ideals vital to the caring person and, at the same time, respects and expects variations of growth and direction in the cared for. "Caring," according to Milton Mayeroff, "is the antithesis of simply using the other person to satisfy one's own needs."[13] Mayeroff, whose understanding of care is strongly influenced by humanistic psychology, views it primarily as "helping the other grow." In caring, "What I care for [a person, an ideal, an idea] is an extension of myself and at the same time is something separate from me that I respect in its own right. To care for someone, I must *know* many things. I must know, for example, who the other is, what his powers and limitations are, what his needs are, and what is conducive to his growth; I must know how to respond to his needs, and what my own powers and limitations are."[14]

Honesty is an essential part of caring. "I must be genuine in caring for the other. I must 'ring true.' There must not be a significant gap between how I act and what I really feel, between what I say and what I feel. To be 'present for' the other, so that the other can be present for me, I must be open to the other...." The process, rather than the product, is primary in caring, for it is only in the present that we can attend to the other. The father, impatient for his child to grow up and become "something" that he is not now, does not really take the child seriously and thus makes caring impossible.

In the broad sense, "being with" characterizes the process of caring; in caring for another person, we can be said to be basically with that person in his or her world. Caring is also motivated, in part at least, by the need to be cared for, such as found in friendship or family relationships. "In a meaningful friendship, caring is mutual, each cares for the other; caring becomes contagious. My caring for the other helps activate his caring for me; and similarly his caring for me helps activate my caring for him, it 'strengthens' me to care for him."[15]

A different perspective on care, but one that also holds together the care for self and for another, comes from Nel Noddings' feminist critique of Lawrence Kohlberg's work on moral development. She argues that the "highest" stage of moral judgment, is "not so much concerned with the rearrangement of priorities among principles," but "with maintaining and enhancing caring." Searching for a norm in what women do, rather than in what men do, she notes that women "do not abstract away from the concrete situation those elements that allow a formulation or deductive argument; rather, they remain in the situation as sensitive, receptive, and responsible agents."[16]

Noddings observes that caring involves two parties: the one caring and the one cared for. Caring is always a two way transaction. She refers to the work of Martin Buber and affirms with him that relationships always involve reciprocity.[17] To care "is to act not by fixed rule but by affection and regard." Thus the actions of the one caring will be varied instead of rule-bound, and his or her actions, while predictable in a global sense, will be unpredictable in detail. "The rational-objective mode must continually be re-established and redirected from a fresh base of commitment. Otherwise, we find ourselves deeply, perhaps inextricably, enmeshed in procedures that somehow serve only themselves; our thoughts are separated, completely detached, from the original objects of caring."[18]

The caring attitude, according to Noddings, has as its prototype the mother-child relationship. It is through this attitude, that we express our earliest memories of being cared for and that our growing bank of memories of both caring and being cared for becomes universally accessible." That is natural caring. Ethical caring, although based developmentally in the original relationship, is different. It may grow out of the natural caring and merge into it, but it differs in being intentional. It may be accompanied by love, but it always involves responsibility for the other—for the cared-for one. "As we care, we hear the 'I ought'—direct and primitive—and the potential for suffering guilt is ever present."[19] Guilt is most likely to appear, however, in caring that is sustained over time. From our perspective here, this means that guilt is an inevitable part of family relationships because of the enduring nature of those relationships. Nevertheless an ethic of caring does not separate the self from the other. Thus, according to Noddings, while it affirms responsibility for the other, it also advocates that one care for oneself.

Many of the things that Noddings has presented in her view of care resonate strongly with the understanding of care and, particularly, pastoral care as it has developed in the modern pastoral care movement. The development of those sensitivities to relationships that have been identified as feminine seem to us to be qualities essential to becoming a good pastor. Noddings' emphasis on being aware of one's own involvement in what one does and the impossibility of evaluating thoughts and acts apart from the one who has them and does them is a central feature of what is best in pastoral supervision. Learning to deal with one's responsibilities for caring and the necessary guilt that accompanies the impossibility of fully carrying out those responsibilities is one of the most important things that supervised clinical experience offers.

In the light of this understanding of care, our concern now is to develop the concept of care as generational. Don Browning, following Erik Erikson, has developed a normative picture of the human being as *generative*. Although derived from the same root word, the concept of *generational* focuses on the placing of human beings in generations—for example, "These are the generations of . . ."—and emphasizes humanity's place and responsibility within the sequence of history, rather than individual productive abilities. Child psychiatrist Arthur Kornhaber has affirmed the importance of the three generational family in his study of grandparenting. "The natural family," he says, "is comprised of people who are rooted in the past, live in the present, and consider and plan for the future. Most people are unaware of the significance of intergenerational relationships," but, he continues, "I can state categorically that a healthy and loving bond between grandparents and grandchildren is necessary for the emotional health and happiness of all three generations."[20] Generationality is a powerful symbol of what it means to be God's creature, even God's ordinary creature.

To be human is to care for one's fathers and mothers and children. Isaac honors Abraham and Sarah; he blesses Jacob and Esau. As creatures who have been given time, our recognition that our own generation is not all there is and is not all that motivates us is strikingly involved in all the family problems and tensions we experience and to which, as pastors, we are to minister. Although we are inclined to think of it in that way, ministry to members of families should not be judged adequate or inadequate by whether it seems to preserve a particular family structure, but by whether it offers care and facilitates caring for our generations. We believe that the generational nature of caring may be clearly seen in two fundamental characteristics of human beings: relationality and temporality.

GENERATIONAL HUMANITY AS RELATIONAL

In surveying the biblical literature on the interpretation of the *imago dei* in humankind, Westermann concludes with Karl Barth that the concept's basic meaning is that of partnership, the ability to enter into relationship. That ability is not something possessed by humanity apart from God, but something given by God in the blessing of humanity. Westermann insists that this idea did not originate with Barth. What Barth did more effectively than others before him was to emphasize that the image was not something possessed by humanity but was the essence of humanity itself. The biblical text is concerned with God's action and God's image in the person, rather than an abstract definition of human nature. The "uniqueness of human beings," says Westermann, "consists in their being God's counterparts. The relationship to God is not something which is added to human existence; humans are created in such a way that their very existence is intended to be the relationship to God."[21]

In biblical understanding, the individual is consistently limited by the humanity of the other. It is not possible to live humanly and not take the other into account. There are many ways in which this affirmation is stated. One of them is Westermann's discussion of the Cain and Abel story. What we are and want, he says, is limited by the very existence of other human beings—symbolically and in actuality our brothers and sisters. Again, he goes beyond Genesis 2-3 in the development of his anthropology, insisting that Genesis 2-3 has not yet said the last word about what ultimately constitutes created and limited humans. Basic to this, he says, "are the negative and positive aspects of existence together as brothers. 'Man' is not just Adam and Eve, but also Cain and Abel."[22] This is quite similar to Barth's description of humankind's limitation in terms of relationship, to the brother or sister in *Church Dogmatics* (vol. III, part 2). He or she is our fellow human being, whom we have been created to be *with*. Our individuality is limited by the *thou* of the other because humankind is fellow-humanity. In the encounter of I and Thou, one can only pretend to be isolated.

Again Westermann is helpful in commenting that a human being must be seen as one whose destiny it is to live in community; people have been created to live with each other. "This," he says, "is what human existence means and what human institutions and structures show. Every theoretical and institutional separation of man and woman, every deliberate detachment of male from female, can endanger the very existence of humanity as determined by creation."[23]

Humankind's relationality can also be seen in Westermann's discussion of shame, which, he says, "is not something that takes place in the individual, but in relationship with others. . . . Being ashamed is . . . a reaction to being discovered unmasked. It is a reaction of the whole person as the blushing which accompanies it indicates."[24] Westermann's understanding of the relationality of shame is consistent with most modern psychological interpretations of this very human phenomenon.[25] To experience shame is to care for how others may feel about us and is, therefore, an acknowledgment of the importance of our relationship to them. That experience is the mark of our humanity. To be shameless is to lack humanity.

From a philosophical, rather than a biblical, point of view, Paul Tillich also affirms the centrality of human relationality in his "ontological polarities, individualization, and participation." Human relationality is part of the ontological structure of being itself. Our individualization is limited by its polarity: participation.

> Participation is essential for the individual, not accidental. In fact, no individual exists without participation, and no personal being exists without communal being. The person as the fully developed individual self is impossible without other fully developed selves. If he did not meet the resistance of other selves, every self would try to make himself absolute . . . there is no person without the encounter with other persons. Persons can grow only in the communion of personal encounters. Individualization and participation are interdependent on all levels of being.[26]

Thus the relationality of human beings, according to a number of important theological interpreters, may be seen as representing humankind's opportunity to be fully human; yet, at the same time, it is the most important limitation of that humanity. Moreover, as we are focusing on the issue, it is also an expression of the necessary relationship between the generations of our lives or, more specifically, to the persons in the generations before and after us.

GENERATIONAL HUMANITY AS TEMPORAL

Our relationality is radically conditioned by our temporality. As relational human beings, we have time but not an infinite amount of it. "God's blessing makes it possible for a person to relate his whole life, in its course from day to day and year to year, to God. One receives from God's hand one's whole life, especially in its daily unobtrusiveness in which nothing particular happens."[27] The God of the first eleven chapters of Genesis is One who is creating, sustaining, and relating to all of life, not just to its more dramatic events and heroic persons. A relationship with this God, according to Westermann, "embraces humanity in the span of existence from birth to death. It includes growth and maturity, the increase and decrease of powers, recovery and strengthening, hunger and plenty." The fact of human temporality is a significant part of Westermann's argument that the anthropology of Genesis must include much more than the creation stories. He notes that it also includes human limitation. "In blessing, one receives from one's creator the capacity for propagation; this includes, however, that people are bound to a short span of existence. One exists as a person only in the span which leads from birth to death."[28]

Barth is another important interpreter of human temporality, for he emphasizes the significance of humankind's movement from the past through the present to the future. "A human self-understanding genuinely orientated by a general picture of man will be halted by the riddle of human temporality, and will have to be content to assert that we must live our life in the absolute uncertainty given with this riddle because we are not asked whether we would prefer a different possibility."[29]

"To be man," according to Barth, "is to live in time. . . . Human life means to have been, to be, and to be about to be. Human life means to be temporal." The same is true, according to Barth, for my fellow human being who "does not confront me as an abstract idea, but for good or evil in his historical reality, in the totality of what he was and is and will be, in this totality as the Thou without whom I could not be a human I." Time was created by God "in order that there might take place His dealings in the covenant with man, which finds its counterpart in the relationship between man and his fellows. It is for this reason and in this sense that time is the form of our existence."[30]

"A man without an awareness of history," continues Barth, "without definite pictures of what was and the patience to learn from them, would be an escapist, running away from reality and God, and quite unreliable in his dealings with his fellow-men." But I am "not only what I was, I am already . . . what I shall be." And God "will guarantee the reality of our future too (however long or short it may be), just as he guarantees it even now and has always done so. . . . There is no need to suppose that we are masters of our future, or that we posit it absolutely in the form in which we conceive it. But we are surely free to live to-day responsibly for tomorrow. Is not this the freedom to pray the fourth petition of the Lord's Prayer: 'Give us *today* our bread for *tomorrow*?'"[31]

From a different theological perspective, H. Richard Niebuhr also emphasizes the importance of time in describing human beings. For Niebuhr, the human self is "time-full."

> The past and the future are not the no-longer and the not-yet; they are extensions of the present. They are the still-present and the already-present. . . . My interpersonal past also is with me in all my present meetings with other selves. It is there in all my love and guilt. The self does not leave its past behind as the moving hand of a clock does; its past is inscribed into it more deeply than the past of geologic formations is crystallized in their present form. As for the future, the not-yet, it is present in my now in expectations and anxieties, in anticipations and commitments. To be a self is to live toward the future and to do so not only in the form of purposiveness, but also of expectation, anticipation, anxiety, and hope. Past, present, and future are dimensions of the active self's time-fullness. They are always with it from the moment it has realized that "I am I."[32]

The self remembers itself. According to Niebuhr, in the encounter with others, the self remembers "its parents and their actions upon it and its responses to them." The future also involves an encounter with others. The present is a time of preparation "to meet the actions on me that I foresee, hope for, or fear." Human anxiety and guilt are not experienced in relation to "timeless being but as relation to a continuous interaction that has gone on and will go on through a long time." The self, claims Niebuhr, comes to present encounters "with images and patterns of interpretation, with attitudes of trust and suspicion, accumulated in its biographical and historical past. It comes to its meetings with the Thou's and It's with an a priori equipment that is the heritage of its personal and social past." Present actions are also made with reference to the future as well as to the past. "Man responding in the present is interpreting what acts upon him as historical being, being in time."[33]

Niebuhr notes humankind's attempts to free itself from the past as having been successful "only in encounters with nature . . . little seems to have been accomplished in the sphere of interpersonal action by means of forgetting the past and making a fresh beginning." One can, however, successfully reinterpret the past, recalling, accepting, understanding, and reorganizing the past instead of abandoning it "if present relations of selves to others are to be reorganized, if the responses of selves to others and to themselves in interaction with others, are to fit better in the total process of interpersonal life, then the past must not be forgotten but remembered, accepted and reinterpreted."[34]

One can see developed in both Barth and Niebuhr the opportunity and limitation of the gift of time. As presented in the Genesis stories, and in terms of the anthropological emphasis we are making, human beings have generations. This means that as they are created and are generated by those before them, they also have the opportunity to create and to produce those who are related significantly to them and who will follow them in time. But their time is limited. They will not see all their generations, only those that are nearest them. In our time, most of us have significant influence only on those generations immediately before and after our own. Because the time we have is not infinite, its importance is greatly enhanced. We are time aware, anxious that we indeed do take advantage of what has been given us for stewardship.

This awareness of time is not just a philosophical matter. It can be seen in the everyday story of Al and Ann and their ambivalence and struggle about whether to have children, their awareness of their aging, and a further, more vague, awareness of a change in the meaning of their sexuality. We only touch on these personal and pastoral issues here. They are further developed in the chapters that follow. Our concern at this point is simply to affirm the generational character of human beings and its implication for practice. When we look at Al and Ann's marital problem, we are also looking at the generations of Al and Ann—their relationality in the context of the temporality.

CHALLENGES TO THE FAMILY AND TO GENERATIONAL CARING

As with almost any thesis, there is an antithesis and various contrapuntal themes that offer critique and correction to the major theme. Our statement that the norm for family living is the function of care for one's generations is useful, but it is also limited. In considering those limits, we would say first of all that some of them are recognized by the norm itself. In affirming that Christian family living is characterized by the care for one's generations, we are stating that care for one generation to the exclusion of others is inadequate and un-Christian. To idealize or overemphasize the marriage relationship or the parent-child relationship, for example, is not to meet the standard represented by generational care. There must be some balance and flexibility in our caring. Thus within the norm itself there is a critical principle that must be attended to, must be related to counter themes, that challenge its adequacy.

The Christian tradition affirms the relationality of human beings and the kind of commitment, loyalty, and care that holds the family together. At the same time, as the following words from the Gospels suggest, it also stands over against any idealization of the family or, for that matter, any other human relationship:

> While he was still speaking to the people, behold, his mother and his brothers stood outside, asking to speak to him. But he replied to the man who told him, "Who is my mother, and who are my brothers?" And stretching out his hand toward his disciples, he said, "Here are my mother and my brothers! For whoever does the will of my Father in heaven is my brother, and sister, and mother." (Matthew 12:46-49 RSV)

Although the point we are making here touches only a portion of the text's meaning, it is an important one. Some of the limits of the family must be considered in thinking Christianly about what is normative for the family.

There are other challenges to the family, which are implied by our generational care norm but which are not actually a part of the norm itself: (1) the relationship of the public and private sphere of life, or how one's life and vocation outside the home are related to one's life at home; (2) the relationship of the family and family members to significant persons outside the family and the relationship between one's kinship and friendship systems; and (3) the relationship of care for oneself and for others, whether friends or family. Each of these challenges can be understood as an expression of Jesus' question, "Who are my mother and brothers?" We understand them not so much as problems that can be solved as issues to be continually addressed in life. We only touch on them here, but they reappear in later chapters.

The article by Hahn, cited earlier, points to the destructiveness of a rigid allocation of men to the public and women to the private sphere of life. Dorothee Soelle's book *To Work and to Love* is a more extensive attempt to address the issue of the public and private spheres in the context of a theology of creation. Soelle and her co-author, Shirley A. Cloyes, argue that work, as it is depicted in Genesis 2, "is not a curse that descends on the human being after the Fall; it is from the beginning, an expression of the human project of liberation, of its dignity and integrity. Through work, human life shifts from passivity to participation."[35] The variations on the theme of how love and work are related in the public and private sphere are integrally related to the way we learn to care for our generations and appear repeatedly in the lives of persons whom we discuss in this book.

Equally significant is how our friendship and kinship are related in our caring (or who is our neighbor and how is he or she related to those who are physically kin to us?) The New Testament presents a tension between family loyalty and the care of those outside the family. The Christian *koinonia* is a community of people who have a particular communion with one another because they have a particular communion with God. Paul refers to the community and describes it as marked with sympathy and concern, which is another way to describe *agape* as caring (Rom. 12; Col. 3–4).

John H. Elliot has recently described the inclusiveness of the New Testament household in a study of I Peter. The early Christians, though mostly Gentiles, adopted the importance of the Jewish notion of household: It was a locus of identification (when people traveled they took their households with them) as well as a defense against outside forces (such as persecuting non-Christians). And the mission activity of the early community was not individualistically oriented. "It was in homes and from homes that the first adherents were sought. It was not merely individuals but entire households who were converted and transformed by the good news of human reconciliation and of the new possibilities of community."[36] The main function of those in the household was to care[37] (*diakountes;* I Pet. 4:10-11). Those who were members of the household were not all in kinship relationships, but whether visitors or slaves, they were called *oiketai*.

The issue of who is a member of one's household, both literally and symbolically, applies not only to the religious concept of the household of faith but also to the broader issue of relational closeness and intimacy. Blood and kin are not essential for an adequate notion of relationship as a context for caring. With whom am I most able to share myself personally, and does the answer to that question relate to the relationship I have with my family? This is an ongoing question for persons who live alone and for those who live together in many different forms of households.

The relation of care for self and care for others is another important challenge to the care for our generations. As we have observed family tensions and problems, it seems inescapable that an adequate concept of care for others requires recognition of the need to care for oneself. This is only implicit in the "Who are my mother and brothers" passage in Matthew, but the needs and expectations of all who look to Jesus, as recorded in the Synoptic Gospels, seem to be in tension with his need to withdraw from the cries of others to care for himself. In the modern literature on care, such as the writings of Noddings and Mayeroff, an inescapable dimension of care is that for ourselves. But this is not an easy affirmation or resolution. There inevitably seems to be some degree of guilt that is a part of our care, because we can never care enough. There is also paradox. The concept of self-care inevitably involves the necessary anxiety of self-concern that Heidegger describes, but it also involves the "be not anxious" and the "care not for yourselves" of the Sermon on the Mount—self-care that transcends care. As we have suggested, these three challenges are not so much problems to be solved as they are ongoing issues to be lived with in the care of our generations.

GENERATIONAL CARE AS PASTORAL

The material in this chapter has ranged widely in our attempt to develop the normative concept of human beings as generational and caring. There will be further development of both these concepts in relation to particular persons and family situations in the chapters that follow. It is not difficult to look at the story of Al and Ann, which has been touched on in this chapter, and see some of the human struggle to care, to be cared for, and to deal in a caring, responsible way for the generations before and after our own.

We have been writing about the family in a way that concerns all persons with Christian commitment, not just those set apart by ordination to be pastors. This approach reflects one of our major assumptions, that in dealing with the family, one's own or another, there are certain basic human experiences that must be dealt with whatever degree of responsibility or level of competence one has. The book is intended to be theoretically and practically useful to all persons who are concerned to view their lives from a religious perspective, not just for those with professional pastoral responsibility. Pastors who attempt to minister to families in some way bring their relationships to their own generations with them, just like anyone else.

In emphasizing our common experience, however, it is important to say that within the faith community or among those who hold Christian convictions about human beings, we are not all alike. There are significant differences between clergy and laity, which we believe are unrealistic to obscure in discussions of "the ministry of all Christians." The modern pastoral care movement has been accused of adopting a "clergy paradigm" and presenting the ministry of pastoral care exclusively in terms of clergy development. Although there are reasons to criticize the emphasis on professional education for care, we affirm what has been learned from the "clergy paradigm" and believe that there is more for all Christians to learn from it than the other way around.

One of the things that has been learned is broadly supportive of our thesis about generational care. Central to the learning theory of clinical pastoral education, but seldom articulated, is the principle that learning to care must take place in three types of relationships: that with peers, that with authorities, and that with those to whom one attempts to minister. The peer relationship is analogous to those in one's own generation. The authority relationship has inescapable parental dimensions, and the relationship with those to whom one ministers—whatever the age or experience of the minister—involves learning to nurture as a parent might nurture a child. The kind of responsibility for learning in these three ways is an important part of what has been learned in the clinical education of clergy, or clergy candidates, that must not be lost in extending this kind of experience to laity.

In our view of ministry, including that of pastoral care and counseling, an important way in which clergy and laity are related to one another is on a continuum of ecclesiastical accountability, responsibility for professional growth, and amount of time available for ministry. What we say to clergy and laity in this book and in our other teaching is essentially no different. The way it can be received by each is, however, quite different. (Perhaps, in the best of all possible worlds, or in an ideal church, there would be no difference, but in our world there is.) Clergy are accountable to bishops and church courts for what they do in their ministries in a way that laity are not. Clergy are accountable for professional growth and development in ministry in a way that laity are not. Clergy have time available for ministry to families that laity do not. What we offer to clergy and laity about the family and ministry to it is essentially the same. What is possible for clergy to do with this information can be significantly greater than what laity can do because of the time and responsibilities given to them.

In responding to Al and Ann's problem with communication, the Christian pastor also responds to how they care for the generation before them (their parents), for their own generation (each other), and for the generation following them (their children or their struggle with what they will pass on to those who come after them). Although their care for the earth and all that is in it is not limited to their family relationships, Al's and Ann's humanity and ours is expressed through the ways that we care for the three generations with which we have direct relationships.

Al and Ann's friends, Ann's sister and her parents, Al's mother, the laity concerned with ministry to families within their church—all of these, in our judgment, might profit from understanding Al and Ann as creatures who care and from responding to them in a caring way. They also need, however, an experience of professional care with one who has studied such care clinically and academically in order to offer caring in a technically skilled way. A professional carer for marriages and families needs to be able to handle the intimacies of family relationships in a way that maintains and facilitates the intimacy.

In this chapter, we have presented the point of view that is essential for the remainder of this work: an interpretation of human beings as having been given the responsibility for the care of their generations. We make no claim that this is an adequate description of what it is to be human, but we do believe that it is an essential part of that meaning. We turn now to the caring for our generations by those whose households include only themselves.

NOTES

1. Celia Allison Hahn, "Men, Women, and the Remarriage of Public and Private Spheres," *The Christian Century* (July 4-11, 1986) 547.
2. Claus Westermann, *Genesis 1-11* (Minneapolis: Augsburg, 1974), pp. 159-60.
3. Jurgen Moltmann, *God in Creation* (San Francisco: Harper, 1985), pp. 29-31.
4. Joseph Sittler, *The Ecology of Faith* (Philadelphia: Muhlenburg, 1961); *Essays on Nature and Grace* (Philadelphia: Fortress, 1972).
5. Joseph Sittler, *Gravity and Grace: Reflections and Provocations* (Minneapolis: Augsburg, 1986), p. 18.
6. Heinz Kohut, *How Does Analysis Cure?* (Chicago: The University of Chicago Press, 1984).
7. Claus Westermann, *Elements of Old Testament Theology* (Atlanta: John Knox, 1982), p. 88.
8. Ibid., p. 95.
9. P. E. Davies, "Care," *Interpreter's Dictionary of the Bible*, p. 537.
10. Rudolph Bultmann, "Flesh, Sin, and World," *Theology of the New Testament* part II.B, trans. Kendrick Grobel (New York: Charles Scribner's Sons, 1951), p. 242.
11. Martin Heidegger, *Being and Time*, trans. John Macquarrie and Edward Robinson (New York: Harper, 1962), p. 42.
12. W. Robert Beavers, *Successful Marriage* (New York: W. W. Norton, 1985), p. 207.
13. Milton Mayeroff, *On Caring* (New York: Harper Perennial Library, 1971), p. 1.
14. Ibid., p. 13.
15. Ibid., pp. 26-32.

16. Nel Noddings, *Caring: A Feminist Approach to Ethics and Moral Education* (Berkeley: University of California Press, 1984), p. 42.
17. Ibid., p. 72.
18. Ibid., pp. 24-26.
19. Ibid., p. 99.
20. Arthur Kornhaber, *Between Parents and Grandparents* (New York: St. Martin's Press, 1986), pp. 3, 17.
21. Westermann, *Genesis*, pp. 151-58.
22. Ibid., p. 318.
23. Ibid., p. 160.
24. Ibid., p. 236.
25. See, for example, Gershen Kaufman, *Shame and the Power of Caring* (Cambridge, Mass.: Shenkman, 1980).
26. Paul Tillich, *Systematic Theology I* (London: Nisbet, 1953), pp. 195-96.
27. Westermann, *Elements of Old Testament Theology*, p. 103.
28. Ibid., p. 112.
29. Karl Barth, *The Doctrine of Creation: Church Dogmatics III* (Edinburgh: T. & T. Clark, 1960), p. 514.
30. Ibid., pp. 521-27.
31. Ibid., pp. 539-48.
32. H. R. Niebuhr, *The Responsible Self: An Essay in Christian Moral Philosophy* (New York: Harper, 1963), pp. 92-93.
33. Ibid., pp. 95-98.
34. Ibid., pp. 102-4.
35. Dorothee Soelle and Shirley A. Cloyes, *To Work and to Love* (New York: Brunner/Mazel, 1986), p. 72.
36. John H. Elliott, *A Home for the Homeless* (Philadelphia: Fortress, 1981), p. 198.
37. William Johnson Everett *(Blessed Be the Bond* [Philadelphia: Fortress, 1985], pp. 2-10) has noted the ambiguity in the usage of four terms that are consistently used in discussions of family and relational life—*individual, couple, family,* and *household*—and has usefully presented a way to think about and to use them more accurately.

CHAPTER TWO

CARING FOR OUR GENERATIONS AS AN INDIVIDUAL

If two lie together, they are warm; but how can one be warm alone? (Ecclesiastes 4:11 RSV)

Shelly: It's a little bit embarrassing to still be a virgin at twenty-five, but somehow, with the guys that I've dated, it never seemed quite worth it.

Pastor: The younger men in your life sound about as disappointing as the older one.

Shelly: Almost.

Shelly had come to pastoral counseling several weeks prior to this particular interchange with the pastor. She had been referred by the campus minister of the local university and, somewhat unusually, had brought her mother along with her. On her first call to the pastoral counseling center, she had indicated that she was depressed by what was happening in her parents' marriage and some other things in her own life. On the second call, the day of her first appointment, she asked if she could bring her mother in because "she's more depressed than I am." The pastor indicated that bringing the mother would be fine and decided when they came in that he would see them together, at least for the first interview.

Since Shelly had been the one who asked for the counseling, the pastor devoted the majority of the first interview to inquiring about how she experienced the family's pain. What the pastor heard in the story was what he had already seen in Shelly's bringing her mother with her. Shelly seemed to have been the one designated as therapist for her family's pain. Bringing her mother for counseling, however, suggested that she was about to retire from that role.

After spending most of the first hour on what was happening in the family system and assessing the roles of mother and daughter within it, the pastor turned his attention to Sue, Shelly's mother, who had great difficulty in talking about how she was experiencing her life situation. She could talk about the family, both her present one and her family of origin, but describing herself, her actions, and her feelings seemed almost impossible for her. The pastor pointed out rather directly that no matter how many bad things her husband had done, the only person Sue could do anything about right now was herself. He noted that her real difficulty seemed to be in being herself and being aware of what was going on in her own life, not the lives of others. He told her that if she wanted to do something about that, he would be glad to see her in counseling, apart from her daughter. She would, however, have to decide each time as to whether she wanted to come back for another session. It was not something, he said, that she had to do because she was sick, but what she might choose to do because she wanted to deal differently with her life.

For some weeks, the pastoral counselor worked individually with Shelly and with Sue. As the oldest of the three children, Shelly had taken on the responsibility of maintaining the family peace and tranquility, which her mother sought and her father despised. Her mother, Sue, was a quiet, pretty, somewhat fearful, woman who had always lived near her parents and devoted much of her life to trying to please them. Shelly's father, Sam, was a successful businessman who started his own fast-developing company. He continued to be the charming and popular person he had been in high school and college, who was drawn to Sue because of her beauty and dependability. He didn't worry about her closeness to her family. In fact, it attracted him because his own family was unstable, and in "Sweet Sue" he seemed to have found what he needed.

Shelly combined the quiet prettiness of her mother with some of the "drive" for success of her father—the father who was always somewhere else. Wondering where Dad was and when he would be home was one of the constancies of her growing up. She was aware of conflict between her parents, her mother's tears and depression, but the actual conflicts were always well hidden. If they became too intense, Dad would leave, and Mother would tell Shelly and her younger brother and sister that everything was fine; Dad was just under a lot of pressure from his work. During Shelly's high school and college years, her mother's depression became worse, and she acknowledged to Shelly that things were not going well in the marriage. She suspected Sam of having an affair. Following her mother's path, Shelly stayed close to home, going to college at the local university, but like her father and in contrast to her mother, she majored in business rather than liberal arts and humanities. She was in her first job at the regional office of a large corporation and had also begun a graduate program in management.

Shelly was attractive enough to be sought after by a number of boys in high school and college, but she had been involved in only one serious relationship—with a young man she had met at the campus religious group. With him, in contrast to the boys she had dated briefly and whom she perceived as sexually exploitive and undependable, she was able to engage in long, serious conversations. He was sensitive and dependable, but not sexually assertive or exciting enough to her to do much with her sexual feelings. Men, for Shelly, seemed either exciting and undependable or dependable and unexciting.

SINGLENESS OR INDIVIDUALITY?

The question of the cynical preacher in Ecclesiastes has been an inescapable one from ancient times down to the present. "To what extent am I alone or together, and, if together, together with whom?" Too often family issues have been discussed only in terms of those who are living together in a household. Persons who live alone—the never married, the separated, the divorced, and the widowed—also have a family life, and it is that life and the issues of individuality and separateness that continue into other forms of family living that we discuss in this chapter.

Singleness, in popular usage, most often refers to persons, relatively early in adulthood, who are dealing with the question of whether they will find someone whom they wish to marry and who will wish to marry them. Without avoiding the importance of this question and this group of people, we attempt to look at some of the more important ways that individuals deal with family care, whatever the circumstances of their singleness. We certainly do not deny that there are significant differences in the meaning and experience of being a single person at different ages in life and in relation to the causes of being single—one's never having married, divorce, or the death of a spouse, and so on. The lives of the persons we discuss will reveal some of those differences. Nevertheless our emphasis is upon the meaning and importance of individuality and relatedness as an issue for human living, whatever one's marital status.

The term *single* is itself a problem, and we have been somewhat ambivalent about using it. It is a term denoting a social status, acquiring its meaning through the negation of the legal term *married.* Thus it suggests that it is contrary to the assumed social norm that everyone should be married. To put the issue more humanly, a single woman in one of the adult church school classes in which we shared some of these ideas said rather heatedly, "I object to being called 'single' because it defines me by what I don't have instead of who I am as an individual." The same person went on to argue that the church ought to be able to talk about human beings in terms of what an individual should be without having to bring in whether the person is married.

We agree with her argument. As a public policy for the church and for other structures within society, an emphasis on individuality rather than marital status, is important, just as the use of the term *Ms* instead of *Miss* or *Mrs.* is an important affirmation that the identification of who one is should not be primarily related to marital status. Because of this necessarily negative understanding of the term *single*, our primary category in this chapter will be the "individual" rather the "single." This solves one problem but involves us in another one: ambiguity. Although most of the discussion is focused on persons who, in terms of marital status, are single, in using the broader category of individuality we are dealing with issues that also involve persons in other levels of society with respect to marriage, the divorced and widowed, and persons of all ages. Focusing on issues of individuality common to all is not a denial of the differences in these varied life circumstances but an emphasis on the common elements of family care. Moreover, because all of us are individuals, what we say about individuality has importance not only for those who live alone, but also for all of us.

In chapter 1, we presented a view of human beings in families, created in relationship, but with limited time for making those relationships fruitful. Here the focus narrows to the ongoing struggle between individuality and relatedness and how this affects the care of our generations. In terms of Christian theological assumption, dealing with how individual persons are related to their generations is not only necessary, but inescapable as well. Theologically, one is never really alone. Nevertheless the reality of aloneness is one of the most powerful human experiences. How can persons "be warm" when they feel separated from those to whom they are related by kinship and to others to whom they might be related in friendship or in marriage? The question of Ecclesiastes is painfully human and is central to what is said throughout this book.

In our earlier discussion of relationship as a central feature of what it means to be generational, we touched on Paul Tillich's ontological polarity of individualization and participation. For practical purposes, what Tillich means by ontological is simply that the struggle between individuality and relationship is structured into all the processes of life and can never be resolved. We now explore some of the ways in which the continuing struggle between individualization and participation are worked out in our lives. This struggle takes place whatever the form of family living, in which a person participates and at every point in life, although the issue seems to be more intense at some points than at others. In family living and caring, the three most important dimensions of this struggle are: (1) how one maintains separation while maintaining loyalty to one's generations—particularly the generation before; (2) how one deals with and differentiates between issues of commitment and loyalty; and (3) how one copes with the necessary losses of life. These issues are a part of our family living at every point in life. Our focus in this chapter is on the first two of these. We address the third in chapter 6.

CARING THROUGH THE DIFFERENTIATION OF ONE'S SELF

The influence of one's family of origin, particularly the influence of one's designated role in that family, can hardly be overestimated.

Shelly: The most I enjoy being with my family is when Daddy's not around. He seems to be the center of all the conflict. Mother is there, trying to stay nice and charming, and there he is saying absolutely nothing. And I'm caught in the middle. It used to be that I enjoyed being in the middle, but I'm slowly getting away from that.

Pastor:	You must have found some different ways of getting enjoyment.
Shelly:	I think it has to do with accepting myself—accepting myself when I'm with them. It's really more like forgiving myself.
Pastor:	You mean forgiving yourself for not making things better for them.
Shelly:	That's right. I can't change either one of them. I can't change the family. (pause) But when she [mother] tells me that Daddy is ignoring my sister—and she probably means he's ignoring her—I don't trust myself *not* to try and make it right. I don't trust myself to be an adult. Instead of arguing with her, I just go along with what she wants. I can't stand her disapproval.
Pastor:	It looks like to me that you've been finding some ways to stand it.
Shelly:	But it's hard. I guess I watched too much TV when I was little. Somehow, I've got this picture of the perfect family, where everybody gets along. Why can't my family be like that? Everybody else's family is like that.
Pastor:	And if they're not, then somebody's got to do something about it.
Shelly:	And that's me. I know that's not the real world, but it seems like it should be.

There are a number of ways one might understand Shelly's loyalty to her family of origin and her acceptance of the "family therapist" role for herself. One might ask, however, even from the point of view of the Christian tradition, whether the way she had chosen was the best one to "honor her father and her mother." From the point of view of the individualization side of Tillich's polarity of individualization and participation, it was clearly a distortion of her potential as a centered self. She was losing herself in a destructive way, and what she needed was further individualization in order to maintain an adequate polarity in her system of relationships.

Most helpful in understanding this task is the work of Murray Bowen, who, in one of the most striking papers in the literature of family therapy insists that the "one most important goal of family systems therapy is to help family members toward a better level of 'differentiation of self.' "[1] In accordance with most of our assumptions about family therapy, Bowen notes that the first method of family therapy was directed at the entire family unit. In contrast to this assumption, he presents his "accidental discovery" that effective family and individual change could take place when persons take responsibility for dealing with their families in a new and more nearly adult way.

Bowen describes an experience that took place in the early sixties, when he began suggesting that psychiatric residents who were studying family therapy become involved in therapy with their spouses. His hypothesis was that these couples would deal with their extended families in the course of their focus on their own marital relationships. The results of this, he says, "were disappointing." About a quarter of the couples made some significant change with families of origin, but most made only a token effort. "Most never really got beyond either blaming their parents or benevolently forgiving them." Instead, they "tended to become *overinvolved* [italics ours] in the relationship in the marriage. . . ." In contrast to the group involved in therapy with their spouses, the other residents simply received group instruction in ways that the self could be differentiated from the family of origin. There was little or no private time with any resident, but to Bowen's surprise, these "residents, and other trainees in the course, were making as much or more progress at change with their spouses and children than similar residents I was seeing weekly in formal family therapy. These observations appeared valid by the most searching criteria I could use at the time."

There are many ways in which Bowen's "accidental discovery" and his subsequent development of this insight has importance for our theological norm for the family: caring for your generations. We mention three of them here. The first significant affirmation is that one can do "family work" as an individual and that much of this family work really has to be done on one's own. It involves the initiative of the family member more than that of the therapist. Second, one can become *overinvolved* in working on relationships in one's own generation, particularly the primary intimate relationship with a person of the opposite sex. Attention to relationships with the other generations can, among other things, take the pressure off this "working" on one's intimate relationship and thus indirectly improve it. Third, the psychotherapist, the pastor, and all of us have work to do with our families of origin if we are to be effective in dealing with our own and the following generations. One cannot assist others in differentiating and in achieving the other goals of effective family living if one has not done at least some of this herself or himself. But what, specifically, does this involve?

Bowen's concepts of family structure and change have many useful applications, but our concern here is with the practicalities of separating from the family of origin and, only indirectly, with the theory. In the appendix of her book, Jeannette R. Kramer[2] has presented a checklist for changing oneself with one's family of origin. It deals with these practicalities and grows out of not only the work of Bowen, but also the practical wisdom of many different psychotherapists. We can touch on just a few of the highlights here. We believe that it is a valuable resource for the counseling of single young and middle adults, premarital guidance, and the pastoral care and counseling of couples. In discussing Kramer's checklist, we use the second person pronoun, as she does, to make the whole process more personal.

First of all, Kramer suggests that you must become an astute observer of your own family, learning facts about it that emphasize "who, what, when, where, and HOW, not why." Following the experience of many psychotherapists, we deemphasize the "why" question because it tends to remove you from the actual data of life and to involve you in speculation. It is important to become aware of family traumas, myths, patterns, rules, and binds and, most important, "which of these have affected you in a significant way—which ones you like and which ones you want to change."

Second, Kramer suggests your making a plan that can be slowly implemented "in an ongoing campaign." This should involve contacting family members on a one-to-one basis, "trying to break the pattern of the way you relate to that person when you are together in the family group. You may wish to start with family members who are farther from the center of the family circle in order to 'practice' this new way of relating before getting to the more important parents and siblings." She notes that a cut off member of the extended family is important in that he or she has somehow broken family rules, and that person's story, in contrast to the "official" family story, "gives you important information about family function. Letters and phone calls can prepare the way for visits, but you should be the one who initiates both the beginning and end of the call." Visits should be planned—at least at first—in relation to how long you anticipate that you can maintain your "new" way of relating without getting caught up in the old patterns. Perhaps "the most important part of your plan is the fact that it is yours and that you have taken responsibility for what happens in the family rather than simply letting it happen to you."

One of the most useful ways of carrying out this responsibility is what has been called by a number of psychotherapists, taking an "I" position. Kramer suggests that this involves "making clear statements about your own thoughts, feelings, and actions without using others to explain the way you are. It is important to be in as much control as possible of your emotional reactiveness, using anything at your command—for example, matter-of-factness or humor, to de-intensify the situation. "Maintain one-to-one communication even if you are with more than one person." Avoid taking sides or listening to one person's blaming another for family circumstances. "Find ways to communicate clearly and openly about matters which are barely or never referred to, making the covert overt." In doing this, "use your own feelings of anxiety, hurt or anger as signals that you are getting sucked into old patterns and that something must be done to maintain your 'new way' of relating."

Kramer concludes the checklist with her own three-point summary of the differentiating process and Bowen's three rules for communication with your family of origin. Both of these "threes" contain much that is useful in caring for one's generations.

Kramer's summary:

1) Make a differentiating move.
2) Expect opposition from the family togetherness forces.
3) Know what you will do in response to the opposition forces in the family so as not to be taken by surprise.

Bowen's rules:

1) Avoid counterattacking when provoked.
2) Do not become defensive.

3) Maintain an active relationship with other key members without withdrawing or becoming silent.

Kramer's book is recent enough that we have not, at the time of this writing, made direct use of the material as we have presented it here. However, we have, over the years, been involved in what Bowen calls "coaching" persons who were attempting to carry out suggestions such as these. Our experience strongly suggests that they are important and that they work. Certainly, they work differently for each person and do not always accomplish the particular change in relationship a person may wish to see in other family members. What this effort seems consistently to accomplish is helping persons overcome powerlessness in relation to their families of origin, particularly in relation to the prior generation. Thus significant change is made in the person's differentiation from the family of origin.

This is the way it was with Shelly. She came for pastoral counseling aware not only of the sadness in her life, but also that much of it was related to her entanglement in her family. She had brought her mother with her for the first session to say, in more objective surroundings, that her mother needed to take responsibility for her own life and not hold on to the dishonest myth that they had a peaceful family. Shelly's individual counseling was, according to Bowen's theory, family counseling, because it focused primarily on her differentiation.

One of her first differentiating actions was to talk individually with the grandmother who had been so dominating in Sue's life and, less directly, in Shelly's. A family rule that Shelly had discussed quite early in her relationship with her counselor was that a member of her family could never leave home—that is, could never live anywhere except in the immediate geographical area—if he or she wanted to remain a legitimate family member. Her grandmother would not, Shelly said, let her cousin ever come home again because she had moved west. The pastoral counselor had wondered with Shelly if this were really the case. The next week, Shelly had talked individually with the grandmother, who had quite simply said, "No." Shelly's cousin had made the emotional cut-off herself. The untrue myth was simply resolved by talking directly about it.

Further details of this event are interesting, but not necessary, here. The important thing for us is Shelly's use of the pastoral counselor's support to gain freedom to talk more directly to her grandmother. (This is something that most pastors can offer to their parishioners without a great deal of counseling training.) In that successful process, she gained the further freedom to move away from home without having to lose her family. In the same session in which she reported this incident, she also reported three dreams. One was a long and involved escape from a place that Shelly was trying to get away from. She related this, as one might imagine, to her escape from her good child role in the family. The second dream had to do with taking a tour over an estate under the direction of an attentive caretaker. She associated this to her relationship with the pastoral counselor, who took care of some of her anxieties as she toured the estate of her family. The third dream had to do with her looking at and feeling some expensive cloth that seemed to belong to her. She remembered her satisfaction in doing this, and the dream seemed important, though unclear. As she reflected on her feelings about this dream, she thought the cloth might be for a wedding dress, its not yet having been sewn suggesting her virginity. Her enjoyment of the dream came from her belief that the valuable cloth was going to be made into something beautiful before long.

As one can see from both Shelly's action with her grandmother and her dreams, she came to counseling ready to do something about her life, and she did. Shelly's situation concretely exemplifies many of the items on Kramer's checklist. Shelly talked regularly, but not too frequently, with her mother about their having responsibility for changing the peaceful and passive course of their lives, each in her own way. She contacted her father and arranged a time to meet with him. In this meeting, she let him know some of her anger and disappointment in him. She made no effort to tell him what to do, but simply told him where she was. She began to change the relationship with her younger sister, telling Sara that she (Shelly) was no longer willing to be the super-responsible one who indulged little sister's irresponsibility. They both, she said, needed to grow up in a different way—Shelly's declaration of independence being that she was no longer going to be responsible for keeping the family from falling apart or for bailing Sara out of tight scrapes. Although there are quite a few things left to do, it is quite evident that Shelly has discovered a better way to care for her generations, including her own.

THE PLACE OF COMMITMENT

This emphasis on separation seems necessarily to raise questions about the place of commitment and loyalty in the care of one's generations. In everyday speech, commitment and loyalty are often used synonymously. For example, a man or woman in a committed relationship will sometimes describe the partner's intimate relationship with another person as an act of disloyalty. This is an understandable usage of the term, but it carries with it an authoritarian claim: the claim of one in a superior role on one in an inferior role or the claim of an institution on an individual. The claim of loyalty in a marriage relationship reflects some of the traditional views of marriage—its institutional importance and the patriarchal structure of the family. If one has a different understanding of marriage—one that is more egalitarian, less institutional, and more personal—then the term *loyalty* is inappropriate for the marriage relationship. It tends to appear when an individual, the church, or a particular society feels threatened or defensive about the stability of the institution of marriage.

The importance and power of the term *loyalty* can better be maintained if it is used for intergenerational relationships that have authority and dependency defined openly as a part of their structure. Dependency is an important part of the marriage relationship also, but, normatively, it is a part of marriage's caring function, not its basic structure. It is a factor of choice, an intentional acknowledgment of need, not a claim that can be made on the basis of the existence of the marriage relationship. In marriage, which we understand as the personal relationship of peers within the same generation, *commitment* is a more appropriate term than *loyalty*. Commitment emphasizes choice and intentionality, rather than prior claim and obligation. Since both terms are so much a part of family caring, further interpretation of them is quite important.

Margaret Farley has helpfully defined commitment in terms of entering into a new form of relationship. "The root meaning of 'commitment,' " she says, "lies in the Latin *mittere*—'to send.' I 'send' my word into another."

> The essential elements of interpersonal commitment *are* an intention regarding future action and the undertaking of an obligation to another regarding that intended action. . . . A remedy for inconsistency and uncertainty, commitment is our wager on the truth of our present insight and the hope of our present love.[3]

Perhaps we can make our understanding of commitment and its differentiation from loyalty more practical and concrete by looking at another person's experience in pastoral counseling.

Tim is forty-one years old, divorced, and, to all external observers, quite successful in his career. He saw a pastoral counselor several years ago and gained some important insight into himself and his family relationships as well as gaining satisfaction from the relationship with his counselor. He comes to counseling this time because, as he puts it, "My work is no longer a safe place." He is unable to shut out the noise of others at work, to maintain his separateness and to focus steadfastly on his immediate and long-term career goals. In spite of being rather consistent in an exercise program, which reduces his stress and tension, he reports feelings of vulnerability and high anxiety and times of intense rage, which he fears may sometimes be uncontrollable.

There is additional stress in his personal life. Toni, a woman in her mid-thirties with whom he has been involved for almost four years, is pushing more strongly for marriage. Although she says she does not want children, she is aware of the pressures of her age and has told him that she is unwilling to wait much longer. His parents have recently moved south from Detroit in order to retire near him, and this adds to Tim's feelings of things closing in on him. He is beginning to see the same kind of rigidity in himself that he sees in his parents, and, as he puts it, "I don't know what they'll expect of me." Because he has interpreted the results of his previous counseling primarily in terms of the insight he achieved, Tim states that what he wants this time is "a new way to look at things." He seems only indirectly aware of how much the relationship with his former counselor meant to him.

As the pastor listened to Tim's story, he was most aware of his struggle with commitment and closeness, both of which seemed to place him in a trap. Tim was intensely aware of the two major failures in his life. Early in his career, he had been promoted rapidly and had been sent from the home office of the company to head their operations in another major city. After the first excitement over his success had worn off, Tim found himself unable to function. He seemed paralyzed, constantly fearing failure, if he were required to make a major decision. Within a few months, he resigned his position and took a demotion in order to return to the home office. He feels himself fortunate now to have moved to a responsible management position in a new company without having lost too much as a result of his previous failure.

His other failure was in his marriage. He had married the "right" woman, one who could compensate for his lack of ability in social situations. Tanya always knew the right thing to do or say. Tim was convinced that he could depend on her and that they were the right team. He found out, however, that what Tanya wanted was to depend on him. The assertiveness he admired in relation to others seemed quickly to become aggression in relation to him. Tanya demanded from him, and Tim felt shame and inadequacy. Because he was so convinced that he had married the kind of person he needed, he struggled to maintain the marriage in spite of what seemed like Tanya's constant rage toward him. Finally, he gave up, with the strong conviction that he would "never get into that again."

In listening to Tim's story, the pastor wondered about Tim's caring and being cared for. What he said about the relationship with Tanya suggested that he had secretly expected to be cared for and that caring was something that one *should* be secretive about. Neither his father nor his mother were open about their feelings. They encouraged him in his achievements, but seldom seemed to enjoy him for himself, rather than for what he had accomplished. Tim viewed both his parents as persons who had been hurt and disappointed in life and whose major concern in parenting was to be sure that their children would not be as vulnerable to hurt as they had been. He put this view of his parents together with a description of his move from being a fat eighth-grader, who "couldn't make the first cut" on the basketball team, to the president of his class in high school, who dated the right girls and did all that was possible to be admired.

One wonders, as did the pastor, whether it is possible for a person like Tim to learn to care and to be cared for when so much seems to depend on protecting oneself from hurt. Is it possible for Tim to make a commitment to another woman, when his prior commitment seems now to have been so ill-conceived and destructive? It seems important to seek a more theoretical understanding of this fear of commitment, which appears in Tim and so many other men today. Like Tim, many men feel that they have already tried intimacy and failed; therefore, they must avoid it in the future. We have found the work of Lillian Rubin helpful in addressing this problem.

Rubin bases her theory of male-female intimacy on psychoanalytic object relations theory and the work of sociologist Nancy Chodorow[4] and psychologist Dorothy Dinnerstein.[5] Rubin sees some of the important differences between males and females, with respect to commitment and caring, in relation to the fact that in most cultures only women mother. Because the mother is the primary caregiver, it is she "with whom we make our first attachment, she with whom we form a symbiotic bond . . . whether a girl or a boy, it is a woman who is the object of our most profound attachment, a woman who becomes our first loved other." As the child leaves the mother's arms, the period of separation and individuation comes into flower. It is a time when "I" and "you" become more clearly distinguishable in the child. It is the time when, if there is what D. W. Winnicott has called "good enough mothering," the child learns to deal with the real fact of separation with enough security that separation is not identified with abandonment. Long after "the conflict between our need for separation and our desire for unity has left center stage," says Rubin, "these issues will live inside us to influence the next act."[6]

In adulthood, when we find ourselves in an intimate relationship, we experience again

> those early struggles around separation and unity—the conflict with wanting to be one with another and the desire for an independent, autonomous self. . . . Of course, as adults we know there's no return to the old symbiotic union. . . . But the child within feels as if this were still the reality . . . the same child who had to separate from mother now withdraws in fear—not just from his wife's expectation of connection but from the seemingly

inexhaustible well of his own dependent wishes and needs that this new relationship threatens to reawaken. (*Intimate Strangers*, pp. 52-53)

The important point in Rubin's discussion for us is her differentiation of the ways in which males and females struggle with the issues of separation and gender identity. Because they are the same sex, it is more difficult for a girl to separate from her mother, "harder for her or her mother to know where one ends and the other begins." With respect to gender identity—the knowledge that says "I am a girl" or "I am a boy"—"the identity between mother and daughter is a help not a hindrance." For a boy, it is a more difficult and complicated issue. In order to identify with his maleness, a boy must renounce his connection "with the first person outside self to be internalized into his inner psychic world." Although they happen at different times, "identification and attachment are so closely linked that the child can't give up one without an assault on the other." Attachment to the mother becomes ambivalent. "He still needs her, but he can't be certain anymore that she will be there, that she can be trusted."[7]

Rubin sees in this process the seeds of the male put-down of women and of the fear that so many men have of being controlled by women. A male child who finds himself "pressed to reject so powerful an inner presence as mother has been in his early life" can live "with it only by disempowering her—by convincing himself that she's a weak and puny creature whose lack of maleness must doom her forever to a subordinate and contemptible place in the world." A girl, in contrast, "never has to separate herself as completely and irrevocably as a boy must." The sameness of her sex with the mother makes the problem of gender identity easier for the girl, whereas the problem of separating is harder. Because a girl never has to separate herself so completely and irrevocably as a boy must, "she experiences herself always as more continuous with another . . . she will preserve the capacity, born in the early symbiotic union, for participating in another's life, for sensing another's emotional states almost as if they were her own—the capacity that, in an adult, we call empathy."[8]

For a woman, the sameness with mother, and the continuity of identification it permits, enables the development of empathic capacity, whereas for a man, "Difference and discontinuity dominate the early developmental period and, therefore disable the growth of these same qualities."

> For women, the issue of maintaining separation dominates; for men, it's sustaining unity that's so difficult—problems that make themselves felt around every important issue in a marriage, from the conflicts we experience around intimacy and dependency to the way we parent our children. (*Intimate Strangers,* pp. 63-64)

We touch on Rubin's theory again in our chapter on marriage. One of the strengths of her formulation, from our point of view, is that it is not a deviation from mainline psychological theory but an expression of it. Using psychoanalytic object relations theory, she interprets an insufficiently explored cultural fact: that in a vast majority of cases and cultures, it is the female who mothers and who is the responsible and experienced carer. That fact has significant effects on the different ways in which males and females form their sexual identities and separate from the parental generation, particularly the prime figure in that generation—the mother. The issues of sexual identity—who one is sexually and how he or she expresses it—and of separation and attachment are obviously not only developmental issues of the past, but they are also involved in one's intimate relationships with the present generation.

Samuel Osherson's study *Finding Our Fathers: The Unfinished Business of Manhood* complements Rubin's work. According to Osherson, men don't have an opportunity as boys to grieve over the loss of their mothers and to complete the process of separation and individuation from women. The result of the boy's separation-individuation struggle is "That men carry about as adults a burden of vulnerability, dependency, or emptiness within themselves, still grieving, reliving a time when going to mother for help as they wanted to was inappropriate, and they wouldn't or couldn't go to father with the confusion, anger, or sadness they felt."[9]

Rubin and Osherson provide valuable perspectives for understanding Tim's struggle with intimacy and realizing that it is similar to that of many men in our culture. Another point of view that also relates the struggles of our own generation with our relationship to the generation before is that of Boszormenyi-Nagy,[10] who describes how parents attempt to correct in the next generation deficits they experienced in their own. Tim's parents, who received a legacy of pain and personal injury due to what they perceived as their own vulnerability, sought to create a toughness in their children, which would insulate them from experiencing what their parents had. Tim had attempted to carry out that official family legacy in his life; but as the pastor's own relationship with Tim deepened, Tim's own caring side and that of his father began to emerge.

The pastor first saw it when he asked Tim about his relationship with his former counselor. Although Tim described what he had received in terms of what he had learned about himself, it was evident from the way he talked about his counselor that he felt that the counselor genuinely cared for him. Tim acknowledged how much that relationship—not just what he had learned—had meant to him. Somewhere in the process of this discovery, the pastor commented:

Pastor: It sounds to me as if you enjoy being special to somebody, and it's clear that you felt that Len (the counselor) genuinely liked you in spite of what a failure you had been.

Tim: (smiling) It seems like that. I called him the last time I was in town, and he really sounded like he was glad to hear from me.

Pastor: I'll work as hard as I can to be sure that that never happens to me, but you can never tell. There may be something about you that's lovable in spite of all the ways you've screwed up your life. I wonder where you got that. Surely, not from your parents.

Tim: Well, I don't know. My father never wanted us to see it. He kept all his tenderness hidden, but I saw him go out of his way again and again to keep from having to fire someone. He covered for his men and tried to help them, but he never talked about that. I discovered it while listening to him talk to them on the phone.

Pastor: Well, I hope no one ever discovers it in you.

The pastor's sarcasm is obviously a means of indirect support and affirmation of Tim's caring side. Direct support or exhortation to do what is desired are seldom as effective as an indirectness that suggests that the counselee be what he or she has actually been perceived to be by the counselor rather than attempt conformity to an impossible goal. Tim's search for his father's tenderness and his own resonates with Osherson's concept of "healing the wounded father." "For many men," Osherson says, "the process of exploring their fathers' lives, empathizing with their pain, gets blocked. They may be put back in touch with their anger at what they didn't get and the wish to be taken care of by a perfect father who has all the answers for them. In describing his own experience Osherson says,

> When I realized how much of my life I had spent distancing my father, feeling angry at and scared of him, the feeling led directly to a wish to hold him that shocked and scared me. . . But when we imagine holding and caring for our fathers and letting them do so for us, we are freeing our own ability to hold and care for others. (*Finding Our Fathers*, pp. 182-84)

Tim's struggle with commitment, caring, and intimacy was facilitated by his relationship with the pastor, by his search to rediscover his father, and—more directly—by Toni's decision to give him an ultimatum about their relationship. She finally was able to risk losing Tim, telling him that if their relationship were to continue, Tim would have to get over his resistance to marriage and get on with it. Tim shared his panic and fear with the pastor, but soon decided that he was willing to risk marriage again, in spite of all the things that weren't perfect about Toni.

Pastor: What happened? You've been running from this for a couple of years. Why did you give in?
Tim: I got sick.
Pastor: (laughs) You had to get sick to agree to marry her?
Tim: (also laughs) It's not as bad as that sounds. While you were out of town, I got the worse case of flu I have ever had, and Toni took care of me. And then she got it, and I took care of her.
Pastor: If I were I a bit more biblical in my thinking, it would look to me as if the Lord struck you down to teach you something.

Tim:	I've got no particular problem with that. I did learn something.
Pastor:	It's pretty useful to discover you're human even if it takes 'til you're forty to do it. How does it feel to know that you're a caring person?
Tim:	I like it.

As the reader may suspect, or know from experience or from what we have said previously, Tim's decision to marry Toni stirred his desire to be closer to his father. In the process of telling his parents about the forthcoming marriage, which he believed they did not feel was a good enough one for him, Tim confronted his father with the father's failure to bless him with his approval throughout his life. Although his father acted as if he didn't understand, Tim was proud of his willingness to face the issue and indicated his commitment to keep at it.

Pastor:	I doubt if you can ever get all you want, but you seem to have discovered how important it is to you to admit you're hungry. It appears to me that you've spent most of your life trying to hide that.
Tim:	It's funny. After I got over worrying about trying to talk to him, it felt good to tell him what I was feeling.
Pastor:	I suspect that you'll find that the same thing will apply to your relationship to Toni. If you've over some of your fear of being trapped by her, you can probably risk letting her know more and more of who you are.

Some of Tim's struggle with commitment and recommitment can be clarified if we return to some of the insights of Margaret Farley and compare them with the understanding of loyalty in Ivan Boszormenyi-Nagy.

One of Farley's key concepts for discussing commitment is "framework." We expect, she says, that human relationships "be governed by certain norms or ethical principles—principles of justice. Frameworks for commitment, then, ought to be subject to norms of justice . . . the frameworks, the *laws* of commitment need to accord with principles like respect for persons, like equality and mutuality and equitable sharing."[11] If "what makes it impossible to go on in a commitment-relationship is the particular framework that structures the relationship, then restructuring—even radical restructuring—may restore possibility." Quite often, just considering making the practical change that seems necessary in the framework of a commitment opens up a "new hope for faithfulness."[12]

Tim's gradual realization that he could commit himself to an intimate relationship involved a change in that relationship's framework. The framework with which he began his relationship with Toni was very similar to the one inherited from his relationship to Tanya, and he had promised himself that he was not going to become involved in the same thing again. Becoming genuinely and hopefully committed to Toni involved a reframing of what commitment meant to him along with gaining a more realistic understanding of his dependency and his ability to care and to be cared for.

Farley describes theoretically what appears to us to have happened to Tim. He was able to discern what was essential to his commitment to love another and what was accidental to it. Frameworks take their meaning and value from the love they structure and mediate. "A just love, committed unconditionally, may require that its framework be lived to the end; but it may also require that its framework be changed."[13] Even if we decide that we are "justified in changing the framework of a commitment, the love underlying that framework still obligates in some way." The realization of this, not theoretically but experientially, allowed Tim to recommit himself. His experience in life and in his pastoral counseling had convinced him that he could negotiate a change in the conditions or framework of his commitments without violating them.

According to Farley, we almost always

> embody our love in a form that will make ongoing demands upon us and allow us to share the lives of those whom we love. . . . Commitments to frameworks are all relative to the love they are meant to serve. As relative, they may be essential to the love, or not. Our faithfulness depends on our discernment of the essential or nonessential connection of the frameworks to the love. (*Personal Commitments*, pp. 124-25)

Another important factor in commitment, which she emphasizes, is memory. "Forgetfulness," says Farley, "is a way of slipping into death. Remembering is a way of growing into vision and love. Paradoxically, it is remembering that can give us a future." Her point is strongly confirmed by our clinical experience. Consistent with our discussion of generational care in the first chapter, Farley emphasizes the importance of time as an issue in relationships. When "the prophets of Israel called the people to remember the past—the promises made to them and their response—they thereby called them to remember 'who you are.' " This kind of remembering

> includes the possibility of seeing new meaning in the past as it unfolds in the present. If we are not to be 'unhitched' from our commitments, the secret is to hold together our past and our future, but to do so in a way that does not leave us with something static and unchanging. Only if we are open to new meanings for the past can we risk flexibility in our expectations of the future. (*Personal Commitments*, p. 57)

Although it may involve many other things, pastoral counseling is a process of remembering. Farley has described what we have experienced with Tim and others in the counseling process: the discovery that commitment can expand, as well as diminish, possibilities.

THE PLACE OF LOYALTY

Having presented some of Margaret Farley's very valuable understanding of personal commitments, it seems important to return to our earlier distinction between commitment and loyalty and develop our understanding of the latter. We have identified commitment with relationships made to persons within one's own generation, relationships that are made by choice and that involve, or should involve, dependency as a choice rather than as a part of the structure of the relationship. Loyalty, in contrast, involves relationships that are not by choice, that are intergenerational or involve some authority dimension, that are by kinship or other circumstance, and that involve the dependency of one person on another as a part of the relationship structure. Although the distinction we have made between the two terms does not come from Ivan Boszormenyi-Nagy, his work is so much identified with the concept of loyalty that some discussion of his understanding of it is essential for the relationship we are attempting to clarify.

Patton, in his work on human forgiveness,[14] uses Boszormenyi-Nagy's work to interpret the specialness of family relationships: why the rage at personal injury by a family member is so intense and why the defenses erected to prevent further injury are so powerful.

Boszormenyi-Nagy is perhaps the most important psychological contributor to the generational understanding of the family, and what we attempt to present from a theological perspective is both directly and indirectly dependent on his work. In their recent volume, Boszormenyi-Nagy and Krasner used the term *context* for "the dynamic and ethical interconnectedness—past, present, and future—that exists among people whose very being has significance for each other." The "context" involves the "consequences that flow from person to person, from generation to generation, and from one successive system to its successive system."

Boszormenyi-Nagy and his associates have tried to integrate historical and systemic understanding of the family, insisting that the consequences of the past "are decisively influential, perhaps even irreversible, but not rigidly *predetermining,* circular, or homeostatic." In affirming the importance of the "fact of personal accountability for relational consequences" or "the *willingness to care,*" Boszormenyi-Nagy's theory seems close to our theological norm for the family: the care of our generations. Moreover, his description of the aim of contextual therapy—making *"interventions based on the understanding of the fundamental connections between formative and all later relationships"*—seems significantly related to some of the more important goals of pastoral counseling. The contextual approach, he says, "asks its therapists to help clients order their life priorities," which are "inseparable from responsibility for perspective consequences, especially for posterity"[15] or, in the terminology of this book, "caring for the generation that comes after you."

Boszormenyi-Nagy's values are expressed explicitly throughout both of his books, but is more strongly and, perhaps, more ideologically, stated in *Between Give and Take.* The following far-reaching statements are illustrative of this:

> Self-sustaining continuity of relationship is a more valid and specific goal of therapeutic intervention than is the simpler goal of change. (p. 14)
>
> Individual freedom is most effectively won through a considera-

tion of balances of fairness between the self and all of the significant others with whom the self is in relationship. (p. 16)

Contextually, marital relationship may often be in the focus of therapy, but never without regard for the inclusion of the prospects of the parent-child ledgers, or without responsible caring about consequences for posterity. (p. 89)

Defining the concept of "ledger" can quickly provide further insight into Boszormenyi-Nagy's theory of the family. "Each person," he says, "maintains a bookkeeping of his perception of the balances of past, present, and future give-and-take. What has been 'invested' into the system and what has been withdrawn in the form of support received or one's exploitive use of others remains written into the invisible account of obligations."[16] This is the ledger in which familial accounts are kept. To understand a family, nothing is more important than to know who are bound together in loyalty and what loyalty means to each of them and to be aware that, through the course of life, vertical loyalty commitments clash with horizontal ones. "Until the Post-Victorian age," according to Boszormenyi-Nagy, "the issues of family loyalty were largely unformulated because they were taken for granted. Our age, on the other hand, denies these issues with the help of the myths of individual material success and endless struggle against the threat of authority."[17] What is needed is a flexibility that incorporates the new loyalty toward one's mate and children into the existing fabric of the larger family system.

The expression of loyalty and the integration of horizontal and vertical concerns is expressed by Boszormenyi-Nagy under the rubric of care and in relation to the parent-child model.

Adequate parenting is one premise of a transgenerational order of being. Repaying parental care is another. Since it can only be accomplished through giving to the next generation, the direction and criteria of repayment between parent and child can only be grasped through a consideration of at least three generations. . . . Simply put, a person receives from his past and his parents, and gives through his children and his future. . . . Acts of caring between people are inevitably private and personal. They are also motivated by the actual consequences that receiving care implies the obligation to offer care. (*Between Give and Take*, p. 100)

The therapeutic effort toward rebalancing familial accounts involves, among other things, rehabilitating family members' painful and shameful images of their parents. "We have not," Boszormenyi-Nagy says, "seen anyone benefit from a therapeutic outcome in which a person only faces, realizes, and expresses his contempt and disaffection towards his parents. In our experience this is a losing game for everyone concerned."[18] Therapy involves each family member, exploring his or her developmental past, which, in effect, allows other members to understand and experience him or her as a person, not just as a parent, mother, or wife. It attempts to facilitate the discovery of the other's common humanness or how—as Harry Stack Sullivan, whose theories of the 40s contributed to the family therapy of the 60s, might have put it—family members are "more alike than otherwise." Such a discovery, in Boszormenyi-Nagy's terms, moves toward rebalancing the ledger and family members' horizontal and vertical relationships.

To demonstrate what he means by family loyalty, Boszormenyi-Nagy reinterprets the meaning of the fifth commandment:

> The ultimate measure of an offspring's honor for his or her parents has to do neither with having to submit to parental values nor having to rebel against them. Filial respect for the past is most creatively embodied in a person's entitlement to take what has been given in the past, assess its merit, and, finally, recast it into more effective modes of offering future care. (*Between Give and Take*, p. 146)

Viewed from our theological perspective on the family, the most striking thing about the work of Boszormenyi-Nagy and his associates is the set of values that he openly embraces and advocates. He affirms the special and inescapable nature of the parent-child and child-parent relationships in a world that tends to see all relationships as if they were the same. It is built into the ontology, or structure, of things to insist on balance and fairness when all evidence seems to point the other way. Moreover, there is no such thing as a one or two generation family. Whatever the composition of our household, all of us live with at least three generational assumptions about family life. Not only *can* you go home again, but you *must*. Jacob must seek the blessing from Isaac whatever the cost.

For both Shelly and Tim there was a high cost, but each, in

different ways, received a blessing. Shelly's blessing can most easily be interpreted in terms of the concept of differentiating her self from her family of origin; however, that concept, though central, seems inadequate to interpret all that was going on. She was inescapably caught in her loyalty to her family and unable to make a commitment to persons in her own generation, with whom she had a choice about relationship. Her efforts toward differentiation led her to a new understanding of loyalty, one which, in terms of Boszormenyi-Nagy's theory, involved freedom won through a consideration of balances of fairness between herself and the significant others in her extended family. She was able to take what had been given in the past, assess its merit, and begin to recast it into more effective modes of offering future care. She began to deal realistically with her loyalties and thus prepared herself for making a commitment.

Although Tim was almost twenty years older than Shelly, he gained a similar blessing. His situation was complicated by a prior marriage. Shame over his failure in it was complicated by similar shame over a failure in his career. He was extremely anxious about avoiding another mistake. Commitment seemed to him to be a trap. Becoming able to enjoy his dependence in his present counseling and acknowledging that that was what had been most meaningful in his prior counseling paved the way for the insight achieved during his "getting sick." Dependency, at this point in his life, was not fatal. It could be chosen, talked about, and enjoyed. On a more cognitive level, he was able to make a distinction between commitment and loyalty. In making a marital commitment to a member of his own generation, he was not obliged to carry out the relationships of the past. As Farley has suggested, although we embody our love in a form that will make ongoing demands of us and allow us to share the lives of those we love, the frameworks for our commitments are relative. Our faithfulness depends not so much on maintaining loyalty to what was said and done in the past as discerning the essential and nonessential in the continuing relationship to and the choice of that person in the present.

In this chapter on caring for our generations as an individual, we have been primarily concerned with the issues of separation and commitment. Whether they are not the most important issues in our caring as individuals, they are the ones we meet most often in our clinical practice. As we noted earlier, the other major issue affecting relational life is the fact of loss, which affects every structure of family living. (We have chosen to deal with it in chapter 6, which is concerned primarily with the process of separation and divorce but also with other major losses in our lives.) In that context, we deal further with the issues of commitment and loyalty as they are related to the marriage relationship and to the relationship between parents and children.

We have, in this chapter, only indirectly addressed what we have called the "challenges to the family," symbolized in the question: Who are my mother and brothers?—the relation of care of self to care of others, the relation of kin and friend, and the relation of our family and work life. All three of these issues can be seen in the stories of Shelly and Tim, and they will reappear in the following chapters. We move now, however, to examine generational care as it appears in the preparation that the church offers for marriage and remarriage: the ministry that has traditionally been called premarital counseling or guidance.

NOTES

1. Murray Bowen, "Toward the Differentiation of the Self in One's Family of Origin." *Family Therapy and Clinical Practice* (Northvale, N.J.: Aronson, 1978), pp. 529-47.

2. Jeannette R. Kramer, *Family Interfaces: Transgenerational Patterns* (New York: Brunner/Mazel, 1985), pp. 327-39.

3. Margaret A. Farley, *Personal Commitments* (New York: Harper, 1986), pp. 17-19.

4. Nancy Chodorow, *The Reproduction of Mothering: Psychoanalysis and the Sociology of Gender* (Berkeley: University of California Press, 1978).

5. Dorothy Dinnerstein, *The Mermaid and the Minotaur: Sexual Arrangements and the Human Malaise* (New York: Harper, 1976).

6. Lillian B. Rubin, *Intimate Strangers: Men and Women Together* (New York: Harper, 1983), pp. 50, 52.

7. Ibid., pp. 54-56.

8. Ibid., pp. 57-79.

9. Samuel Osherson, *Finding Our Fathers: The Unfinished Business of Manhood* (New York: The Free Press, 1986), p. 7.

10. Ivan Boszormenyi-Nagy and G. M. Spark, *Invisible Loyalties* (New York: Harper, 1973); and Ivan Boszormenyi-Nagy and B. R. Krasner, *Between Give and Take: A Clinical Guide to Contextual Therapy* (New York: Brunner/Mazel, 1986).

11. Farley, *Personal Commitments*, pp. 36-37.

12. Ibid., p. 90.

13. Ibid., p. 99.

14. John Patton, *Is Human Forgiveness Possible?* (Nashville: Abingdon Press, 1985).
15. Boszormenyi-Nagy and Krasner, *Between Give and Take*, pp. 8-10.
16. Ibid., pp. 38-40.
17. Boszormenyi-Nagy and Spark, *Invisible Loyalties*, p. 149.
18. Ibid., p. 95.

CHAPTER THREE

GENERATIONAL CARE PRIOR TO MARRIAGE AND REMARRIAGE

And Jacob served seven years for Rachel; and they seemed unto him but a few days, for the love he had to her. (Genesis 29:20 KJV)

Preparation for marriage has taken many forms. Jacob's service to Laban is only one of them. Although this ancient story has far different assumptions about marriage preparation than what we have today, if we look at it symbolically, instead of literally, it may have more to say to us than we might expect. The social situation in which we live has radically changed, but the basic questions a couple needs to consider prior to marriage are not really so different: What must I know prior to this marriage? What must I do? At times, the church and its clergy have been very definite and clear about how to answer these questions. At other times, there has been a great deal of uncertainty and confusion about them. Our time appears to be more like the latter.

SOME RECENT HISTORY

Our attempt to describe premarital care and counseling in the light of a Christian anthropology of care is clearly different from the way this ministry has been practiced in recent years. *Premarital counseling,* the most common name for this ministry, most often involves what a pastor does prior to officiating at a wedding. Actually, the time immediately prior to the marriage, when most couples receive premarital pastoral care, is likely to be a time of denial of any problems at all in the relationship and, therefore, is a highly inappropriate time for "counseling," a concept that presupposes awareness of "having a problem." Premarital pastoral care may also refer to consultation that is offered by a pastor to couples who are concerned about the way their relationship is developing.

It appears to us that premarital pastoral care has developed more out of the church's anxiety about the apparent instability of the institution of marriage than out of a pastoral concern for individuals. In fact, it might not be going too far to suggest that the identification of premarital guidance as "counseling" may be attributed to the church's attempt to locate the problem of marriage in the couple rather than in its own view of marriage or effectiveness in blessing it.

During much of the first half of this century, the role of the pastor in premarital work was understood as judging the fitness of the couple for marriage in relation to the church's understanding of impediments to a valid marriage, such as too close a degree of kinship, failure in a prior marriage, and significant differences in religious background and commitment. More recently, most Christian communions have deemphasized this judgment role in favor of a teaching role that emphasizes preparation for marriage. In spite of this change of emphasis, however, some judgment on the part of the pastor about the fitness of the couple seems to be inevitable. Built into both the legal and ecclesiastical rituals that take place in relation to a marriage are judgments of the legal, physical, and spiritual fitness of the couple for marriage. Some kind of judgment about the couple by the pastor, therefore, is implied whether it is emphasized. Moreover, the minister who offers premarital guidance in connection with his or her performance of a marriage ceremony is, in the performance of that ceremony, making a statement about the church's view of what marriage is, and it is part of the minister's responsibility to make an accurate and appropriate statement.

As an accepted form of ministry, premarital counseling had its beginning in the United States during the 1920s. Premarital counseling literature, prior to 1950, encouraged ministers to believe that if they did effective premarital work, the divorce rate would drop dramatically. Although this concern diminished in later literature, there seems to have been a continued assumption that effective premarital care, coupled with faithful church attendance, could help reduce the divorce rate. The procedure that ministers were to follow was largely instruction, for lack of information was assumed to be a couple's major problem.[1]

A noticeable shift in the emphasis of the premarital guidance literature occurred during the decade of the 1950s due to the strong influence of pastoral psychology, with its heavy emphasis on counseling and psychotherapy. Premarital pastoral care began to focus more on the nature of the relationship that marriage involved rather than on information necessary for a successful marriage. Premarriage ministry was to help a couple achieve an intense interpersonal involvement and exchange through an open and free communication of feelings. The major purpose for meeting with couples was to prepare them for marriage by anticipating various aspects of the relationship. The assumption seems to have been that with proper premarital counseling—that is, if the pastor provided the right information in the right way, and if the couple made sufficient effort, it should be possible to move in the direction of perfecting the marriage and therefore divorces would be reduced.[2]

In our judgment, the view of human nature that is implicit in most twentieth-century premarital counseling literature has tended toward a kind of theological optimism and works righteousness, holding a somewhat romanticized view of marriage as a structure unaffected by sin and human limitations. In contrast to this, we see the function of premarital guidance, like the human nature with which it must deal, as considerably more limited. It involves, quite simply, assisting a couple in: (1) surfacing assumptions about themselves, their families of origin, and the religious community which—at least through the minister—they are asking to bless their marriage and (2) developing a significant relationship with the minister and, it is hoped, with the religious community that he or she represents.

We do not disagree with the predominant understanding of the pastor's role in premarital care as a teaching one. As we interpret it, however, it does not, as many of the premarriage manuals suggest, involve instructing the couple on what they should know and do in order to be appropriately intimate with each other and thus avoid divorce. The pastor's teaching role is both interpretive, in the sense of reviewing the data of the couple's lives and interpreting them from a perspective of generational caring, and consultative, in that the acceptance of the pastor's way of viewing life and relationships is clearly not required. It may be accepted, rejected, or perhaps deferred for use until a later time. In stating that the pastor functions in premarital guidance in an interpretive and consultative way, we are suggesting that the traditional judgment by the pastor of the couple's fitness for marriage should be shared by the pastor with the couple. The observations the pastor makes should be presented in such a way that the couple can incorporate them into the already existing judgments that they are making about each other and about the church they have asked to bless their marriage.

The type of interpretation and consultation offered by the pastor is determined first of all by whether the pastor offering the premarital guidance is also officiating at the marriage ceremony. If the pastor is performing the ceremony, he or she has as much responsibility for accurately representing the church as for offering consultation to the couple about themselves. If premarital guidance is being offered apart from officiating at the ceremony, then the situation has been defined as focusing upon the couple's concerns in judging the appropriateness of their intention to marry each other.

We believe that the structure for premarital care, which we present later in this chapter, can be adapted for use both by the minister who offers premarital guidance in connection with performing marriages and for the minister who, apart from involvement in the marriage ceremony, consults with couples who are aware of some problem in their relationship. In each case, the pastor will be involved with an interpretation of what marriage is and where the couple is in relation to it. In the case of the parish minister who is involved with the way a particular church expresses its understanding of marriage in its ritual practices, the interpretation of the church's views will necessarily be more explicit, acquainting the couple with a Christian view of marriage as well as helping them marry each other. This is not a demand for conformity to certain beliefs, but it is at least an introduction to Christian understanding. For the premarital counselor who consults with a couple about their relationship, the views of the church appear more implicitly in his or her assumptions about what is normative for marriage and, therefore, for a good relationship.

The specific issues to be addressed within the structure for premarital interviews we propose are: (1) the anxiety and ambiguity of marital choice; (2) care for the prior generation, experienced both as the parental church and as the couple's families of origin, by understanding their traditions and hidden agendas; (3) care for the present generation and the development of peer relationships in love and work; (4) care for the future generation by confronting the issue of how they will contribute separately and together to those who come after them.

THE ANXIETY AND AMBIGUITY OF MARITAL CHOICE

Our beginning this chapter with the story of Jacob's premarital preparation is not to suggest that our approach to this topic has scriptural warrant. We are simply asserting that the ancient story can still be a powerful symbol for the modern struggle to marry the "right person." Despite radical cultural differences between our times and biblical times, there are common concerns about the family that extend through all generations of human beings. It is not difficult to imagine, for example, some of those in unhappy marriages today reflecting on Jacob's story and wondering with Jacob, "How might I have avoided marrying Leah?"

The modern Leah can be of either sex. In fact, as pastoral counselors, we have more frequently heard some version of that question from women than from men. It was a question that concerned both Mary and Milo. Engaged for almost a year, they were aware of a problem in their relationship. During Mary's initial telephone call, the pastor had set the structure for what he called a premarital evaluation. He indicated that his usual practice was to have two sessions with the couple together, a session with each person separately, and finally a feed-back session together. After the feed-back, there would be no further couple sessions, but each would have the option of individual counseling if they wished it.

The covert or overt agenda for those who consult the pastor for premarital guidance is how "to avoid marrying Leah." If the agenda is only covert, the couple's concern is that the church may somehow offer more help in reducing marital risk than may a secular official. If, as in the case of Mary and Milo, they are aware of a problem, behind their concern is the anxiety about possibly making a grave mistake. Unless the pastor, for some personal reason, has a similar anxiety—that he or she must officiate a successful marriage or damage his or the church's effectiveness, he or she comes to the couple with a quite different agenda: (1) providing a relationship in which they can experience being cared for and (2) communicating to them the ways he or she experiences them as persons called to care for their generations.

Mary and Milo stated that they had come to the pastoral counseling center because of a relationship problem. Central to each of their concerns was the anxiety of their choice of each other, or, to use the symbol from our biblical story, a dread that, left to their own devices, they might "marry Leah instead of Rachel." One of the problems of marital choice today is that it appears to involve so much responsibility. In the days of family arranged marriages, there was someone else to blame if things went badly. The apparent freedom offered couples today to make their own choices is a dreadful one. So little is arranged by others that everything appears to rest on the adequacy of the couples' choice. In a time of sexual freedom and extensive career preparation, a time when the determinisms of family expectations and sexual and social needs are less pressing, few people have to get married. Instead, they have to choose to.

This choice is often made more difficult by the couple's feeling that they really know too much about each other. The anticipation of satisfaction through further intimacy may have been lost. Sexual freedom can complicate life as well as simplify it. The sexually experienced couple know enough about each other that it is difficult to anticipate how marriage can make anything better. In the case of a remarriage, a person often knows so much about what can go wrong and how bad it can be that the positive features of marriage are obscured. Most couples need help in accepting the human paradox, that knowing a great deal about another in a relationship does not resolve the ambiguity in the relationship. Instead they tend to be involved in a kind of idealistic perfectionism that suggests that if we can't make the relationship perfect, we need to find another one that is. The exercise of choice in selecting a mate involves the toleration of a great deal of anxiety and learning to live with the ambiguity and imperfectability of human relationships. A major function of premarital pastoral care and counseling, therefore, is relieving some of this anxiety through a relationship with a parental figure who has nothing at stake in the success of the marriage. The pastoral counselor is one who can say matter of factly, "You seem surprised and disappointed that there's something wrong with your relationship." In so doing, the counselor suggests some of the natural ambiguity in human relationships.

In Mary and Milo's situation, Mary was anxious about Milo's apparent need for power and his materialistic tendencies. Milo, on the other hand, described himself as enjoying the good things of life and said that he felt Mary disapproved of him. As the pastoral counselor listened to each of them in their first hour together, it appeared that Milo was right. Mary did disapprove. She and Milo had been going together a year and a half, and, somewhat to her surprise, Mary felt let down. She thought she had found the perfect man for her. She had "won out" over several competitors for Milo, but now she felt disappointed and worried about her choice. He did not seem capable of sharing the kind of life she wanted to have.

As Mary and Milo talked about each other and their relationship, they both agreed that he was more comfortable with things as they were than she was. Everything seemed to have come more easily to him, while she was a striver—doing well but not quite comfortable when she wasn't working for something. She worried more about what people thought about her than did Milo. She got depressed more easily and worried that he was taking things too lightly. Sexually, "just once is enough for him," but Mary wanted more. It is not clear, however, that she was seeking only sexual satisfaction. She seemed to be looking for an intimacy she didn't have, while Milo seemed irritatingly satisfied with the way things are.

These patterns in their relationship and their individual personalities emerged rather quickly when the pastor invited them to talk about why they had come and what they wanted. Only occasionally did he have to ask for a story or incident to illustrate the generalization being made. Although Mary took the lead in describing her discomfort, Milo was able to acknowledge his concern about Mary's "extremes"—the intensity of her feelings and the way she seemed to criticize his friends. Mary seemed to have a significantly greater capacity to support and almost seemed to enjoy it when Milo was "down." Milo, on the other hand, became impatient with her depression and wanted to cheer her up or get away from her.

What we are discussing here are the things that rapidly emerge in the couples who, aware of a problem, come for counseling. These are the same things that are not talked about directly and are seldom acknowledged by the couples who come to a parish minister to get married. Moreover, we believe that the minister has no responsibility for trying to get a couple to talk about such things unless they want to; they can see all that they are ready to see by looking at their respective families of origin and the relational patterns exhibited there. In order to deal with the resistance to looking at their own relationship, which appears in couples "just coming to be married," and to avoid accentuating the anxiety of the "problem aware couples," the pastor moves rather soon in her or his premarital work to the couple's view of their prior generation.

CARING FOR THE PRIOR GENERATION: THE FAMILIES OF ORIGIN

In one of the most helpful documents in premarital pastoral care literature, Kenneth Mitchell and Herbert Anderson insist that "you must leave before you can cleave."[3] They argue that the most important task of premarital care is assisting the couple in appropriate disengagement from their families of origin. They note what many pastors, even those most intent on "doing counseling," have seen for years: Couples whose primary concern is just to do what they have to do to be married in the church are usually reluctant to examine their own relationship. Their discussing their families of origin, according to Mitchell and Anderson, is less likely to produce resistance and more likely to yield fruitful results.

The fruitful results we have seen from examining the relationships and patterns of the prior generation are bringing to the surface assumptions about what marriage is and what the couple's particular marriage is likely to be. Adapting for their purposes the work of family system theorists such as Bowen and Framo,[4] Mitchell and Anderson describe their family system approach to premarital pastoral care and suggest a variety of methods for implementing it—for example, discussion of family myths and traditions as well as the roles of various family members and the explicit and implicit rules for family behavior in the respective families. Discussing Murray Bowen's concept of triangles and some of the specific triangles in the families of origin of the couple is another way of involving a couple in an examination of the way family systems function. (See C. Margaret Hall, The Bowen Family Theory and Its Uses [Northvale, N.J.: Aronson, 1981].) A method we have used for this is asking couples to write or tell a story about the past—for example, the myth of the parents' marriage or some other marriage that is significant to the couple. The discussion of such stories can be significantly revealing of assumptions about marriage and the family without being directly critical of the couples' present relationship. (See Kramer in the previous chapter for further ideas to facilitate discussion of the families of origin.)

More important to us than direct facilitation of separation from the families of origin is discerning the patterns of care that exist or existed in the prior generation. How did the various members of the couples' families care for one another? What kind of expectations about care and loyalty were generated? How may the expectations of the prior generation conflict with the expectations of intimacy with one's intended spouse? What negative and positive images of caring in the marriage relationship does the couple have? Much of this can be elicited through the discussion of a genogram or detailed family history, whichever seems more congenial with the pastor's way of structuring a conversation. Most important to remember is that this is not simply gathering information for information's sake but enabling the couple to see how influential the parental generation is in their relationship to each other. We believe that this kind of approach can open up possibilities for the care of the prior generation, rather than unconscious acting out of the "invisible loyalties" we mentioned in the previous chapter.

CARING FOR THE PRIOR GENERATION: THE CHURCH THAT BLESSES MARRIAGE

The church, particularly its tradition, is part of the prior generation for the couple considering marriage. Their being married in or by the church, or even seeking *pastoral* counseling, appropriately involves the couple in caring through an understanding of the parental generation of the church they are involved in caring for the parental generation of their families. To claim the church's blessing for a Christian family requires caring enough to understand some of the ways the church has struggled with family issues in trying to make the faith relevant to life. It seems essential, therefore, whether the pastor is directly involved in interpreting the meaning of the church's rituals, to be aware of the various views of marriage, which have influenced the couple's coming to the pastor and church for its blessing. It is also important for the pastor to be aware of assumptions influencing the way he or she gives that blessing.

We do not propose to survey here the vast literature on the Christian family but to find a means of ordering some of the data that consciously or unconsciously influence how we offer premarital pastoral care and counseling. William Johnson Everett's book *Blessed Be the Bond* is quite helpful for our purposes. According to Everett, the churches' attention to a Christian understanding of marriage "has either dwelt in the lofty ideals derived from faith positions or enthusiastically grabbed onto whatever therapeutic device might seem to help people struggle through their difficulties."[5] With him, we are concerned with avoiding both.

Everett goes on to describe Christianity's view of the family as basically ambivalent, on the one hand honoring it, on the other, seeing it as an impediment to the holy life. "Nature and grace point to two different vantage points for approaching marriage. Each Christian tradition "finds its own way of relating the two." He identifies four major Christian options in which the issues of nature and grace in marriage are worked out: sacrament, vocation, covenant and communion.[6] We present them briefly, recognizing that in doing so we do some injustice to each.

The *sacramental* view grounds the social and ecclesial institution of marriage in the basic structure of life lived as faith. This view emphasizes God's grace, working through nature and marriage as an order of creation. It is more concerned with the integrity of the symbol than with the justice of relationships. It places greater emphasis on the expectations of the church and less on the natural dynamics of love. It claims the presence of redemption, but denies the personal reality of brokenness and perversity in life. The sacramental view tends toward the reduction of marriage to an institutional form. Households and families exist to socialize people, uncritically, into the faith through the regular routines of their lives.

Covenant is a major biblical symbol for the divine-human relationship and was only later applied to marriage. It is sometimes unconditional, sometimes conditional. It seems almost inescapably related to the legal concept of contract, although some writers emphasize the contrast between the two concepts. The entry into covenant generally appears to be free. Once having entered it, however, a person's freedom appears to be significantly limited. Covenant has some of the characteristics of *call* in that it involves binding oneself for the creation of a higher purpose; yet, it also serves as a model of God's order, a new and distinct community among other communities. The family is to be a new world as well as to build it. Because the covenant symbol is based on God's covenant with God's people, by analogy it is more applicable to the parent-child relationship than to the marriage relationship.

Marriage, understood as *vocation*, is a response to some purpose beyond its nature. It begins with God's gracious call, rather than (as with the sacramental view) with an order of creation. Marriage as a process of nature is clearly subordinate to the grace that comes through a response to God's call to renew the creation. Married people and families are to serve God by carrying out their vocations. Marriage and the family facilitate this by stabilizing and supporting those involved. The equality of the couple comes through their common call to discipleship, but (as in Barth) the roles they carry out in that call may be static, socially determined, and apparently less affected by grace than the model itself suggests.

The symbol of *communion* stresses the resonance of two natures and the mutual participation in both a world they hold in common and the qualities each has as a person. The symbol has its origin in mystical experience and involves grace, operating through given structures of personality. "In taking nature seriously it stands close to sacrament, but lacks the external or permanent symbolic structure typical of sacrament." It is less likely to stress the influence of church over nature, and demands the sociological condition of equality, psychologically presupposing an orientation toward growth and fulfillment, rather than control or the carrying out of presupposed functions. The communion model seeks to energize persons in their marriage and family relationships, "So that they can accomplish their vocation, live out their covenant, and participate in the sacrament of life." Rather than trying to transform them directly or approach them as instruments or members of a community, the communion model "tries to give them the power to reveal themselves to each other so that in the resonance between their real selves they might be transformed to higher levels of living."

Everett sees communion as a "master metaphor," more relevant for the egalitarian marriage of our time, and which can illuminate and clarify the intent of the other three. We agree with Everett that each of these views of marriage has something important to say to a couple who, in some way, have chosen to be married in accordance with Christian ritual and understanding. We are less sure than he is that the *communion* view of marriage does, in fact, provide a master metaphor. Having some familiarity with all four views is important for the minister who offers premarital pastoral care, because each of them contributes to one's being able to talk about what marriage ought to be.

The pastor, as one representing the tradition of the church, is in effect saying to the couple: "In what way is your relationship developing in a sacramental way? In what way do you share a common call and direction in life? In what way is your covenant together related to the larger covenant of God with his people? In what way are you developing as equal partners in your intimacy with one another? Which of these normative symbols for the marriage of Christians is most present or is missing from the way you understand your relationship?" We see the pastor's dealing, either explicitly or implicitly, with questions such as these as one of the means by which he or she engages the couple in a conversation with the previous generation, part of which is the tradition of the church that assists them in marrying or in contemplating marriage.

CARING FOR THE PRESENT GENERATION: BECOMING A PEER

The conscious agenda for persons seeking premarital care involves their relationship to the present generation and, as in the case of Mary and Milo, a determination of whether they are enough "like" each other for their relationship to seem like "marrying Rachel rather than Leah." In sending Jacob to her brother to find a wife, his mother, Rebeccah, was hoping that he could find someone like them: "If Jacob marries one of the Hittite women such as these . . . what good will my life be to me?" (Gen. 27:46). But how much does the prospective mate need to be like the other? A perfectionism about this and other relationship issues is likely to be more destructive than helpful. Relationship inventories, though interesting and sometimes anxiety reducing for the pastor, seldom yield much practical help. They are more likely to offer the couple static categories for describing themselves, rather than functional descriptions that can be modified with further experience and understanding.

We see the development of care for one's own generation—how one learns to become a peer with one's prospective mate—as best understood in relation to two crucial issues: (1) the development of a common world of meaning with significant others and (2) in maintaining an appropriate balance between relationships with peers outside the home, at work and in friendship, with the intimate relationship with one's mate. Because of their importance in premarital care and for persons in other family circumstances, we discuss them here in some detail.

The first of these issues, becoming a peer through a common world of meaning, has been described by Peter Berger, who turns to the ancient wisdom of Genesis and suggests that the Yahwist account of creation, with its giving to humankind the task of naming the animals, is a powerful symbol for the essentially human task of ordering the world in meaningful relationship to oneself.

> Just as the individual's deprivation of relationship with his significant others will plunge him into anomie, so their continued presence will sustain for him that *nomos* by which he can feel at home in the world, at least most of the time. . . . The plausibility and stability of the world, as socially defined, is dependent upon the strength and continuity of significant relationships in which conversation about this world can be continually carried on. . . . The reality of the world is sustained through conversation with significant others.[7]

Marriage "is a crucial nomic instrumentality in our society." It "is a *dramatic* act in which two strangers come together and redefine themselves." Like Lillian Rubin, but from a sociological rather than a psychological perspective, Berger describes the participants in the marriage relationship as strangers, for "unlike marriage candidates in many previous societies, those in ours typically come from different face-to-face contexts" or "from different areas of conversation." He contrasts our mobile society with the more stable ancient one and comments that unlike an earlier situation, in which "the establishment of the new marriage simply added to the differentiation and complexity of an already existing social world, marriage partners in today's society are embarked on the often difficult task of constructing for themselves the little world in which they will live."[8]

Although it is commonplace to think of today's marriages as being more personal and intimate than the family arranged marriages of the past, Berger proposes that in those more stable societies a couple with limited social and romantic contact might have more to share than a couple today because of their common cultural background. From his point of view, we understand Mary and Milo as having difficulty in creating a social world together. Moreover, viewing Berger's reinterpretation of the creation story theologically, one might hear God's command to marrying couples as: "Create a world of meaning in which your anxiety and loneliness can sometimes be overcome and the pain of human living eased by your caring for each other."

THE CHALLENGE OF WORK

The second issue in becoming a peer with one's mate or prospective mate, balancing responsibilities between work and home, is particularly important at a time when marriages increasingly involve spouses who both have careers outside the home. It is almost equally important, however, when only one member of the couple is working outside the home. Both the man and the woman usually have significant conflicts between the desires and responsibilities of love and work. From the perspective of a liberation theology of creation, Dorothee Soelle and Shirley A. Cloyes argues that "God created us as workers and lovers. To be created in God's image means to be able to work and to love. . . . To talk about our sexuality and our work is to talk about the fundamental activities of our adult lives."[9]

Work, as it is depicted in Genesis 2, "is not a curse that descends on the human being after the Fall; it is, from the beginning, an expression of the human project of liberation, of its dignity and integrity. Through work, human life shifts from passivity to participation." They take E. F. Schumacher's concept of "good work,"[10] in contrast to "meaningless, boring, stultifying, or nerve-wracking work" and insist that it is the equivalent of being able to care. In "good work" we discover who we are through doing good work; we take responsibility for ourselves and for others, and we lay the foundations for the future of our society and of ourselves (see Soelle and Cloyes, *To Work and to Love*, pp. 72-89).

Using systems theory, family therapists David Ulrich and Harry Dunne have addressed the love and work issue and have attempted to show

> how individuals move back and forth between the work and family systems, how each system affects the way the person functions in the other system, and how the person may seek to achieve balance between the systems and still step back far enough from their combined effects to preserve a zone of spontaneous functioning.[11]

In work, perhaps more than in any other part of life, differences between the family and child come to exist, be recognized, and developed. A person becomes an individual apart from his or her family and a peer with other adults in the world by escaping the role designation set by his or her family of origin.

Ulrich and Dunne claim that

> While individuation may hinge on what one does, the broader task of individuation is one of balancing. If the process is to be fully successful, the balancing must proceed simultaneously on several fronts. In regard to work choice, one may at least attempt to find some integration of what the family wants, what the available employees want, and one's own preferences. [The balancing task also may be profoundly impeded by the way one's role has been designated in the past.] If one feels compelled by virtue of family designation to be the weak one, the strong one, or the wet blanket, then even the most heroic efforts at balancing of roles may continually collapse. (*To Work and to Love*, pp. 191-92)

In order to accomplish the balancing task, one must identify and acknowledge "the *legitimate* claim imposed by one's origins, as a precursor to discarding those claims that have lost their legitimacy or relevance. Without this acknowledgment of one's origins, the attempt to establish one's own position in the here-and-now is likely to be void of meaning." An important key in the development of an appropriate balance between work life and family life is the small peer group of the workplace, which, Ulrich and Dunne argue, is qualitatively different from the structure of the family of origin. "The peer structure is not like a sibling structure; there is no rank assigned by age. One of its vital qualities is that of playfulness; the members can be playful without threatening anyone with too much closeness or loss of face." Such a structure does not lend itself to being encumbered by the usual family baggage.[12]

KINSHIP AND FRIENDSHIP

Becoming a peer with one's partner of the same generation also involves the development of friendships. Lillian Rubin borrows a concept from D. W. Winnicott, and refers to friends as transitional objects. "Friends are those who join us on the journey to maturity. Like our work experience they "facilitate our separation from the family and encourage our developing individuality by providing the contact and comfort needed for the transition from child-in-the-family to person-in-the-world."[13]

She contrasts kinship and friendship by noting that because our kinship relationships rest on bonds forged in earliest childhood years, they have an elemental quality that touches the deepest layers of our inner life and stirs our most primitive emotions. They are, therefore, likely to be more tumultuous than our friendships. "Friends *choose* to do what kin are *obliged* to do . . . friends accept each other so long as they both remain essentially the same as they were when they met . . . If they change or grow in different or incompatible ways, the friendship most likely will be lost."[14]

Friends seem to us to be more understanding than family, but, as Rubin says, we pay a price for that understanding. The price we pay is the lack of a sense of entitlement that is crucial to a secure and committed relationship. Friendship, however,

> is strictly a private affair. There are no social rituals, no public ceremonies to honor or celebrate friendships of any kind, from the closest to the most distant—not even a linguistic form that distinguishes the formal, impersonal relationship from the informal and personal one. (*Just Friends*, p. 4)

Even in this brief discussion of friendship, one can see some of the most important elements in the kind of peership relation that marriage, at least potentially, is. Marriage is somewhere in between the *obligation* relationship of kinship and the *choice* relationship of friendship. In marriage, there is a public ritual, reminding the partners of the dimensions of obligation of their relationship and its confirmation by the community. But marriage is clearly distinguished from those other relationships by its active dimension. The traditional concept of "performing one's marital duties" has usually referred to an active sexual relationship. More symbolically, it speaks the truth that when marriage is what it ought to be, something intimate and personal is going on in the relationship. The partners are actively choosing to be involved with each other—with the freedom of friendship and the constancy of kinship.

These, in our judgment, are the major issues to be considered in the premarital care of those preparing for marriage or remarriage. The pastor's agenda with a couple touches directly and indirectly on how they are learning to care through development of a common world of meaning and how they are emerging into peership with each other through their relationships in the world of work and/or in their friendships. To the intended spouse, both work and friendship are potentially competitive with the relationship, but commitment to the marriage relationship does not mean resolving one in favor of the other. Rather, it means finding an appropriate balance that stimulates the development of the other. Becoming a peer with one's friends and one's colleagues at work makes peership and mutual challenge and stimulation with one's mate more nearly possible. This suggests that for a spouse who may not work outside the home, if peership with one's marital partner is to be developed and maintained, it is essential that there be a meaningful involvement in life apart from one's family. These are the kinds of issues that the pastor attempts to discuss as he or she focuses on the couple's caring for their own generation.

CARE FOR THE FUTURE GENERATION

The amount of time that is devoted in premarital interviews to a consideration of the future is usually much less than that devoted to examining the patterns of care for prior and present generations. However, concern for the future is an essential part of premarital consultation in whatever context it takes place. Of the four theological symbols for marriage that we discussed earlier, both vocation and covenant have a future dimension. Covenant bases God's promises for the future on his faithfulness in the past and, applied to marriage, conveys an image of the couple's moving into the future in covenant with each other. The image of common calling has an even more specific future reference. The couple has a vocation together in relation to both their anticipated careers and commitments to family. That vocation represents something that they are doing together apart from all others in the home and in the world outside the home.

Both the physical fact and the symbolic meaning of creating children together expresses most clearly the commitment to care for and to invest in the future. Children, like few other things, are something given to the world that can be influenced but not controlled. Children may yield indirect benefits to their parents, but having children to benefit oneself is destructive rather than creative. In his inaugural address at Eden Theological Seminary, Walter Brueggemann[15] raised the question: "Will the faith have children?" In this address, he notes the preoccupation of the Old Testament with the securing of an heir and with the assurance that one generation will not perish. He proposes a structuring of biblical faith around the metaphor of "Sarah's hope and Rachel's grief." Although Brueggemann's concern in his address and ours in this book are quite different, the power of what children mean to the generations is central to both, as the symbols of Sarah's hope and Rachel's grief express.

In a time when the decision to have a child involves persons in the morality of population control in a world with limited resources, that decision seems even more important. There is a seriousness about it that is different from perhaps any other time in history. Whatever the result of the decision, there appears to be a powerful human need in both sexes to express who they are through the nurturing of a child. There is probably more anxiety in a couple's discussion of this, both with the pastor and with each other, than there is about their sexual intimacy. As parenting is delayed due to extended career preparation, the anxiety about whether you can have a healthy child, and if you can, should you, becomes more intense. Pastors who fail to discuss the issue of children with the couples to whom they offer care and guidance are failing to recognize an important part of what each person is as a human being. To make a caring decision about how one participates in the generation that comes after is a central part of what it means to be human and, explicitly or implicitly, an expression of one's faith.

But what are the alternatives to having children for those who deal responsibly with the decision not to have them? Our major contention about Christian family living does not allow for failing to care for the future generation, but there must be ways of caring other than physically having children. We believe this issue is an important part of the pastor's premarital work. Anthropologist Mary Catherine Bateson argues that

> In this period of history . . . all of us who . . . want to be responsible to the future need to be sure that we have a relationship with at least one real, flesh and blood child. People need not give birth to children to be in touch with them. When they decide they are not going to have children, or when their children are grown, they ought not to cut themselves off from children altogether.[16]

She insists that it is not old fashioned to think about parenting and kinship and concern for children as among the central ethical issues. "If we do not remain related somehow with the fundamental biological orientation to the future through reproduction we run the risk that our other choices will become more concerned with gratification and exploitation and comfort than with responsibility." It is not enough, she says, "to be brothers and sisters in this world. That is only acknowledging our common origin. We must also say that together we will be parents. . . . We will knit ourselves to one another by metaphors of kinship in common nurturance of the ongoing life of this planet."[17]

Bateson's exhortations are important and should, perhaps, be a part of the assumptive world of most pastors. The development of practical alternatives are to be personal and direct, rather than simply doing something through someone else. Perhaps all that can be said at this point is that the question of how the two together are caring for the generation that comes after them, in some form, should be an important part of the pastoral agenda for premarital work.

PREVIOUS MARRIAGES AND PREMARITAL AGREEMENTS

Our view of premarital pastoral care makes it intentional in making no major theoretical distinction between preparation for marriage and preparation for remarriage. Some of the issues in remarriage have been addressed indirectly through the situations of persons whose stories appeared in chapters 1 and 2. The church, in the earlier years of this century, considered marriage preparation for those who had been previously married to involve a great deal of investigation of the prior marriage. Much of this concern seems to have grown out of the need of the church to think of itself as responsible for all the marriages at which a pastor officiated and that it needed to maintain the purity of its sacraments or blessings. The Roman Catholic practice of seeking cause for annulment still demonstrates this concern by collecting evidence, to prove that one of the partners in the prior relationship was in some way flawed and, therefore, not able to contract a valid marriage.

We would view the examination of the prior marriage today as operating out of an assumption that *both* partners were seriously flawed and that their relationship and the breaking of it was sinful. We understand the task the pastor has with persons who are considering marrying again to be that of recognizing their own responsibility and sin in causing the termination of the marriage, not simply blaming it on the other person or on external circumstances. The prior relationship needs to be discussed as a part of the history of the person coming for remarriage, but not as the major determining factor in evaluating the present relationship.

The question of premarital agreements is not an issue that fits nearly under the rubric of caring for any of the generations. Such agreements are the way in which—usually through a legal contract—a couple agrees to structure their future together in the light of their past, a past that includes at least one previous marriage and continuing responsibilities. Typically, a man will ask his intended spouse to sign an agreement that states that in the case of a divorce, his financial or other responsibilities for her will be limited. Such an agreement appears to violate the intention of the traditional marriage vows, which speak of a common life of sharing in sickness and in health, in wealth or in poverty.

This issue cannot adequately be dealt with in the space available here. What seems most important to us, in the context of premarital pastoral care, is that both the vows that state what marriage ought to be and negotiated agreements about what is realistically possible should be recognized as part of the marital commitment. In the case of a second marriage, in which vows have already been broken, is it better to marry only if one will affirm that he or she really will abide by them this time or on the basis of what now seems possible between imperfect people with the prayer that the relationship may exceed its expectations rather than fail to reach them? Our answers to these questions seem clear.

A STRUCTURE FOR PREMARITAL PASTORAL CARE AND COUNSELING

As we have indicated, we feel that it is particularly important to have a clearly defined structure for the type of pastoral relationship that develops when a couple is considering and/or preparing for marriage. We propose such a structure as a clinical "case" that, like most cases, raises as many questions as it answers. This seems appropriate because so much that is being written about premarital counseling needs to be questioned. We feel that this particular structure is appropriate both in the more specialized setting of the pastoral counseling center and in the parish. The option to have individual pastoral counseling is appropriate in the parish if the pastor has the time and training to do it well. Further elements in this structure for premarital care differ depending on whether there is a request for premarital evaluation in response to a perceived problem, or premarital guidance is provided by a pastor who will be performing a wedding ceremony.

Parish Context Structure	Counseling Center Context
The first interview is spent in getting acquainted with the couple, the history of their relationship, and their assumptions about marriage and what a marriage ceremony should be. The pastor shares with them some of her or his assumptions about marriage and the particular customs of this parish. The assignment of preparing a genogram for each family of origin is given.	The first interview is spent in hearing each person's view of the perceived problem in the relationship and how their anxieties about it affect them. How do they understand marriage, and how does their present relationship fail to exemplify that understanding? The assignment of preparing a genogram for each family of origin is given.

The second interview is spent in discussing the genogram, the couple's perception of each set of parents and other significant persons of the prior generation, how they see themselves and their potential mate as relating to these significant persons, and comparing features of the respective families of origin.

The third and fourth interviews* are spent in getting in touch with each person separately, hearing something of his and her history outside their families, their values, their hopes, their beliefs, and their relationships with significant others of their generation, hearing any individual concerns they may have about themselves. The pastor discusses with each person anything brought up in the individual session that he or she may want to mention in the feedback session in order that the confidentiality of that session will not be violated.

The second interview is spent in discussing the genogram, the couple's perception of each set of parents and other significant persons of the prior generation, how they see themselves and their potential mate as relating to these significant persons, and comparing features of the respective families of origin.

The third and fourth interviews are spent in getting in touch with each person separately, hearing something of their history outside their families, their values, their hopes, their beliefs, and their relationships with significant others of their generation, hearing any individual concerns they may have about themselves. The pastor discusses with each person anything brought up in the individual session that he or she may want to mention in the feedback session in order that the confidentiality of that session will not be violated.

*These interviews may be omitted if the pastor senses that the couple resists making use of them. If they are used, care must be taken in the feedback session in order that the confidentiality of the individual sessions will not be violated.

The fifth interview with the couple together focuses on their thoughts and fantasies about their life together, their plans for children, or other ways of caring for the future generation. There is feedback from the pastor as to how she or he sees the relation-

The fifth interview with the couple together focuses on their thoughts and fantasies about their life together, their thoughts about having children, and other ways of caring for the future

ship and each person's contribution to it and a final discussion of views of marriage and the marriage ceremony. generation. There is feedback from the pastor as to how she or he sees the relationship and each person's contribution to it. The pastor again offers an option of individual counseling if either should want to explore something that has emerged in the evaluation.

In the telling and interpretation of these stories, the couple has the experience of using their imaginations together, an important ingredient in creating a life together. As we have suggested in the interview agenda noted above, the discovery or rediscovery of the story of the religious tradition from which they come and of the one they are asking to bless their marriage is also an important part of preparation for marriage. As is often the case, even with couples from the pastor's own parish, assumptions about their religious tradition are not what one might expect. In order to bring together the couple and the tradition in an honest and meaningful marriage service, religious assumptions and traditions need to be explored and interpreted. It is the minister's responsibility to interpret what the religious community has said and is saying about marriage in the wedding service. Most often there needs to be an interpretation of the history of the various elements, their meaning, and how they may be related to the couple to be married. Optimally, this interpretation may elicit a discussion of the couple's view of the elements in the marriage service, sometimes restating them so that they may be participated in with honesty and conviction.

Again, we have presented such a specific structure for the premarital interviews not to suggest that it is the best one for any particular pastor. Our purpose is simply to be specific enough that our proposals can be understood. They may then be accepted or used to develop a procedure that is more appropriate for other pastors. Mary and Milo and most couples in their situation are not asking for a counseling relationship of indeterminant length. They are told, therefore, how long, in the pastor's opinion, it will take to address their specific concerns about the proposed marriage. When that has been done, the couple's relationship with the counselor will be terminated. We believe that lengthy premarital counseling is inappropriate because it unduly involves the parental generation (which the counselor is whatever his or her age) in the developing relationship of the couple. It continues the dependency of the couple on the prior generation at a time when, in the very fact of contemplating marriage, they are making a public statement about their maturity.

Our final reflection suggests that the minister's responsibility in premarital pastoral care can appropriately be described as providing a hermeneutical bridge between the couple's present life situation, their families of origin, and the way that the church has historically offered blessing to a marriage. Like other forms of family living, marriage preparation involves the care for our generations and the determination of how that care may affect the contemplated marriage.

Notes

1. Theron S. Nease, *Premarital Counseling Literature in American Protestantism (1920-1971)* (Princeton, N.J.: Princeton Theological Seminary Ph.D. dissertation, 1973).
2. Ibid.
3. Kenneth R. Mitchell and Herbert Anderson, "You Must Leave Before You Can Cleave: A Family Systems Approach to Premarital Pastoral Work," *Pastoral Psychology*, vol. 30, no. 2 (Winter, 1981) 71-88.
4. Murray Bowen, *Family Therapy in Clinical Practice* (Northvale, N.J.: Aronson, 1981); James E. Framo, *Explorations in Marital and Family Therapy* (New York: Springer, 1982).
5. William Johnson Everett, *Blessed Be the Bond* (Philadelphia: Fortress Press, 1985), chapter 4.
6. Ibid.
7. Peter L. Berger, "Marriage and the Construction of Reality," *Facing Up to Modernity* (1977) 7.
8. Ibid., p. 10.
9. Soelle and Cloyes, *To Work and to Love*, p. 115.
10. E. F. Schumacher, *Good Work* (New York: Harper, 1979).
11. David N. Ulrich and Harry P. Dunne, *Love and Work* (New York: Brunner/Mazel, 1986), p. 16.
12. Ibid., p. 86.
13. Lillian B. Rubin, *Just Friends: The Role of Friendship in Our Lives* (New York: Harper, 1986), p. 34.

14. Ibid.
15. Walter Brueggemann, "Will Our Faith Have Children?" *Word & World*, vol. 3, no. 3, 272-83.
16. Mary Catherine Bateson, "Caring for Children, Caring for the Earth," *Christianity and Crisis*, vol. 40, no. 5, (March 31, 1980) 68.
17. Ibid., p. 70.

CHAPTER FOUR

GENERATIONAL CARING FOR MARRIAGE

And the man and his wife were both naked, and were not ashamed. (Genesis 2:25 RSV)

For Al and Ann, like many of those marrying in the United States today, theirs was a second attempt at a successful marriage. Second marriages are important to the church in its understanding of marriage because they help to underscore the fact that marriage is a genuinely human institution that often fails, not one the church can preserve by its blessing or by the minister's "saving it" through her or his pastoral counseling. Second marriages are not the norm for what marriage should be, but they serve as a useful reminder of the way things are and the necessity that Christian ministry must deal more with what is then with what ought to be. Pastoral care and counseling exist to care for persons, not to preserve structures. Certainly, structures are necessary for a fully human life, but they are not ends in themselves. They are, rather, a means for facilitating full human living.

The point of view that we have been developing about the family and the pastoral care of persons in families began with a biblical picture of the human being created by God and given time and space to care for God's creation. In following God's command to be fruitful and multiply, humankind has used God's gift of time to live in relationship and to care for the generations before and after. Relationship itself—the way we most fully express our humanness—is also a gift of God, a response to our loneliness; the partner of the opposite sex is one for whom we yearn because of both her or his likeness to us and difference from us. Although the marriage relationship provides an informative paradigm for other relationships, we do not understand it theologically as an enduring structure to be preserved for itself. Rather, it endures and fulfills its purpose when the human capacity for caring is continually expressed and developed through it.

VIEWS OF MARRIAGE AFFECT OUR CARING FOR IT

As might be expected from what has been said thus far, the concept of marriage we have developed here is best defined by the process of care that goes on within it, not the form it takes or how long it lasts. As the image the Napier and Whitaker book title, *The Family Crucible*,[1] suggests, lack of adequate structure within a family is a major cause of family pain and dysfunction. However, a strong structure is important so that the "heat" of caring can be adequately contained and facilitated, not to preserve the structure itself.

In contrast to this view, traditional Christian views of marriage and the family have focused more on structure than on function. The sacramental view, most often associated with a catholic understanding of the church, emphasizes the institution of marriage and the church's involvement in it more than the persons involved in the marriage. The covenantal view, most often associated with the reformed tradition, emphasizes the word of the covenant more than the process of keeping it.

A major difficulty in emphasizing the structure or institution of marriage, rather than its function, is that it tends to venerate and value what has happened more than dealing with what is happening now. The church has often been better at grieving over the failure of first marriages and trying to locate the fault for the failure than it has been in caring for persons preparing for and struggling with second marriages. Within most Christian communions, even those that do not view marriage as a sacrament, there remains an idealism about marriage and a feeling that second marriages are never quite as good as first ones. There also remains a conviction that the first marriage is the only valid one, or at least the only one that can be joyfully recognized by the church without acknowledging that the first blessing "didn't take."

Some years ago, I (Patton) read an article submitted for publication in a pastoral journal. Because of its writing problems and faulty research design, I rejected the article, but I remember it far better than most of the articles I do accept. I cannot recall the exact title of the article, but it was about the continued coital intimacy of the divorced "born again" with their former spouses. The authors had surveyed participants in single adult groups of several large evangelical churches, comparing the sexual behavior of divorced persons who described themselves as "born again" to those who did not. Among the "born again," they found that a large number of divorced women continued to have intercourse with their former husbands. Although there were too many variables in the study to be able to give an adequate explanation for this, one of the reasons suggested was that these divorced persons did not really believe in divorce, or they felt that they might be divorced legally but not in the sight of God. Our clinical experience with less conservative persons has confirmed the view that there are quite a few divorced persons who do not really believe that they are divorced and whose views about marriage and divorce influence their behavior sexually and otherwise.

One's view of marriage clearly influences how one cares for one's own marriage relationship and how pastoral care and counseling is offered to others. Our functional norm of caring for your generations does not preclude either a sacramental or a covenantal view, but it seems closer to the view of marriage as vocation. This requires an understanding of Christian vocation that goes beyond Luther's use of the concept to justify the *status quo* and to proclaim the partial truth that everyone can be a Christian in his or her present place and status. It is closer to Rosemary Haughton's understanding of the partners' in marriage being equally responsible for making a future, at home and in the world of work, both separately and together.[2] As the *J* story of creation suggests, marriage is a practical response to human loneliness and a conviction that things go better when they are shared.

In contrast to the symbols of sacrament, covenant, and even communion, vocation, as we understand it, is a process conception of life and marriage that claims that its meaning is discovered on the journey rather than in the way that the journey was begun. The road conditions for the journey and the ways of coping with them are as important as its point of origin and destination. The ongoing choice and commitment of the marriage relationship has the practical function of making it easier to deal with the road conditions, including the behavior of the kids in the back seat. Marriage, understood as shared calling, is not an attempt to live up to ideals but a commitment to be intimate in the real world.

John Barnett, an Atlanta psychiatrist, has used the symbol of the

Fall to describe what he perceives to be the necessary disillusionment involved in the life of a marriage. Viewed in this practical way, an experience of the Fall may involve the fear of having married Leah, the chaos of the kids in the back seat, or a variety of other realistic, but disturbing, human experiences. According to Barnett, three courses of action are available to married couples in the throes of the Fall and, as the symbol suggests, the Fall in marriage is experienced by everyone.

> First is the choice of getting rid of the real person intruding into the marriage and holding on to the fantasied ideal of a marital partner. Second, there can be a shoring up of roles and a development of apathy in regard to marital growth. Third, a couple can move toward continued demythologizing of their relationship and actively engage in the turmoil of establishing real people in a real marriage.[3]

This third way of demythologization and realism seems most likely to be possible with a shared vocation symbol for marriage. To give up "longstanding deeply ingrained mythology and seek relationship based on personal realities certainly does not insure the finding or enjoying of such relationship," says Barnett, but the realism and risk can make the marriage exciting even though it can never be fully secure. It seems consistent with a norm for family living that involves the caring for one's generations, including one's own.

Although this view of marriage is convincing to us, we present it more to argue for the importance to the process of care of clarifying one's own view of marriage, not to claim the superiority of this particular point of view. Awareness of what view of marriage they do hold is both theoretically and practically important for pastors who are attempting to offer pastoral counseling to Al and Ann and to address the tensions and disappointments in their own marriages.

CARING IN AL AND ANN

Recall the situation of Al and Ann at the beginning of chapter 1. They have come for pastoral counseling because of, as she puts it, Ann's inability to get Al to talk with her. At age forty-one, she says she craves a deeper intimacy in their relationship, and in her frustration at not having it, she finds herself attacking Al in order to stir him up enough to "get something out of him." How the pastor responds to Ann's hurt and anger will, at the moment, be more immediately informed by his skill and experience in working with troubled couples than by his theological view of marriage. In our judgment, however, that theological view indirectly informs every intervention he makes. It has become a part of the interpersonal skills he has available for interaction.

In their seventh session together, Ann began to cry, and Al looked confused. They had been talking about one of the familiar issues in their relationship, Ann's compulsive working around the house and her inability to get Al to help. The pastor wondered why she was crying now; they had been through all this before. So he asked: (looking at Al) "Do you know what Ann is feeling or where her emotions are coming from?"

The pastor's question has several purposes behind it and can accomplish a number of things. First, the pastor notices and calls attention to Ann's feeling and thus says, implicitly to her, "Your tears are important." Rather than doing this directly, however, the pastor speaks to Al. It would certainly be possible to interpret the pastor's action as disrespect for Ann's feelings, the two talking in an apparently unfeeling way *about* her rather than to her. The pastor's decision, in one sense made intuitively and in another made on the basis of an understanding of each person's family relationships and psychological development theory, is that in spite of Ann's tears Al is the one most in need of help at the moment; he is most in need of having his opinion respected.

In many ways, the pastor knows more about what is going on with Ann than does Al. Asking this question of Al, however, has the effect of saying to him that it is both appropriate and important that he understand his wife's feelings and the events to which they are related. The question offers both respect for Al and a clue about what he needs to be more aware of. Most likely, without this attention given to his view of Ann's feelings, he would choose to ignore them and hope that they would go away and not bother him. One cannot know now whether Al picks up the clue; that can only be determined in later interviews, when Al begins to talk about his increased sensitivity to Ann's feelings. The interaction with Al is obviously intended to be an educational one, not unlike a mathematics teacher's asking a question in order to tell the students what to study for a test.

Al answers the pastor's question by cautiously suggesting that Ann's tears may have something to do with her parents' coming visit.

Pastor: Oh, (turning to Ann) then it has to do with more than just painting a room. You're doing something for your parents. I knew you must have been feeling something important. (The pastor and the couple sit for several moments in silence.)

The pastor does not leave Ann and her feelings for long. He takes Al's matter of fact explanation of the fears (the parents are coming) and—in the light of his understanding of Ann, psychological theory, and Christian anthropology—he underscores the importance of the event and Ann's feelings about it. Painting a room to get ready for one's parents is not just painting a room and being frustrated about how long it takes or doing it right. It says something about what human beings are really like—Christian anthropology.

We pause a moment to ask the reader, "Does this seem like making far too much of a very simple interaction?" Surely pastoral counseling of married persons and families must deal with more important things than this—tears, painting, and family visits! Sometimes it does. As most pastors know, ministry to families may involve all those things that the tabloids, confession magazines, and soap operas tell us about. In our judgment, however, the apparent degree of pathology or chaos in the family is not directly indicative of the importance of the issue for pastoral caring. Although it is certainly possible that in our interpretation of this particular interaction we are making too much out of too little, it seems worth the risk of doing this in order to emphasize how much persons reveal about themselves and their views of human life in the apparently simple things they say.

As valuable as verbatims, recordings, written transcripts, and even videotapes are for the learning of counseling and psychotherapy, they sometimes suggest that the pastor or psychotherapist is only responding to the words that were said prior to Ann's response. This is actually only a small part. A caring and useful response to Al and Ann is one that is responsive to the whole person and family, not just to what is said by one person. It is a response to their history, their presenting problem, how their personalities seem to be structured, the theory of personality underlying that understanding of psychological structure, and—for the religiously committed persons—a theological view of what human beings are, not just what they appear to be at the present time.

Now, about room painting and Christian anthropology—Ann is painting the room to care for her prior generation, to express her being a part of the generations of Adam and Noah and Ann. The agenda—with her mother particularly, but also with her father—is unfinished, and her intimacy with Al, the care for her own generation, is significantly related to her ability to come to terms with care for the prior generation.

Al: I just wish I could make her stop being sad.

Pastor: I don't think sadness is the main thing Ann is feeling now.

Al is uncomfortable with Ann's feelings, and his usual response is trying to "make her feel happy" and, thus, return to a normal non-threatening state or to get away from the feelings and Ann by ignoring her or physically absenting himself. The pastoral counselor's intuitive response, intuition informed by a theoretical point of view, is to suggest to Al that there is another way of understanding and responding to Ann's feelings. He suggests that sadness is not the main thing Ann is feeling (Actually, it probably is, but to Al, sadness is something that people shouldn't have; therefore, to suggest immediately that sadness can be a good thing would probably be incomprehensible to him.) The pastor pulls his punch and suggests that sadness and some things that Al might accept as good exist side by side.

Pastor: (Turning to Ann) What I think is going on with you is sad, but it's more than that. There's a good feeling in the sadness, feeling full, or like something important's going on.

Ann: (nods in agreement)

Pastor:	(speaking somewhat lightly to Al so he won't retreat further from the feelings present in the room) You know, another thing that I think is that Ann probably doesn't want you to cheer her up but to be near her when she's feeling emotional like this. Have you ever thought of trying to do that? I really think that's one of the things she's been asking you to do.
Al:	I don't think I could do that. I'm not sure I could.
Ann:	(somewhat angrily) He just doesn't seem to care. He's so concerned about himself.
Pastor:	Ann, I don't mean to be taking Al's side, but I really do believe he cares. He just doesn't know how to do it very well. (Looking at Al and smiling) I don't know if you agree with me or not, but my impression is that although you're good at a lot of things, this is not one of them. I don't have any doubt that you care a lot. It's expressing it that's the problem.

Several observations, an intuitive, almost unconscious relating of the observations to both psychological and theological theory, and decisions made about how to respond to Al and to Ann are all a part of this interaction. The observations were of Ann's filling with emotion and Al's anxious and defensive look. The question, "What's going on here?" was given a tentative answer from psychological theory, and this was placed in a tentative theological framework.

INTERPRETIVE PERSPECTIVES FROM THE SOCIAL SCIENCES

What other theories are helpful for interpreting what is going on with Al and Ann and other couples like them? One of them is Lyman and Adele Wynne's theory of intimacy. The Wynnes have argued that intimacy "recurs most reliably, not when it is demanded as a primary or continuous experience, but when it emerges spontaneously within a context of basic, well-functioning relational processes." The Wynnes define intimacy as a *"subjective relational experience* in which the core components are *trusting self-disclosure* to which the response is *communicated empathy.*" It is important to recognize, they say, that "self-disclosure, in itself, does not necessarily generated intimacy. An intimacy experience has not taken place, in our definition, until there is empathic feedback, that is until acceptance and acknowledgment are communicated, verbally or nonverbally, as an indication that this trust is justified.

Like Ivan Boszormenyi-Nagy, the Wynnes take the general philosophical position of Martin Buber and argue that intimacy and I-Thou experiences "cannot be willfully induced or long sustained." Preoccupation with intimacy as a goal, "as with simultaneous orgasm, interferes with its attainment and also distracts, at the very least, from attention to other forms of relatedness." Intimacy occurs most consistently in ongoing relationships of a multidimensional nature. It can be experienced in brief unidimensional encounters with relative strangers, but such "highly sporadic, intimate disclosures in 'one-time only' relationships seem possible *because* of the unlikelihood of a further relationship and the attendant opportunities for betrayal." Intimacy in ongoing relationships is of a different order.

The Wynnes theorize that intimacy involves four sub-processes that unfold sequentially. First is the process of attachment/caregiving, or complementary affectional bonding, the prototype for which is the parent-child relationship. Second is the communicating process, in which there is a common focus of attention and the exchange of meanings and messages. Third is a joint problem-solving and the sharing of everyday tasks. Fourth, the final sub-process is mutuality, understood as the integration of the precluding processes into an enduring pattern of relatedness. It is important to note that mutuality "incorporates both distancing, or disengagement and constructive re-engagement." Although these processes unfold sequentially, they are circular and recurrent, rather than linear, in relationship to one another. Even after mutuality has been attained, relatedness often returns, focusing on earlier processes for various lengths of time. But, say the Wynnes, "until attachment/caregiving is incorporated into a relationship system, the relationship is not likely to become enduring and reliable."

Having stated the relational context in which intimacy most likely can occur, the Wynnes argue that in spite of the centrality given by Western culture to being intimate, intimacy is not in itself a primary relational process. Rather it is a corollary of the more basic relational processes. Moreover, although mutuality increases the likelihood of intimacy, intimacy can occur before mutuality has developed, for example, in the problem-solving activities of preadolescents in the chum stage of development. Intimate experience is "a supplementary, but not essential, process for strengthening the bonding that has been crucial for the survival of the human species throughout the ages."[4]

What both men and women look for underneath the sexual attraction and stimulation offered by the other is the same kind of experience that was originally offered by the mothering parent—not in the same degree, but with the same quality and constancy. Lillian Rubin, whose work we touched on in chapter 2, has argued that the different experience one has with one's mother as a child offers a different experience for men and women seeking to be intimate as adults. She points out how this difference may appear:

> Stop a woman in mid-sentence with the question, "What are you feeling right now?" and you might have to wait a bit while she reruns the mental tape to capture the moment just past. But, more than likely, she'll be able to do it successfully. . . . The same is not true of a man. For him, a similar question usually will bring a sense of wonderment that one would even ask it, followed quickly by an uncomprehending and puzzled response. "What do you mean?" he'll ask. "I was just talking. . . . "[5]
>
> [Men, in contrast,] have integrated all too well the lessons of their childhood—the experiences that taught them to repress and deny their inner thoughts, wishes, needs, and fears; indeed, not even to notice them. It's real, therefore, the kind of inner thoughts and feelings that are readily accessible to a woman generally are unavailable to a man. When he says, "I don't know what I'm feeling," he isn't necessarily being intransigent and withholding. More than likely, he speaks the truth.[6]

Rubin's observations resonate generally with our clinical experience and specifically to our understanding of Al and Ann. When Ann complained that Al never told her anything, she felt he was intentionally withholding. Most of the time he was not; he was doing—in terms of Rubin's theory—what he as a male had learned to do, with the additional feature provided by his particular family history of being the only child of a woman who also had a "difficult to get to" husband. Al had internalized his father's way of dealing with a woman. He tuned her out. There were other factors in each person's history that accentuated the conflict over intimacy. Ann's family had generally done everything at a faster pace than Al's, and it was easy for her to grow impatient with him. He had had a stuttering problem as a child and had overcome this by slowing down in his speech and generally being calculating about everything he said. His first marriage had been characterized by what he perceived as his wife's excessive dependency, something he wanted to get away from, whereas Ann's had been characterized by her husband's lack of dependability and his not being there when she needed him.

Ann was not satisfied. She asked for more, and Al continued his pattern of avoidance. The task of pastoral counseling was to help them break this pattern of Ann's demanding and Al's avoiding. This was not done by focusing exclusively on what was happening in their relationship with each other. Often, counseling begins there, but pastoral counseling is most effective when it moves among several perspectives, following a model suggested by Karl Menninger for psychoanalytic psychotherapy but adaptable to a number of other forms of human interaction. Menninger, in discussing the process of interpretation, states that the therapy moves from a contemporary situation to the analytic situation to the childhood situation. A complete interpretation involves all three.[7]

Placed in the context of the work with Al and Ann, and in relation to our anthropology of care, Menninger's comment suggests that their struggle to care for each other in everyday life is brought into and experienced in the counseling room and in relation to what is going on with the pastoral counselor. It is then related to their stories of caring and being cared for in relation to the prior generation and to their present life. The exploration of the past is not so much for explanation as for the recovery of some of the feelings of those relationships. It is not particularly important for Ann to be able to explain the way Al is. It is important to empathize, or feel, with his struggles to deal with his mother and, as Gerkin, following Gadamer, has suggested, to fuse horizons of interpretation with him.[8] That process certainly might involve explanation, but it is explanation in the sense of bringing closer in relationship, not explanation as it is so often used, as a means of objectifying and pushing away.

In this horizontal fusion, understanding and closeness might first happen between one member of the couple and the pastoral counselor, as it did when the pastor noticed and interpreted Ann's feeling when Al was trying to ignore it. It is not enough, however, for the pastor to interpret back to Ann that her sadness was not something she wanted to get rid of but to share. The pastor's responsibility is to assist Al in seeing this himself and to learn how to respond to it. The goal, therefore, is not for the pastor to satisfy the couple's needs but to show them how to satisfy each other's needs. This instruction, however, is more experiential and affective than it is didactic. It grows out of what actually happens in the counseling room. It is important to emphasize that the kind of marital intimacy that Rubin discusses and that Berger sees as the sociological purpose of marriage today is developed not only by focusing on relationships with one another, but also through the mutual care for the parental generation—talking about it, doing it together, and reflecting on its success and failure.

CARE IN MARRIAGE FOR THE FUTURE GENERATION

Intimacy is developed in a marriage and is discovered in the counseling room not just by focusing on the marriage relationship *per se* but in the care of the future, as well as the prior, generation. Most pastors who have experience in ministry to a marriage have heard more than once the statement, "I just wish he could be with me like he is with the children." Undoubtedly, this is said much more about men than it is about women and for the reason noted by Chodorow: "Boys come to define themselves as more separate and distinct, with a greater sense of rigid ego boundaries and differentiation. The basic feminine sense of self is connected to the world, the basic masculine sense of self is separate."[9] With his children, however, although there may be a sense of awkwardness and not quite knowing what to do, men can allow themselves to operate less carefully. The boundaries that are strictly maintained with the spouse are much more permeable with children.

Both the skilled pastoral counselor and the intuitively sensitive pastor can see in a father's relationship with his children a readily available example of what the emotionally starved wife is looking for and can find ways of suggesting this to the husband. We have observed again and again how a husband who simply does not understand what his wife wants, much less how to provide it, has moved out of that angry *impasse* when we found a way to shift the discussion to his relationship with one or more of the children. Although a husband's jealousy of the time his wife gives the children is more frequently heard as a complaint than the other way around, the husband's jealousy is most often focused on his wife's not having time for him. In the wife's complaint, the focus is seldom on the time spent but on the spontaneous, unguarded quality of the relationship—something her spouse has with the children, but not with her.

George, who had become a securities salesman after completing his military obligation, felt that giving in to his feelings was destructive to his career objectives. He had grown up with little parental affirmation and support and had learned to trust only the affirmation that comes from yourself when you've succeeded on your job. Pastoral counseling with him and his wife, Geri, was most effective when the pastor was able to get George to talk about his two daughters and his joy in playing with and taking care of them. Tending to speak only in generalizations about most of his life, he could talk concretely about particular events that he had shared with his children. It was then that the pastoral counselor could "catch him" expressing his feelings and could attempt to help him distinguish feelings and point out when he was sharing them. The pastoral counselor's most useful comments to him were something like, "Did you know that the feeling you just shared with me about the children is what Geri wants you to share with her?" or "It's the child in you that she's asking you to share with her."

Men like George can feel comfortable in their playfulness with children, but appear threatened if asked to share that with their wives. They may know how to relate sexually to their wives—or at least think they do—but are fearful that showing the caring or playful side of themselves will make them too vulnerable and undercut the person they are trying to develop in their business life. The pastor's most effective interventions—and for the parish minister these can be informal conversations as well as counseling—are those that maintain a balance between supporting and affirming the successful, competitive self that George is trying to develop and suggesting that he has a more personal intimate self within in him that needs further development. As difficult as it can be to get beyond the defensiveness of someone like George, when it has been done, some of the most satisfying interactions are those in which the pastor is able to laugh with him about his interpersonal awkwardness and, if things go really well, to cry with him about the sadness of his life.

The issue of caring for the generation after is an issue not only for couples with children, like George and Geri, but also for childless couples like Al and Ann. The issue is not the same, but it is an issue, and an important one. Al and Ann married in their late thirties. Al's first wife had a two-year-old child when they married, but their marriage did not produce a child. Ann had never been pregnant. Her first marriage had seemed so shaky that there was never a right time. Al and Ann began talking about having a child early in their relationship, but again the time never seemed quite right. It was hard for Ann to accept the disruption in her career that a child would make, and when they did decide that she would stop taking her contraceptives, pregnancy did not occur. As she approached forty, Ann decided that she was too old for both pregnancy and birth control pills, so she asked Al to get a vasectomy. In his quiet way, Al agreed without saying much about his reluctance. He had not shared with Ann how much his first wife's child had meant to him and had not grieved over her loss. He knew what it was like to care for a child, but not how to talk about his feelings of caring.

When he got the vasectomy, which everyone had told him was a very simple procedure and easy to recover from, he found the whole thing very painful. The recovery took longer than he had been told, and when he did attempt to resume sexual relations with Ann, ejaculation was painful to him. When it stopped being painful, sex simply did not feel as good as it had before the operation, and after a while, as Al put it, "My heart just wasn't in it anymore." He tried once or twice to say something about it, but he was not used to talking about things, so he just gave up and tried to ignore their sexual relationship as best he could. Ann didn't know what he was feeling, so she assumed he had lost his desire for her and tried to hide her feelings of rejection by blaming Al for all sorts of things.

The issue for pastoral caring and the mutual caring in a marriage is recognizing the importance of the question of parenting for virtually everyone. There are a variety of other issues related to that one, such as the great significance of the body's sexual function and the importance of that function for a personal identity and self-evaluation. Vasectomy, as a surgical procedure, is very simple, but without a comfortable way for the injury that it imparts to be discussed, its results may be a major disruption in the quality of a marital relationship. The couple whose sexual relationship becomes externally regulated by a fertility specialist in order to increase chances of achieving pregnancy suffers a similar injury. Sexuality, rather than a joy, can become a dreaded responsibility. Psychologically, we have seen such injuries most often hidden away and not noted as a part of the presenting problem in counseling.

Osherson deals extensively with men's difficulties as a result of their failure to become fathers. In a particularly interesting section of this discussion, he speaks positively of some of the results of this problem in relation to his theme of "healing the wounded father":

> Reproductive difficulties can help heal the wounded father within our hearts by leading us to understand that pain and vulnerability are a part of life, not a badge of failure. A man can come to see that he can do everything right, try as hard as he can, be ingenious, alert, and smart, and life can still knock him on his ass. He may learn the reality of his interconnection with those he loves: the importance of comforting and allowing yourself to be comforted.[10]

The important thing for the pastor, and for the specialized pastoral counselor as well, is not to become an expert on the details of sexuality in order to give advice, but to know enough to understand. A key element in that understanding is taking seriously, though not literally, the bibical injunction to be fruitful and multiply. The need of persons to contribute to the carrying on of their generations is not something that can easily be ignored.

PASTORAL COUNSELING OF COUPLES WHO CARE

Something of the type of pastoral intervention that can take place in response to marital problems has been seen in the discussion of Al and Ann, but our concern here is to present, though briefly, an overall approach to ministry with troubled couples. We describe the process in terms of both intervention in the marital system and providing a caring pastoral relationship:

Stages in the Pastoral Counseling of Couples

SYSTEM INTERVENING	PASTORAL RELATING
1. Structuring to become involved in the marital system	1. Asserting pastoral responsibility for each person in the marriage
2. "In-betweening" or pulling partners apart	2. Pain-sharing with each person
3. Supervising relationship observation	3. Providing a pseudo-marriage or "in the room" affair
4. Consulting on marital communication	4. Giving pastoral blessing to the remarriage
5. Exiting the system	5. Learning to say good-bye*

Although, like most models of a human process, this one distorts as well as reveals, this way of thinking about the therapeutic process seems important in caring for persons in a troubled marriage. The most obvious distortion is the impression given by almost any sequential system that the constituent elements are approximately equal. In this particular case, they are far from equal and vary significantly with every couple. The first two stages in the process are usually the most lengthy and involve the most effort by the pastor or therapist. The most important principle operative within the structure is responding both to the marital system and to the persons involved in it. The aggressive,

* Adapted from *Pastoral Counseling: A Ministry of the Church*, by John Patton. Copyright © 1983 by Abingdon Press.

responsible, *administrative* dimension of caring is expressed in the former, and the tender, solicitous nurturing dimension is expressed in the latter. To be a pastor is to look at the whole picture, not just at troubled individuals within it; therefore, the first response of a pastor to persons involved in a troubled marriage is more to the system they are involved in than to the persons themselves.

What this means in practice is that much of what the pastor has learned about listening to individuals does not seem effective with a marital or family system. (We use the word *seem* advisedly because it is more the way a person goes about the process that is different, not what is actually going on.) What most pastors have learned to do, quite appropriately, in their counseling courses and pastoral experience is to listen. In working with a couple instead of an individual, the importance of listening remains primary; it is the way of listening that changes. What the pastor cannot afford to do is to sit passively and soak up what the couple does when they are in the room with the pastor. This may be very helpful with an individual who needs to unload something that has been bottled up within, but if the same individual is allowed to ventilate feelings that have to do with the marriage relationship, it will be counterproductive and destructive—counterproductive in the sense of simply repeating the unsatisfactory way that the couple is already related, destructive in shaming the less verbal partner in front of an authority figure, as is the pastor.

In the first interview with Al and Ann, the pastor began with the question he habitually uses at the beginning of a couple or family session: "What hurts?" The value of that question is that it focuses on the pain of the person responding rather than on what she or he thinks her or his spouse has done to cause it. Typically, Ann did not wholly ignore the question in her response, but she quickly moved from her feelings to the poverty of the relationship and what Al had done to cause it.

Ann: I get irritable. We just have no communication. I can't get him to talk to me. He won't respond to anything, and I get angry.

At this point, had the pastor simply listened, it is likely that Ann's anger would have begun to build as she began to blame Al for what had happened. She would have attempted to shame him before the pastor, and Al—in spite of his quiet passivity—would have responded angrily and attempted to justify himself by blaming her. We speak of what would likely happen so confidently because we have experienced it so frequently ourselves and have heard it on the tape recordings of our less experienced students.

Family therapist Robert Beavers describes the same process in terms of ambivalence and projection. Unlike many therapists, Beavers is quite explicit about his central values and, in effect, his anthropology—or that which he understands as essentially human. "Avoidance of choice can be seen as an elemental part of human emotional illness. The wry aphorism, 'When adversity comes, take it like a man, blame it on your wife,' captures the flavor of this human tendency to avoid the responsibility inherent in being alive, that is, the responsibility of making personal choices." The anxiety about personal responsibility and choice results in ambivalence—that internal process of swinging back and forth between alternatives and, to reduce this anxiety, projection, or viewing the problem as coming from outside, takes place. "Though the battle is merely shifted [in perception] from an internal source to an external one, the threat to the integrity of the self is removed."[11]

If one looks at Ann's answer to the question of her pain in the light of Beavers' view of the human condition, one can see in it her struggle with responsibility and choice or, using our anthopological framework, her struggle to care and be cared for. One can see it also in her anxiety of having to face up to all of this and, therefore, her blaming the problem on Al. The pastor's task, then, is to become involved in the system and to relate pastorally to each person in it.

Pastor:	Ann, could you go back to your feeling? You're telling me about Al, and I want him to do that. What is it that you have been feeling?
Ann:	(cries softly)
Pastor:	(waits a few moments and then turns to Al) Where is your hurt?
Al:	She's very critical of me. She just doesn't let up. It seems I can't do anything right.
Pastor:	And you feel?
Al:	I don't know. Frustrated I guess.

In this situation, the pastor is able to interrupt Ann and to refocus the question with relative ease, whereas sometimes the projection on the other and the anger that escalates as the other is blamed requires strong and forceful intervention before it can be stopped. What is most important to emphasize is that it is essential that it be done; otherwise, the destructive projection of blame on the other, which goes on regularly at home, simply recurs in another place—this time with an audience. In Al and Ann's situation, the pastor merely has to intervene quietly by restating the question, responding sensitively to Ann's feelings, and then involving Al in the process with the same question. Al responds similarly to Ann, by pointing to what she does to him, but in doing so acknowledges the problem that Rubin has identified in the male developmental process: the difficulty in knowing his feelings.

What the pastor is dealing with early in this relationship with the couple is the difference in their relative ability to know and to share their personal feelings and their problem with boundaries (knowing where one person stops and the other begins). Beavers relates the boundary problem to ambivalence about choice and the way that persons deal with anxiety by putting it outside themselves onto others they are close to. The pastoral task, in the short term, is intervening in the system in a way that breaks up the old projection on the other or, as Beavers puts it, "clarifying the boundaries between family members." The long-term task is assisting Al in recognizing and sharing his feelings. These tasks correspond with what Patton describes as the first two stages in couple intervention: (1) entering the system and taking pastoral responsibility for the persons, and (2) "in-betweening" and pain-sharing. Since what he refers to as stages does not mean that one has to be fully accomplished before another is begun, one can see the activity of the so-called second stage in this very early interaction.

Pastor: (responding to Al's identification of his feeling as frustration) Try to tell me what the frustration is like. Does is remind you of anything that you've ever experienced before?

Al: Well, my mother used to get on me a lot. She still does. It's more like that than anything else.

Ann: I'm not your mother!

Pastor: It's hard for you to have Al identify you with his mother, but I'm not sure why it is so hard.

The pastor "in-betweens" by not letting the angry outburst toward Al continue. Although he could respond to Ann's anger, anger is seldom the primary feeling a person experiences, so the pastor responds to Ann's embarrassment at being likened to Al's mother and attempts to explore it. All the while, the pastoral counselor is attempting not to be seen as identifying with either person, but responding to and caring for the pain in both.

Ann: It's just one more case of his responding to something besides me, his not hearing me.

Pastor: I think Al is just trying to do what both of us are asking him to do: tell us what he's feeling. He's not saying that you're like his mother, but that sometimes when he's with you what he feels is like it felt with her. There really is a difference. (turns to Al, who nods in agreement)

At this point, the pastor attempts to interpret Al's behavior to Ann. The difficulty in doing this comes in maintaining a sensitivity to her feelings, while at the same time suggesting a way of understanding what is going on in Al. This is possible because earlier in the relationship the pastor demonstrated himself to be trustworthy, responding as fairly as possible to each person and insisting with all his personal authority and firmness that one point of view not supersede the other. He suggested to Ann that just because she stirs "mother" feelings in Al does not mean that he sees her primily in that way. Furthermore, he took Al's response, which Ann interpreted negatively, and reframed it positively, commenting that Al is trying to do just what she wants him to. The implicit suggestion is that neither Al nor their situation is impossible; it is simply one that requires understanding and practice.

What is happening in the session is that the interaction is beginning to move from "in-betweening" and "pain-sharing" toward "supervising relationship observation" and an "in-the-room affair." There has been enough breaking up of the old patterns of interaction through the pastor's getting in between the couple and insisting that they relate to him, and there has been enough communication to each person that the pastor does understand their pain that they are becoming free to look at what is going on in the room rather than just bring in things from outside. What is going on now that was not possible earlier is that the pastor has a significant relationship with Al, one that allows the pastor to step back from and supervise Ann in observing and understanding; he also has such a relationship with Ann that he can assist Al in learning from that relationship.

At the risk of being misunderstood, we continue to use Patton's phrase, the "in-the-room affair" between the pastor and one of the spouses, to describe further what is going on in the pastoral counseling process. Even though it has been misunderstood, the phrase has the value of calling attention to itself and, thereby, emphasizing its importance. We are using *affair* to describe a situation in which a married person, because of the relational poverty of the marriage, becomes intimately related to a person or activity outside the marriage. When the brokenness that contributed to the affair can be accepted, the couple can be more open to the true-to-life experience of learning from what has gone wrong rather than vainly trying to fix things without that recognition.

By changing one feature of what takes place in an affair—secrecy to openness—an "in-the-room affair" can take on positive meaning. For example, in sharing Al's or Ann's pain and understanding something of the way they have been experiencing life, the pastor becomes intimately involved with each one in the presence of the other, thereby illustrating that it is possible to appreciate and to understand that person with whom each is having so much difficulty. That relationship, like an affair, provides something that was missing in the marriage, but because it takes place openly, it can be observed, learned from, and later practiced in the primary relationship of the marriage.

If the term *affair* needs to be understood in this specialized way, the term *intimacy* does also. Earlier in this chapter, we discussed Lillian Rubin's and Lyman and Adele Wynne's views of intimacy. What we say here is consistent with those views. *Intimacy* does not mean sexual involvement, but the fact that the term has been associated with sexual expression is instructive. It does point to some of the same things that sexual activity does—willingness to be seen as one is, risking shame in order to express oneself, attending intensely to the needs of the other—all of these features appear in an intimacy that is not physically sexual. What intimacy means in the context of the pastoral relationship is also very similar to what Berger described as creating a *nomic* world. In their disappointment with each other and the distrust that went along with it, Al and Ann were not free to create a meaningful world together. It was possible, however, to do that temporarily with a caring person of the parental generation—the pastor. (The pastoral role and function mean that the pastor, whatever his or her age, is always of the parental generation.) Another way of describing intimacy is by doing some reframing, or changing the meaning of a phrase that is usually used negatively in the practice of family therapy: the *double bind*. That phrase has been used to describe a pathological relationship in which a person is repeatedly controlled cognitively, affectively, and behaviorally by another person, usually a parent or parent figure. In order to try to escape the bind and the possible punishment, the bound person becomes dysfunctional.

Intimacy, in contrast to this, involves persons who understand themselves to have equal power with each other and allow themselves to be influenced, if not controlled, cognitively, affectively, and behaviorally by the other person. As peers in the relationship, they have the freedom to move away from each other at any time. If this freedom is no longer present, what had been intimate becomes a destructive bind that must be broken some way, usually by divorce. A double bind is a relationship with a person one cannot escape. Intimacy is that same thoroughgoing involvement with someone one can escape, but chooses not to. At its best, pastoral counseling offers *an escapable intimacy*, which provides support and satisfaction as well as the opportunity for learning how to relate more effectively. The characteristics of intimacy that we have described here are essentially the same as those that make commitment and recommitment possible in a relationship. They transcend the obligations of loyalty and activate the possibility of choice. If this kind of experience and learning from it do indeed happen, the couple become sure enough of themselves and of the pastor's intervention, if needed, that they can use the counseling session to practice their intimate communication with each other with the pastor's consultation.

Prior to one of their last sessions together, the pastor noticed that Al and Ann were actively involved in talking with each other when he went out to invite them into his office. After they had seated themselves in his office, he commented:

Pastor: The two of you looked like you were involved in something pretty interesting when I came out to greet you.

Al: Oh, it was nothing very important. We were just talking about our visit to see my mother during the holidays.

Pastor: My guess is that was important. What happened?

Ann: He was able to tell her that he didn't want to do something she told him to do, and I don't think he's ever done that before. I mean, he's not done it, but this time he told her, "No," and why.

Pastor: (smiling) I was right. It was important. How did that feel, Al?

Al: OK, I guess. No, it was a little funny. I don't like to tell her no, but what she wanted didn't really make sense, so I told her I wouldn't do it and explained why.

Pastor: And she fainted or had a heart attack?

Al: No. She acted all right. She didn't act up like she used to. I guess I was a little surprised.

Ann: He just didn't make so much of it himself or worry about hurting her, and it worked out.

Pastor: I think I would leave out the word *just*. It seems like a big thing to me. Al's changed some of what's been bothering him in his relationship to his mother. I wonder if he can say no to you, too, or is that different?

Ann: I'd rather he say whatever he's feeling. I might not like it, but then I know where he is.

Pastor: The other interesting thing about this experience is that you seem to have gotten some satisfaction in sharing it and talking about it together. I'm impressed.

Ann: I'm proud of him.
Pastor: And that feels pretty good.
Ann: It sure does.

Now, quite obviously, things don't always work out as well as this interaction seems to, and certainly there will be other pain and struggle to deal with. The pleasantness, in contrast to the earlier unpleasantness, however, is not nearly so important as Al's new form of care for his prior generation, his and Ann's increased ability to talk about the experience, and Ann's willingness to affirm him for what he did do instead of holding out for some greater achievement. The pastor is able to move from a supervisory to a consultative mode of interaction, commenting on and underscoring what is working well. Although not all of his consultation will be in the form of positive support, something to affirm and appreciate makes later suggestion and critical comment easier to accept. We have called this type of interaction, whether the pastor's comments are more positive or negative, consulting on marital communication and giving pastoral blessing to the remarrying that is taking place.

Some explanation of the term *remarrying* seems in order. What this term means to us is not a public ritual at which the minister officiates. It is, rather, the pastor's announcing to the couple through the process of counseling that what they are doing in communicating with each other and in sharing ordinary life experiences with affirmation, rather than blame, is in fact the "in life"—in contrast to the "in ritual"—way that persons marry and stay married to each other. It is, experientially, one of the central meanings of commitment: choosing to be with and to work through the issues that emerge in the process of their life together.

Not long after the session in which this interaction took place, Al and Ann terminated their counseling. Certainly, there was a great deal more to learn from counseling both as individuals and as a couple, but they decided not to do this, choosing rather to try things on their own for a while. In this case, the good-bye process was uncomplicated. In a longer term relationship, in which one or both of the individuals has been intensively involved with the counselor, it takes more time. With Al and Ann, the pastor simply suggested that each of the three of them reflect on what had happened during the course of their time together, looking at both what seemed to have been accomplished and what seemed to have been left undone. Thus the opportunity was given to note important issues still unresolved in the relationship, and the couple was made aware that they could come back again without things having to get so bad as they did the first time.

SOME CONCLUDING REFLECTIONS ON GENERATIONAL CARE IN MARRIAGE

Having suggested some resolution of Al and Ann's marital tension, we find that it seems important to reflect on what has been said about their particular situation in the light of the Christian anthropology of chapter 1 and the understanding of marriage given in this and the preceding chapter. First, we acknowledge what is most obvious in our work and the work of others. When "case material," or specific human events, are brought together with theory, they never fit neatly together. Human events never fully illustrate the theory, and the theory does not interpret or explain all that happens in concrete human experience. In spite of that, we believe that one can see theory enriching the understanding of human life and pastoral practice and specific event challenging and broadening the scope of the particular theory.

With respect to the human event that we have focused on in this chapter, we see that Al and Ann do indeed have a "communication problem," but the vocation of the pastoral counselor includes an understanding of human beings that does not allow her or him simply to deal with that. Although in the verbatim material we can see a good deal of explicit work on clarifying and suggesting means of improving communication, underlying the whole counseling process is the pastor's assumption that the deeper pain of both Al and Ann is related to the inability to care for their generations. They are human beings created in and for relationship to God and their fellows, who have been given the gift of time to carry out their vocation to care. Like Adam and Noah, they are a part of generations with responsibilities to the generations on either side of them in the stream of history.

Not everyone can literally carry out God's call to Eve and Adam within the world views of the Genesis writers. That vocation, however, transcends the literal meaning of having children to populate the world and taming its wildness through cultivation. Rather, it can be understood in our time to mean doing whatever needs to be done to care for the world that God has created and, with respect to the family, caring for the relationships of our own generation and those before and after us. What this means practically is that the issues of family life that confront the pastor—and this includes issues with her or his own family—need to be dealt with not only as problems to be solved, but also as expressions and frustrations of the human calling to care.

Ann is angry with Al not only because of his lack of communications skills or seeming indifference to her, but also because she needs his help in caring for her parents, to move the inequities of the parent-child relationship toward one that includes the mutuality of persons who care for one another as adults. They are frustrated in their sexual intimacy. Intercourse is infrequent and not particularly satisfying. They may need some attention to specific sexual techniques, but more likely, and certainly more within the pastor's vocation, they need attention to feelings about their childlessness and how, having dealt with that loss, they can still contribute to the next generation.

With respect to their own generation, their need is for communication skills on one level, but on a deeper level their need is for respect and understanding of how they are alike and different as male and female and how they may be intimate without losing their individuality and distinctiveness. They need, further, to be aware of and to experience the ways in which, in spite of their own imperfections and the imperfections of their spouse, they repeatedly choose or recommit themselves to each other.

An issue that is evident in most marital cases of tension and conflict and is an important part of the theological picture of humankind's vocation to care is not obvious in what we have presented about Al and Ann. It is the issue of the relationship between love and work. At some point in most marriages today, there is significant tension between the vocation to care for one's family relationships and that to care for the world outside the family. Further digging into Al and Ann's story would reveal that tension, but not as strongly as our overall pastoral experience has revealed it in others. Much of the work in the pastoral care of marriage can involve assisting couples in their understanding and acceptance of their vocation and the vocation of their spouse to care for the world—that is, to carry out a useful task outside the family and for the benefit of the community as a whole. We have dealt with this issue in some detail in the chapters on singleness and preparation for marriage, but that should not suggest its lack of importance here.

The image of nakedness without shame, with which we began this chapter has primarily been used in Christian history as symbolic and the pre-Fall state of human innocence, but it also suggests an important truth about intimacy in marriage. The marriage partner is, normatively, the "bone of my bone and flesh of my flesh" from whom one does not have to hide. He or she is the person with whom one has shared the vocation to care for the earth and to make a life together and for others. Thus it is not only shame in relation to each other from which the couple should be free, but also shame in relation to the generations before and after. They are able to live without having to be ashamed of how those responsibilities have been carried out. Finally, that comfort in nakedness or freedom from shame comes from each one's having carried out his or her vocation to care for the world as well as for the family, for those outside the immediate circle of kin as well as for those within it. Although our sexuality is an essential expression of the intimacy of the marriage relationship, it is not a sufficient expression. What is also required is our pride and respect for the other because of his or her fulfillment of the human vocation to care in a different, but significant, way for those outside the marriage relationship.

NOTES

1. Augustus Napier, *The Family Crucible* (New York: Harper, 1978).
2. Rosemary Haughton, "Marriage: An Old, New Fairy Tale." In J. J. Burtchaell, ed., *Marriage Among Christians* (Notre Dame, Ind.: Ave Maria Press, 1977), pp. 131-50.
3. John Barnett, "The Natural History of a Marriage," *Pilgrimage*, vol. 9, no. 1, (Spring, 1981) 12.
4. Lyman Wynne and Adele Wynne, "The Quest for Intimacy." *Journal of Marital and Family Therapy* (1986), vol. 12, no. 4, 383-94.
5. Lillian Rubin, *Just Friends*, p. 69.
6. Ibid., p. 71.
7. Karl Menninger, *The Theory of Psychoanalytic Technique* (New York: Basic Books, 1958), pp. 147-51.

8. Charles V. Gerkin, *The Living Human Document* (Nashville: Abingdon Press, 1984), p. 137.

9. Nancy Chodorow, *The Reproduction of Mothering: Psychoanalysis and the Sociology of Gender* (Berkeley, Calif.: University of California Press, 1978), p. 169.

10. Samuel Osherson, *Finding Our Fathers: The Unfinished Business of Manhood* (New York: The Free Press, 1986), p. 112.

11. Robert Beavers, *Successful Marriage: A Family Systems Approach to Couples Therapy* (London: W. W. Norton, 1985), pp. 34-35.

CHAPTER FIVE

GENERATIONAL CARING IN THE NUCLEAR FAMILY

God setteth the solitary in families (Psalm 68:5a KJV)

The Jenningses were one of the "refreshingly normal" families in the congregation. Bill and Lucy were elders, and their two children, Carol and Rick, took an active part in church activities. Bill was in his early forties and held a responsible position with the local power company. Although he had no advanced engineering degrees, he had made the most of his military training in electrical work and had progressed to an important supervisory job in the company. For seven years, he had gone to night school and obtained a bachelor's degree. Lucy was in her late thirties and combined her family work with secretarial work in another church in town. In her spare time, she was the "cab driver for the kids," helped out with the Boy Scout troop, and did volunteer work at the hospital. Carol, sixteen, was known as the most beautiful girl in the youth fellowship. At school, she was a cheerleader, worked on the school paper, and was a good enough student to set her heart on going to an Ivy League college. She wanted to be a doctor or maybe do something with children.

Rick was a spirited thirteen-year-old. While his grades were not as good as Carol's, he had a special sensitivity that was admired, particularly by his father. While he sometimes seemed to brood, he was also capable of real extroversion and playfulness. He was in a rock band that played mostly to itself in the garage of one of his best friends. Lucy used to say, "If this were the fifties, he would be a beatnik. If it were the sixties, he would be a hippie. Right now, we just hope that he doesn't come home with a safety pin in his nose. He's a good kid, but he does try me sometimes. Bill seems almost to encourage his antics. Not with anything specific. It's just that adoring smile he gets on his face when Rick comes up with one of his stunts."

In this chapter, we discuss generational caring in what has been called the intact, or nuclear, family: a household of two parents and one or more children. It may also include members of the parental generation of the nuclear parents (grandparents) as well as possible brothers and sisters and aunts and uncles.[1] The family has been described as a crucible.[2] Indeed, the household that consists of two or more generations—the so-called nuclear family—can exhibit a high intensity of heat in relationships that severely tests patience and emotional resources. More often than not, the testing is more subtle than dramatic; yet, the trials and tribulations of caring for and being cared for are constant. In the day to day life of a family, the issue of generational care is a constant process.

Bill Jennings was the eldest of two children from the Midwest. His father was an artist who had worked as a youth in the WPA. Though usually dependable, he had the reputation of being eccentric. He had died in an automobile accident while Bill was in the Army, leaving enough money to support Bill's mother, who was a school secretary, and his younger sister, who is now married to a dentist in Chicago. Bill was always close to his mother and played the role of the "good boy," almost as if to balance the role played by his artist father. Recently, Bill's mother had moved into his and Lucy's home. She had had some minor strokes, and he and his sister had decided that it would be best if their mother spent time at each of their houses, six months at Bill and Lucy's and six months with Bill's sister and her husband.

Lucy also came from the Midwest. Her father was a fairly successful independent contractor in house remodeling. Her older brother now owned the family company, and her parents lived a very comfortable life in a condominium in Florida. She described the family as close, in that they cared very much for one another, but they didn't see as much of one another as Lucy would like. Her mother and father were always keen on teaching independence, and, while loving and generous to their grandchildren, they tended to practice what they preached. Lucy's mother worked in the home until Lucy's brother went to high school. From then on she did the bookkeeping for Lucy's father's business and volunteer work.

One day, while Lucy helped with hospital patients from the congregation who wanted to receive communion, her pastor, Gail, noticed that Lucy seemed torn between needing to go home and wanting to talk. She had noticed several times that Lucy said she had to get home; yet, she persisted in chatting with the pastor in the lobby. Finally, Gail suggested that they take a few minutes to have tea together in the hospital snack bar.

Pastor: It's nice to be able to sit just for a few minutes during the day.

Lucy: Yes, just to sit. The tea tastes good. But, I do have to go soon and see how Mother is. I mean Bill's mother.

Pastor: Is it difficult to have her with you right now?

Lucy: No . . . well yes . . . sometimes. It's just that I don't know sometimes. She is a nice person, and we have always gotten along pretty well. She does have her own notions of how the kitchen should be run, but mostly she gets in the way. It is my kitchen.

Pastor: Two mothers in the house is one too many, heh?

Lucy: Well, it's not terrible and it won't be forever. It's really that I don't have time to myself like I used to. I'm used to being able to do what I want while the kids are in school. Now I have to take into consideration how long I can be away for fear she will have another stroke. And she and Carol are having some problems. She spends so much time worrying about Rick and scolding him, she almost dotes on him. Bill does, too, so Carol gets fed up with it all and locks herself in her room—that is, when she doesn't have an excuse to get out of the house.

Pastor: Sounds like Carol may be a bit jealous.

Lucy: I never thought of it that way. Maybe . . . she has always been the fair-haired child. Do you know she is thinking about going to Brown! Bill and I will have to pull off the financial miracle of the decade to be able to afford that. It sure would be nice, though. Bill sure works hard to make it happen. (silence for several moments) It's hard to believe that the children are growing up. You know, Gail, we have done a pretty good job of it, though.

Pastor: You sure have. I hope Sean and I can do the same.

Lucy: (laughing) Do you have a mother-in-law, too?
Pastor: Come to think of it, I do. I'll come to you if I need any help.

Although the Jenningses appear to be the mythical family of the American dream, they have problems, too. They are an intact family who work hard in their community and who care for one another in the rather quiet sequence of their daily lives. Over the time that they have together, the Jennings family will have to accommodate to change, solve problems, and deal with issues of affection and sexuality, autonomy and dependence, relationships within the extended family, and relationships with non-family members. It appears that they have done fairly well. They don't need pastoral counseling, but they do need pastoral care, such as that offered in the hospital coffee shop. What it is, in the life of the family, that needs to be cared for and how that caring takes place is the subject of the remainder of this chapter.

UNDERSTANDING THE NUCLEAR FAMILY

We understand the family to be dynamic, in flux, and, therefore, always somewhat ambiguous. Trying to understand the material boiling in the family crucible of even a "normal" family, like the Jenningses, requires dynamic categories that reflect the energy of the family system. Dynamics is generally understood as the study of energy components. It involves the conflicts among dimensions, the tensions and counterbalances among forces, and the variety of equilibriums within a structure or system—in our case, the family system. We have chosen two sets of categories to interpret family dynamics, we understand one set as primarily theological[3]—authority and covenant, communion and vocation, and solidarity and creativity[4]—and the other as primarily psychosocial—dependence and individuation, loyalty and delegation, and homeostasis and heterostasis.

These categories have not been arbitrarily chosen. They describe the two basic energy components of family dynamics: centering and moving out. A family is a dynamic entity that finds its locus of attention between the tension of the family household on the one hand and the outside world on the other. This tension has been termed *centripetal/centrifugal* by several family theorists.[5]

Families that are centripetal seek their identity and satisfaction mostly within the family household, while centrifugal families find most of their satisfaction outside the household. Optimally functioning families would be placed on some kind of midline between the two poles, while dysfunctional families would be on one extreme or another. Our theological and psychosocial pairs illustrate the tension between the poles. First, we address the theological dynamics of the family.

AUTHORITY AND COVENANT

Our central assumption about families is that human beings are God's creatures, entrusted with the care of the earth. The seat of all authority is the author of creation. The Nicean Creed states it: "We believe in one God, the Father Almighty, Maker of heaven and earth and of all things visible and invisible." Calvin puts it another way.

> Thence we shall learn that God, by the power of his Word and Spirit, created out of nothing the heaven and the earth . . . and since all things are subject to corruption, has, nevertheless, provided for the preservation of every species till the last day . . . that on some he has conferred the power of propagation, in order that the whole species may not be extinct at their death; that he has thus wonderfully adorned heaven and earth with the utmost possible abundance, variety, and beauty, like a large and splendid mansion, most exquisitely and copiously furnished.[6]

The authority possessed by God, following Calvin's understanding, was in part handed over to human beings through the Church Universal and to civil authorities in order to care for the earth. However, authority is not just imposed. It is also shared and, at some level, participated in by all. For there to be any authority at all, there must be some tacit acknowledgment of it by those under that authority. Authority that is imposed or is *authoritarian* is essentially understable. Paul Tillich makes this point clearly in his discussion of the "history-bearing, centered group." In his section of the *Systematic Theology* dealing with "History and the Kingdom of God," he describes this type of group as able to keep the members united and to preserve its own power while maintaining contact with other power groups. "In order to fulfill the first condition a history-bearing group must have a central, law-giving, administering, and enforcing authority."[7] The centered group must also be able to maintain its integrity in its intercourse with other groups. The role of authority is essential in fulfilling these two conditions.

> The support is based on an experience of belonging, a form of communal *eros* which does not exclude struggles for power within the supporting group but which unites it against other groups. This is obvious in all statelike organizations from the family up to the nation. Blood relations, language, traditions, and memories create many forms of *eros* which make the power structure possible." (*Systematic Theology*, III, p. 309)

Eros, as used by Tillich here, is human striving for ultimate fulfillment for the *summum bonum*. The communal *eros* is that which strives to maintain its power *vis á vis* the power of other communities that could threaten it (*Systematic Theology*, I, pp. 280-81).

The authority of the family is expressed structurally. Some kind of authority conveying hierarchy is essential for family living. The very decision to have children is a decision to exercise authority. Children do not come into the world as equal partners with their parents. They are unable to survive on their own in either a physical or a social sense. They are dependent for years, more so than any other creature in God's creation. As one writer has put it: "The family is the only social system that creates some of its members from scratch [infants]."[8] Thus the authority of the group is central. The family, as a social system, can survive only if new members are taught the rules and orders of the system, lest they be swallowed up by other systems. Or, as Tillich has emphasized, a centered group maintains its own members so that it can be in contact with other centered groups.

The Jennings family, like other families, is a history bearing group, struggling to maintain its centeredness. Children, especially in their early years, are dependent and under the authority of the parents. Tasks are learned, social skills are honed, and boundaries are clearly set, both in a hierarchical sense (parents and children) and in a horizontal sense (those who are my family and those who are not). The boundaries are permeable, allowing for some movement between them. Too rigid boundaries result in isolation, thereby denying Tillich's second condition for being a centered group: contact with others.

The authority of the family is functional as well as structural. It is found in the identity of the family as family. The Jennings family's decision to have Bill's mother live with them, at least part-time, was at least tacitly a decision based on the authority of the family to care for the needs of its members even when those members have not been recent or long-term members of the nuclear household. In this sense, the authority became articulated as a covenantal one.

Families, over the passage of time, add members through childbearing and lose members through death and growing up and moving away. Centered families (that is families on the midline between centripetal and centrifugal) also deal with contacts with other groups and group members (non-kin). The task that has to be completed is allowing for the flux of the coming and going of others while still maintaining a central identity with a common history of traditions.

In the previous chapter, we discussed four common religious symbols for marriage. Some stressed the institution of marriage, while others emphasized commitment and loyalty working themselves out in the family caring process. All four symbols are important, but the symbols of covenant and vocation are functionally more important for our theory of caring for your generations. The symbol of covenant seems most important to describe the family, the symbol of vocation to describe marriage as the central feature of the family covenant.

The symbol of covenant seems inescapably hierarchical and finds its most typical expression in the Deuteronomic covenant.

> The relation of the God of Israel to his nation is based on a covenant. The covenant demands justice, namely, the keeping of the Commandments, and it threatens the violation of justice with rejection and destruction. This means that God is independent of his nation and of his own individual nature. If his nation breaks the covenant, he still remains in power. (*Systematic Theology*, I, p. 227)

A most important part of the covenant is the place of the will and the intention of those who enter into it. As William Everett has put it, "The actors and the powers they bring to the covenant drama are very important. Whereas sacramental symbols tend to emphasize conformation to a structure of true authority, covenant stresses the exercise of power in creating a new world."[9] Covenant implies a negotiation between the parties in the covenant about that which is covenanted for. It requires true relationship and the acknowledgment of differences and, therefore, also involves considerable creativity. There is no easy match of ideas and personalities. Covenants call for work.

How children fit into a covenanting community is not entirely clear. Early on in the life of a child, he or she is more under the power of authority. His or her will is more imposed upon, rather than invoked. As the children grow and take on more and more responsibilities, the more generalized authority of the family takes precedence over the hierarchical one. It is at this point that children take on more and more a covenantal relationship with other members of the family.

> Everyone has definite duties to perform, though these are renegotiated as the child grows older. Perhaps the best example of this is the Puritan claim that the family was a "little commonwealth." The family was molded around a civic ideal for which the members were to be trained through family disciplines. In its modern form, rooted in bourgeois culture, it is found in the parent-effectiveness model advanced by Gaulke. (*Blessed Be the Bond*, p. 49)

Taking Bill's mother into the Jennings' nuclear family was based on the already existing authority and integrity of the family and the making of a new relationship based on a new covenant. Bill and his sister covenanted to share the responsibility of caring for their infirm mother. The members of the Jennings nuclear family also covenanted with one another to care for her, though the implications for this were not always clear. As the conversation with the pastor has revealed, Lucy had to struggle with having another mother in the house. Covenanting requires negotiation and flexibility. Bill's mother also participated in the covenant by coming into the household as an outsider, yet at the same time as a member of the family.

COMMUNION AND VOCATION

The concept of communion is paradoxical. It encompasses two seemingly opposite qualities: individuality and profound union.

For there to be communion at all there must be the participation of two (or more) centered or individualized persons, unique in their identity in the perception of others and willing to be in touch and in communication with others who also hold out their uniqueness. According to Bernard Haring, the Trinity offers us a good example of the paradox of communion. The Trinity illustrates the interpenetration of three entities, though there is also a separateness among the three members.[10] Following this line of argument, Everett believes that the paradox of the Trinity also implies the hierarchy of the patriarchal family. From the Father comes the Son, the Father's heir, and this is made possible through the feminine Spirit. "The primary unit is not the Father, the Son, or the Spirit, however. It is the godhead. Sociologically, it is the family or household community."[11]

Tillich has a more egalitarian attitude in his understanding of communion. For him, communion is the result of individualization's reaching its perfect form in the "person." Communion is only possible in two or more perfectly centered persons, who have no desire to destroy the individuality of the other. The existence of other selves promotes a resistance to our own selves, and the human's propensity for absolutizing the self is called into question. "One individual can conquer the entire world of objects, but he cannot conquer another person without destroying him as a person. The individual discovers himself through this resistance. If he does not want to destroy the other person, he must enter into communion with him. In the resistance of the other person the person is born."[12] Communion, then, is the active participation of selves in all their individuality. There is a separateness as well as union. It is also human participation for participation's sake. There is even a mystical religious quality about it.

Communion involves the private life of the family. When communion occurs in a family, it is the shared intimacy of individual selves participating in it in their uniqueness as well as in their similarity. It is important to note that communion is not to be confused with sameness or what some family therapists call *enmeshment*. Lucy, Bill, Carol, and Rick all have their own particular idiosyncracies. Rick's eccentricism, possibly not unlike that of his paternal grandfather, irritates as well as pleases.

Constant in all of this is the family's identity as the Jenningses, capable of solving problems and living life in its redundancy.

The dynamic that must be considered in tension with communion is the public dynamic of work or vocation. *Vocation* is a term used to denote the use of one's abilities in the public maintenance of creation. Luther put it best: "God himself will milk the cows through him whose vocation that is."[13] The term *vocation* has more often than not been associated, particularly in the Roman Catholic tradition, with the public vow to the priesthood or religious order. This is a far too narrow understanding of the term. It is through humanity's calling that creation is cared for, and, according to the reformed tradition, all work fits into the holy order. God's intention for us is to tend to the earth and to work for its betterment. Therefore, all work may be considered as part of this duty. The minister's vocation is the public work of healing souls. The milkman's vocation is to milk the cow. Both vocations, as well as all others, find their source in a creator God.

The Marxist critique of capitalism has demonstrated that there is no more painful alienation than to be cut off from the intent or product of one's labor. In work experienced as the expression of one's vocation, however, there is a unity of the public quality of producing a valued product and the private sense of immersion in one's own creativity and the purposes of the creator God. Such is the point made by Soelle and Cloyes in discussing the creative activities of children as preparation for "good work" later in life:

> One of the most misguided things a parent can do is to interrupt a young child immersed in an activity. When children are genuinely absorbed in a task, they display an intense love for work. Children can teach us about what respect for the worker means, namely, honoring the forgetfulness of self that occurs during concentrated periods of good work and the human need to finish the task at hand. Immersed in good work, we forget time and space, even hunger and thirst. . . . Good work releases the divine element in us by which we rediscover the source of our creativity and our connection to all living things. (*To Work and to Love,* pp. 96-97)

Communion and vocation are aspects of our private and public selves. One denotes the willful union of individuals who participate in each other's lives with intimacy. The other denotes the public quality of tending to God's creation, not for the sake of the self alone but for the sake of all that has been created. There can be a mystical quality to them both.

SOLIDARITY AND CREATIVITY

Solidarity represents maintenance, while creativity represents change or newness. Solidarity is in part the communal consciousness of individuals that allows for a sense of coherence between the individuals themselves. It is the sense on the part of each individual that the community (the family) is united in one or more respects. The uniting principles can be interests, aspirations, sympathies, or ideals. James Fowler, in his essay on the theology of H. Richard Niebuhr, describes this phenomenon through Niebuhr's understanding of the ethical stance of the community of faith in response to God the redeemer. Fowler understands solidarity to be a triadic structure. Individual human beings sense the superordinate value or goodness that transcends them as individuals. If the individual also perceives others who share this sense of the superordinate, one places oneself within a community of faithfulness. There is reciprocity among all three points of the triadic structure.[14] In a real sense, the household becomes a household because of a solidarity around important principles, legacies, and, of course, through kinship. This understanding of the household as being in solidarity is not unlike the notion of household as described in John Elliot's work on the Gentile Christian communities, who understood themselves as *koinonia* (household) and *oikou tou theou* (household of God) or *oikos pneumatikos* (household of the spiritual).[15]

Solidarity can take on many rather subtle forms. In an article investigating the similarities between a child's private speech and an adult's petitionary prayer, Childs has pointed out that both have social ordering qualities that allow for persons to live with order and cohesion.[16] Prayer is not just an individual's placing himself or herself in communion with God. It is also a way of understanding the self in relation to others who pray. "Prayer just may be a primary vehicle for our understanding of the relationship of all who pray and who understand themselves as part of God's creation. This may well be what the Roman Catholic tradition means in its understanding of the solidarity of all who pray and the communion of saints."[17] In a sense, this is an ethical stance. The household is bound together in terms of something greater than itself, and this gives it (the household) a sense of maintenance and continuity over time.

The dynamic held in tension with solidarity is creativity. According to Herbert Anderson, "Creation is an open system in which God's creative activity continues to be that of making something new."[18] God's creation is an open system in which novelty and change is ever present. Pascal's comment notwithstanding ("The more things change the more they stay the same"), creativity plays a role in the passing of time. Differences are confronted and adapted to, or they are resisted; yet, even in resistance there is a tacit acknowledgment of change and creativity. In terms of the family, then, creativity and change are in tension with solidarity, though both are needed. "The family must be an open system. . . . The privatization of the family, which is intended to be protective, ultimately leads to moral bankruptcy. One can say, therefore, that in a sense a family 'sins' by being closed."[19]

The Jennings family was caught in the tension between solidarity and creativity. Carol exemplified this in many ways. Her understanding of her household was compromised with the entry of her grandmother. Her solidarity with the community, in which she played the special role of the "good girl" with heaps of attention, was challenged when Grandmother paid what Carol thought was inordinate attention to "less good" younger brother, Rick. Yet, the very act of allowing Grandmother into the household was an act of solidarity to the larger, or extended, family and was itself a creative act.

All three of the dynamically related pairs we have described seemed to be in play in the Jennings family. Although relatively stable, it is far from being a static institution. Like other families, it is always in flux through the passage of time. New members can enter and leave. Family identity is maintained and challenged. Issues of control and the compromising that can occur are ever present. Through all of this, God's command to care for the earth is worked out, but it is not accomplished without ambiguity, conflict, and ambivalence. Nonetheless it is worked out.

THE PSYCHOSOCIAL NATURE OF THE FAMILY

The modern social sciences have given us a multiplicity of ways of investigating the family. There are sociological approaches, economic approaches, approaches based on individual personality, historical approaches based on general systems theory, dyadic approaches, and approaches based on group theory. We have found object relations theory and family systems theory to be most helpful in understanding the individual within the family community. Care for the generations has both individual motivations and systemic qualities.[20]

It seems useful to us to look at families using three pairs of psychosocial dynamics that are somewhat analagous to the three pairs of theological dynamics discussed earlier in this chapter. These three pairs are dependence and individuation, loyalty and delegation, and homeostasis and heterostasis. Our primary perspective in using these pairs is vertical as well as horizontal. By this we mean that our investigation is intergenerational, rather than intragenerational, or the investigation between two members of the same generation. It is just as important to understand these dynamics as they come in to play between a person and his or her parents or his or her children as it is to see it in play among marital partners, siblings, or peer groups.

DEPENDENCE AND INDIVIDUATION

The total dependence of the child on the parent before birth continues after birth as well. While this dependence is mostly for physical comfort, feeding, and cleaning, there is also a social dependence. The child's needs for affiliation are met by the gentle touching and caressing of the parent. For several years, those years just prior to school age, the child needs to be near a nurturing and caring object. The child is also dependent on the parent for social skills. It learns the boundaries between the me and not-me, that there are others in this world who have wills and desires of their own. The parents are responsible for helping the child learn how to adapt to the resistance of the existence of others, set the boundaries of social protocol, and afford the safety of membership in the family unit. As the child grows, ideally he or she begins to tend to his or her own needs, though some form of dependence is always present. It is not unusual in our time for children to be financially (and, therefore, really emotionally) dependent well into their twenties and sometimes longer.

Probably the primary way that dependence is expressed in the family unit is through its hierarchical structure. Functioning families operate on a structure in which there are clear boundaries between the generations, with clear control and authority placed on the parents. According to Salvador Minuchin, the leading proponent of structural family therapy, the boundaries must have some permeability, particularly as the children grow and assume more responsibility for their own behavior. Too rigid a boundary can lead to family dysfunction just as can too permeable a boundary in which children can play the parental role and the parents can be dependent and passive.[21]

While dependence and interdependence of family members is a natural and desirable reality, it can also have its more pathological side. In both Bowen's notion of the undifferentiated family ego mass [22] and Lyman Wynne's notion of pseudomutuality,[23] the identity of each family member is so dependent on some close emotional relationship with each other member that there is a fusion of identity. Such families tend to have little contact with others outside of the nuclear family because contact with others threatens the integrity of the fused family. To use Tillich's terminology, they cannot be "centered communities." There is a fear that others can take over, and to be independent in relationships with those outside the family is to be subject to its being divided and, therefore, conquered.

In tension with the notion of dependence is the notion of individuation. "Basically, individuation denotes the formation of individual characteristics and psychological boundaries. The evolution of life over millions of years toward ever more highly individuated species has been beset by two opposing dangers: over- and under-individuation."[24] Over-individuation leads to isolation and separateness, while under-individuation leads to boundaries that are too soft, making the family prone to fusion. The process of individuation involves developing ever newer levels of communication and reconciliation. Family members, especially children as they grow, become other directed, especially in the adolescent years. Both the parents and younger siblings must adapt to this process and, to use the terminology of

Helm Stierlin and his associates, there must be a reconciliation on this new level of communication. "At certain times and in certain ways the otherwise firm and protective boundaries must open up so separateness can be reconciled with togetherness, individuality with solidarity, autonomy with interdependence."[25] Healthy family members are able to have a sense of separateness while still maintaining emotional contact within the family unit. Identity is maintained both as a family member and as a member of other social units, such as clubs, peer groups, and marriages.

Issues of dependence and individuation can be clearly seen in the Jennings family. In fact, the two main issues that have been presented in their story have a great deal to do with how to tolerate individual differences and at the same time stay in relationship. In the relationship between the two siblings, Carol and Rick, the tension between their differences from each other appears to be most intense. While both are and have been dependent on their identity with their parents, both, too, are moving toward separation. Yet, the relationship between the two will probably be the most long-lasting of all the subsystems in the family system.

> Of the three major family subsystems, the sibling subsystem is potentially the most enduring, with many sibling dyads in existence for 80 or 90 years. . . . As the individual grows older, the family system and the individual's roles within that system changes. Beginning in the role of child in the family of origin, the individual "rises" in the system to assume the roles of spouse and then parent in the family of procreation and finally the roles of grandparent and possibly great-grandparent. At the same time, certain roles (e.g., dependent child) are relinquished with the passage of time.[26]

Carol grew impatient with Rick's development of his independent personality, the eccentric, and while this personality development may have been due in part to some systemic loyalty to his paternal grandfather (to be discussed later in this chapter), the tension was compounded in Carol's perception of her grandmother's doting on him. With Carol's waning central position of the good girl being threatened, she regressed to a more infantile 'whining' position that probably later was translated to redoubled efforts at being good. While she had the identity of being the self-motivated prize student and beauty queen, she was dependent on the family for maintaining that identity.

Bill's mother found herself in a particularly difficult position. For most of her married years, she was dependent on her husband, as unpredictable as he may have been. She also had to be self-sufficient, particularly after her husband's death. Then, in her later years, because of her own failing health, she moved into her child's home in a somewhat dependent position. This reversal has not been an easy one, and her systemic attempts to grasp for her old identity as a head of a household resulted in the tension between Lucy and her in the running of the kitchen. Lucy, herself, had trouble with this move on Grandmother's part to have authority over her. For Lucy, after all, adults were to be independent, as taught by her parents, so she had to resist Grandmother's authority move. Bill, meanwhile, is caught between being parent and child. Thus the stress in the family unit, which Lucy shared with the pastor, is not surprising.

LOYALTY AND DELEGATION

According to Boszormenyi-Nagy, loyalty and delegation are concepts that inbue the person with the ability to make choices and decisions. "In essence, loyalty [and delegation] always means making a preferential choice. Loyalty implies that a person has a choice between two alternatives. Otherwise, loyalty would be a superfluous word and could be replaced by dyadic terms like adhering, liking, or agreeing."[27] (It is important to note here that Boszormenyi-Nagy does not make the distinction between loyalty and commitment, which we have made in chapter 2, that identifies loyalty with "vertical" relationships between generations and commitment with horizontal relationships with generations.) Marriage accentuates the conflict between loyalty to one's family of origin—the prior generation—and commitments to one's own generation, one's spouse, one's job, and one's peers.

This triangulated collision of loyalty also finds full play in the vertical plane. Bill and his sister's decision to care for their aging mother consisted, in part, of a sense of loyalty to the person who had for a great deal of their life nurtured and cared for them. However, taking Grandmother into the house conflicted with Lucy's perception of Bill's loyalty to her. While on one level the act of taking Grandmother in was fine with Lucy, it did seem to conflict with the notion of her own sense of what should have been a primary loyalty Bill had to her. In addition, it also seemed to collide with Lucy's own notion of loyalty, taught to her by her independent parents. Lucy learned very early on from her own parents that adults should take care of themselves. Taking Grandmother in seemed to compromise Lucy's participation in her loyalty to this family legacy. In addition, Bill's mother's presence in the kitchen threatened Lucy's independence and control over her house.

The children, too, were caught in the ever-widening web of loyalty conflicts. Carol in particular found herself in conflict with her grandmother. While adult kin have a certain responsibility of authority over more dependent children, Carol was caught between her loyalty to her parents and to Grandmother. Grandmother's doting over the unpredictable grandson increased Carol's loyalty and dependence on her mother in particular.

The stress in the family over loyalty issues both on the vertical and the horizontal planes was apparent: Bill for his mother and wife; Lucy to her parents and her parents' notion of how adult parents should be. All of this stress was expressed, in part, by Lucy's hesitancy to go home from the hospital visit. The pastor heard the story and could well have been guided in her pastoral care of Lucy with this notion of family loyalty.

The second tension of this pair, delegation, is closely connected with the notion of family loyalty. The meaning of delegation is derived from the term *delegate,* one who is trusted with the carrying out of a mission. "Delegation . . . involves the interplay of both centripetal and centrifugal forces. Both meanings of the Latin verb *delegare* are appropriate: "to send out" and "to entrust with a mission." The keystone of delegation is the loyalty bond that binds the delegate to the delegating individual."[28] Delegation, then, is a response, either conscious or unconscious, to the power of authority over and one's loyalty to a significant individual with whom there has been an intensely close relationship.

The bond that generates the action of delegation is usually the parent-child one. On a very simple level, delegation can be understood as an act of loyalty and even gratitude for the caring given us by our parents. While we agree that there are very few pure human motivations, at least part of the reason many people enter helping professions is in response to the caring that they received from their parents. As Stierlin has put it: "Delegation gives our lives direction and significance; it is the sheet anchor of obligations reaching down through generations. As delegates of our parents, we have the possibility of proving our loyalty and integrity and of fulfilling missions reaching beyond purely personal levels" (*The First Interview with the Family*, pp. 23-24). If loyalty is the call, then delegation is the vocation.

While delegaton has some very positive dimensions, the term has been generally understood by most family therapists, Nagy being the most prominent, as being pathological. There is no question that the so-called identified patient or client in a dysfunctional family is more often than not a delegate or scapegoat—that is, the bearer of the pathology of the family system, rather than a pathological individual. The teen-age boy who chronically gets in trouble with his drinking and sexual activity may be the delegate for his father's secret desire for sexual excitement. Under the guise of helping the son, the father may desire all the details of the son's sexual exploits. It is important to remember that the father himself is also the child of parents who may have delegated some of their family system's pathology to him. The delegation pattern may have begun several generations ago. While it is helpful to have some understanding of delegation as a pathological phenomenon, it is more important to understand it in positive terms.

Many of the Jennings family's positive and enviable qualities, for example, were undoubtedly responses to positive and altruistic lessons learned from generations before. The call to care for all things on the earth was not just a call to one generation alone. Carol's wanting to be a doctor or to do things with children, while possibly laced with some narcissism, seems consistent to the notion of service to the community, instilled by her parents and beyond. Lucy's independence was a legacy of her own family of origin. Rick's delegated role, too, is an interesting one. His eccentrism and his occasional brooding seemed to be encouraged by the cuing given him by his father. Even his grandmother's worrying about him seemed to the envious Carol to be more like doting rather than disapproval. Could we not look at his behavior almost as some kind of family protestant principle: Conformity must always be questioned lest it become dull and flat acquiescence to what is. It appears that in many ways he was carrying on the legacy of his "bohemian" paternal grandfather, who was admired by Bill but, for reasons that are not entirely clear, could not afford to have the spontaneity for himself. Possibly Bill's own loyalty to his mother forced him to be "responsible," thereby necessitating his giving up another quality he found attractive.

HOMEOSTASIS AND HETEROSTASIS

For years the notion of homeostasis has been an essential building block for family theorists and therapists. It was first introduced as a concept applicable to the family by Nathan Ackerman in 1958, one of the founders of the family therapy movement. Using some principles from both the physiologist Walter Cannon and Newtonian physics, homeostasis "refers to the vital principle that preserves the intactness and continuity of the human organism, the capacity for maintaining effective, coordinated changing conditions of life."[29] The term *homeostasis* means literally to stay the same. It is the concept that allows for some understanding of the ability of organisms (and by implication the family organism or system) to maintain stability in the face of incoming stimulation from the environment and internal stimulation and stress. Pressures from both within and without threaten the integrity and continuity of the organism; yet, somehow there is some device that protects them both. A biophysiological example of homeostasis is temperature control. The body has the ability, within limited parameters, to maintain a temperature around 98.6 degrees. If the temperature is elevated due to fever or environmental heat, the body sweats and lowers the temperature. In cold, the body shivers, thereby producing heat; there is some kind of internal thermostat. Of course, humans and some other animals can alter their environments with clothes and shelter to augment their own internal device.

It is argued that families, while not really organisms in a biological sense, also have internal stabilizing devices that maintain their integrity and continuity. The concept of homeostasis is helpful in understanding how a family maintains its identity and continuity through the life cycle that must necessarily be threatening. Much of the threat comes from loss. Loss of a sense of freedom and independence comes in marriage; loss of a certain amount of spontaneity and mobility comes with children being born; loss comes when children leave the home; and, of course, there is loss in death and divorce. Families, somehow, are able to continue their corporate identities through these life cycle losses while also facing external threats, such as social unrest and economic uncertainty. One homeostatic stabilizing device that families use is the family myth. A family myth is "a set of beliefs based on a distortion of historical reality and shared by all family members that help shape the rules governing family functioning."[30] Such notions as all members of the extended family take care of their own or that in a family the women are the caretakers and the men are taken care of are familiar family myths that serve a stabilizing function.

Homeostasis in its extreme form, while protecting continuity and integrity, can also limit behavior, sometimes at great expense. The classic example of the child who becomes symptomatic either through physical sickness or through acting out behavior when the parents are in tension is an example of pathological homeostasis. The child's symptom can serve to divert the marital couple from their differences in their tending to the child's problem. The cost of this homeostatic function can be considerable. The child suffers the consequences of the symptom, and the parents are denied the time to resolve their marital difficulties.

As useful as the concept of homeostasis is, particularly in understanding family structure and dysfunction, it is not adequate to interpret family change. Lynn Hoffman has observed that many families who come for treatment with distress in one or more members have seemed to be "stuck at an outmoded stage. Perhaps it is this being stuck that made the early version of the homeostatic model so convincing to therapists working with troubled families."[31] There is also, however, a non-stuckness, a basic disequilibrium, which may be seen in family systems, particularly in observing what is going on in a family system over a significant period of time. We are using the term *heterostasis* to describe this dynamic push toward change, in contrast to homeostasis' staying the same.[32] Again, following Hoffman, "any small instability can amplify, causing the system to pass beyond its limits and in an almost magically way reappear in quite a different state."[33] The notion that families can and do enter into new states of complexity and identity is an important one. The ability to change in creative ways is one of the exciting aspects of what it means to be a part of the human family.

Booker T. Washington, and his family subsequent to him, is one example that immediately comes to mind. His remarkable ability to alter his oppressed heritage and existence against all odds can be understood as a result of a family heterostatic process just as much as through his individual will and intellectual genius. The notion of heterostasis can also be helpful in dealing with pathological homeostasis. In a homeostatically stuck family "the task of the therapist is to try to push the system away from equilibrium, forcing it to search for a different solution; and above all, recognizing the importance of chance in determining which instability will be the determining one." From instability, then, new solutions are found in dealing with problems.

In the Jennings family, homeostatic functions are more apparent than heterostatic ones. The Jenningses seem to have some clear corporate identity even through the normal challenges to it. The coming of Bill's mother into the nuclear family—though creating stress, as well it should—seems to be incorporated without placing the family into a pathological rigidity. There is room for change, of course, thereby allowing for some novelty mostly through the medium of Rick's behavior, though this, too, has some homeostatic qualities through his delegation role. According to the theory of heterostasis, should they become too rigid and at the same time threatened with considerable instability, radical change would be more possible.

THE PASTORAL CARE OF THE NUCLEAR FAMILY

The pastoral care of the nuclear family has been an important function of the church, probably since its very beginning. Most pastoral care of families is quite different from the family pastoral counselor or family therapy. In the latter, a parent comes to the pastor or counselor with rather specific problems that the family needs help with. More often than not, the problem is seen as seated in the behavior of one family member, usually a child, and the parent is asking for help in dealing with that one person. It is rare that a parent presents a problem as being a family one.[34] Dealing with the problem as a family usually has to be insisted on by the pastor or counselor. At any rate, family therapy, or family pastoral counseling, involves a very clear cut presenting problem in which someone is asking a professional to intervene.

Family pastoral care, on the other hand, is less problem specific and, though it can uncover specific problems that counseling could help, it is usually preventive or educational in its nature. In many ways, the pastoral care of families is also observational. The pastor with a particular interest and some training in family systems theory will have more of a feel of what to "look" for or to be aware of. Problem behavior in the youth fellowship may be more than just rebellion on the part of an adolescent. It may also be symptomatic of marital or family dysfunction, to which the pastor can respond. He or she can become more aware of actual family function through conversations with other family members, which begin with what the pastor already knows about: the problem behavior at the church.

If the pastor senses from conversations with family members that one or more of them would be open to a family interview with the pastor, the pastoral role carries with it a natural opportunity to suggest a meeting with all the members of the family household. Pastors can visit with or invite entire families to visit with them without necessarily conveying the threatening idea that there's a problem to be dealt with. There are two very useful methods available to the pastor to facilitate the pastoral care of families. The first is the genogram. The second is a form of pastoral conversation with family members, called *tracking*. Both of these methods are familiar to pastoral counseling specialists and family therapists, and they are useful for the generalist in family pastoral care. An additional value of these methods is that neither assumes that there is pathology or family dysfunction to be addressed. They can be used to talk indirectly about problems in a way similar to what was suggested in our chapter on premarital pastoral care.

The genogram is a device developed by students of Murray Bowen; it has most recently been refined and standardized by two of them.[35] It is a graphic family tree that diagrams families by noting each member by way of indicating their relationships by way with one another. Included in the notations are ages, names, and date of marriages, divorces, and deaths. Men are represented by squares and women with circles, with their ages within the corresponding shape. Horizontal lines connecting people indicate marriages, and vertical lines coming from the horizontal ones indicate children from those marriages. From the basic nuclear family, extended family members are sketched, including grandparents, aunts, uncles, and cousins. Also indicated are geographical locations of family members. Very important to the completion of a genogram are indications of emotional relationships among family members. Jagged lines drawn between people indicate tension, while dark or multiple lines indicate an intense relationship (either closeness or fusion).

The genogram is not an end to itself, for it is really just a schematic diagram that has to be fleshed out through discussion while the genogram is being created. For family therapists, it is a useful technique of family assessment, exploring repeating patterns of relationships and unearthing possible losses that have gone unmourned. For the family, it can be a useful method of discussing family legacies, myths, and traditions. Although many families are puzzled by being asked to draw a genogram, they usually find it quite fascinating. A great deal of reminiscing goes on, with children learning about their families and extended families by listening to their parents. Because still-births and sometimes miscarriages are also included in the genogram, children may learn about siblings they never knew they had, and parents are given a chance to mourn adequately.[36]

As a fairly easy method to learn, the genogram is particularly useful for family life programs in the church. After as little as a half-hour of instruction and possibly an example, families can easily go off by themselves, armed with newsprint and magic markers, to create their own genogram. While the family learns about its legacies, the genogram offers the pastor information about relationships within the family that can be of considerable use in his or her pastoral care.

Tracking is simply a method of conversation between a caregiver and the family. From our own point of view it has at least three valuable functions. First, it allows the pastor to join with and to get inside of the family presenting itself in the pastor's office. Second, it allows the pastor a way to diffuse a family crisis by putting order in what the family perceives as chaos. Third, because it sees family crisis as the crisis of a system and not one of individuals (usually the presenting problem bearer), it takes the onus of responsibility from the presenting problem bearer and the pastor and places it squarely within the arena of responsibility of the family where it belongs.

Tracking, which was first developed by structural family therapists, adopts symbols that the family uses. "The language, life themes, history, values of the family, all come to represent aspects of the family's identity. The family's relational structure is packaged within these symbols of what the family is."[37] These symbols are to be found in the family conversation and are used by the counselor to communicate to the family that the counselor is joined with them. He or she understands their language and through this influences the family transactions in such a way that, as Minuchin claims, the pastor "leads by following."

Tracking is more than adopting the family symbols of communication. It is also the literal tracking of an event that has brought the family to crisis. By a rather painstaking and deliberate series of questions, a pastor and a family can learn how the family first got into crisis and how it is attempting to deal with that crisis. Because the questioning is rather precise and painstaking, it asks the family members to think and to reflect on their experience, rather than just emoting as people in upheaval are prone to do. It defuses the crisis by making it an object of analysis rather than purely a subjective experience.

Another value of tracking is that it takes the center of attention away from the so-called identified problem bearer and places the responsibility on the entire family system. Rather than seeing a crisis as the problem of one family member, it spreads it around. This also gives the family a graphic way of seeing that the solution to the problem is not the responsibility of just one person but the responsibility of the entire system. Such was the case in Lucy Jennings' call to the pastor one Monday night. She asked if she could bring Rick into the office as soon as possible. It seemed that there was a crisis going on with something that Rick had done. Carol had locked herself in her room and Grandmother was sulking. Bill and Carol had gotten into a fight about how to deal with the problem, and it appeared that things were going to come unglued. The pastor suggested that everybody in the family meet in her office the next day.

Pastor: So. What's happening?
Lucy: Rick. (staring at Rick with a look that could kill) He did his thing again.

Pastor:	So, Rick did his thing again.
Bill:	(laughing) Sounds almost dirty!
Lucy:	Bill, it is not funny.
Pastor:	So, Rick did his almost dirty thing again. (silence as the pastor watches each family member. Lucy is bolt upright in her chair. Bill, with legs crossed, sheepishly looks at the floor. Carol slouches like a rebellious adolescent. Grandmother looks confused. Rick sits, smiling dumbly.)
Pastor:	So how did Rick do his thing?
Lucy:	Last night, after practicing with that mob he calls a band, he came into the kitchen door with that thing . . . that, that, that lock of hair on the back of his neck . . . it was dyed purple.
Pastor:	His thing was purple. Who saw it first?
Lucy:	I did and I almost dropped what I was cooking.
Pastor:	So you saw it then—what happened?
Lucy:	I called Bill. At first he didn't know what I was talking about. But then I showed it to him.
Pastor:	How did you do that? Did you turn Rick around?
Lucy:	No! Rick started dancing around the kitchen. You couldn't miss it.
Pastor:	What did you do, Bill?
Bill:	I didn't know that doing something was an option. I mean there it was.
Pastor:	So you just stood there.
Lucy:	No, he didn't. He started chasing Rick, trying to grab that thing.
Pastor:	Well, one thing you do with things is to grab them, I guess. Then what happened?
Lucy:	Let's see. . . . Then Mother came into the kitchen to find out what all the commotion was about.
Pastor:	Mary, what did you do?
Mary:	Land sakes. There was Rick doing one of his stunts again.

Pastor:	What did you see?
Mary:	Well, Bill mostly with that grin on his face holding on to this purple thing.
Pastor:	Yes, the thing again. Then what happened?
Lucy:	Well, then Carol came down from upstairs where she was doing her homework.
Pastor:	And what did you do, Carol?
Carol:	Nothing. There's nothing I could do.
Bill:	Well, what she did was scream that she was sick and tired of Rick and all the stuff he gets away with. Then she stalked up the stairs and slammed the door.
Pastor:	Then what happened?
Mary:	I said that I would handle it, and that's when Lucy yelled at me.
Pastor:	Oh. Why?
Mary:	She said that Rick was her son, and that I should keep my nose out of it.
Pastor:	Oh. Then what happened?
Mary:	Well, then Bill and Lucy went at it. Lasted for about an hour.
Pastor:	What did you do, Rick?
Rick:	I watched television with Grandma. I figured to let them take care of it.
Pastor:	You mean your thing?
Rick:	I can wash it out.
Pastor:	Oh. I wonder what the thing really is?

Perhaps the most striking thing about family interviews is how simple they appear on paper as compared to how they feel to the participants. The participation of an "outsider" in the family dialogue and dynamics, even quite briefly, creates a disequilibrium that can contribute to change in the system. In this case, through the method of tracking, the pastor uses the family's symbols to join with them in breaking a rather complex interaction that took some sixty minutes to unfold into manageable pieces. It was done step-by-step, and while the Jennings family was rather cooperative in answering the questions, the pastor could have maintained appropriate control of the interview even if they hadn't. By insisting that one person speak at a time and asking specific questions, the emotion subsides and the information needed by all to understand the situation is gained.

The pastor used the family symbol "doing his thing" or "his thing" to join in with the family, and to let them know she heard them and respected their unique way of communicating. In addition, by her slow, painstaking method of questioning, she was able to get the family members to analyze the transaction without the flooding of emotional energy. Tracking helped the family not to *be* in crisis but rather had them take a *step back* from crisis and look at it. Finally, by having each family member identify his or her role in the crisis the onus of responsibility was taken away from Rick and placed where it properly belonged: It was a family transaction and a family crisis, and the solution to it rested with them all.

PROBLEMS IN THE PASTORAL CARE OF FAMILIES

Probably the greatest problem in dealing with the pastoral care of families is the misguided idealization of its form over an understanding of its function. We have pointed to this problem in our understanding of marriage as being a covenantal relationship first and a sacramental one second. We appreciate the power of the idealized family as a "haven in a heartless world."[38] Nevertheless the greatest threat to the integrity of the family today may be the idealized notion of the family as the only locus of intimacy. As with the families of antiquity, the generations of Noah, families are social units that allow for the human's basic need for relatedness. However, if that relatedness is left exclusively to the family unit itself it becomes privative, stylized, and ultimately alienating.

We agree with Lyman and Adele Wynne that the quest for intimacy exclusively within the family can be stultifying.

> We do not agree with the goal of *maintaining* intimacy. If couples give primary or continual attention to maintaining intimacy, they paradoxically will achieve it less; their expectations will be illusory and their efforts misdirected. Maintenance of continual intimacy

(even if possible) feels stiflingly symbiotic to us and would impose a continual burden on each partner to deny his or her own selfhood in the effort to support the other. Relationships thrive when the distance between a couple waxes and wanes as different relational or individuating processes come into play. ("The Quest for Intimacy," pp. 383-94)

Moreover, the idealization of the family concentrates its interest on the private dimension of life (love) to the exclusion or diminishment of the public dimension (work). The calling to care for the earth demands responsibility not only for the family, nuclear or extended, but also for the care of the children of God outside the family in the public sphere. The stress on the structure of the nuclear family (father, mother, children, and maybe other kin) also contributes to the ignoring of others in less traditional family structures (childless families, single parent families, and blended families) who also care for their generations. If, as we believe, the function of the family should be emphasized over its structure and that function is to offer a medium for satisfying human relatedness, other forms of family life must be affirmed and cared for, rather than ignored because they are seen as deviations from the Christian family norm.

Feminist critics of the family have raised important questions about the idealization of one particular family structure. The family as one subsystem of the greater social system is influenced by sex and gender domination. In a recent and important *prolegomena* to a feminist critique of family therapy, Virginia Goldner makes this very point: "Indeed, many feminist scholars now take as a point of departure the axiom that human history can best be understood in terms of three semi-autonomous systems of domination: class, race/ethnic, and sex/gender." Citing a rather large volume of literature by authors such as Chodorow, Gilligan, and Mahler, Goldner argues that the family is essentially a conservative institution that protects the patriarchal social *status quo*. Moreover, she says, family therapy theory and techniques tend to aid and abet this *status quo*. The systemic therapies tend to lift the family out of history to see it as a system of transactions devoid of political and gender interests. Feminists, according to Goldner, "reject the idea of the family as some kind of freestanding entity organized on its own terms." Rather, they offer us a view of men and women as members of two distinctive social groups, who, because of the sexual division of labor in all societies, have very different relationships to both the public and private spheres, and, therefore, to the family. "Given their different contexts, men and women enter relationships on such different terms that intimacy between the sexes is be *inherently* problematic and disturbed."[39] Goldner believes that this rather pessimistic evaluation of the family and of family therapy can be turned around if family theorists and therapists and counselors (and clergy as well) abandon the "context is all" notion of family functioning and turn to other resources, such as individual psychotherapy and social psychology.

One final problem that must be pointed to is that as care givers all pastoral workers should have some realistic notion of their own family relationships and family attitudes. One's own family role will undoubtedly be played out in one's other social roles. An unself-reflective act of ministry with a family can be full of more mischief than caring. Our own blindspots in understanding our own generations will make us blind to the similarities in others.

SUMMARY

In this chapter, we have looked at generational caring within the nuclear family. It is within the family crucible that generational caring comes into full play, precisely because two or more generations actually occupy the household. We have examined three "theological dynamics" that point to the ambiguities and the stabilities of family life. God has called us to live in the family not only under authority, but also with the freedom to make commitments in the context of our loyalty to God and others through covenant. We are called to communion not only in our most personal relationships, but we are also called to the public exercise of our vocation. We are not only called to faithfulness and solidarity, but are also challenged to creativity and resourcefulness.

From the social sciences, we have examined three psycho-social dynamics that are somewhat analogous to the theological dynamics. Families are domains of dependence and of individuation. They are mediums for the dynamic of loyalty and of delegation of style and public function. They are also to be understood as having stabilizing qualities, as the notion of homeostasis demonstrates, and they have the capacity of sudden and dramatic change, understood as heterostasis.

The genogram and tracking have been discussed as tools that are helpful in the pastoral care of families. These devices, commonly used by family therapists, are methods easily learned by pastoral generalists and can be of considerable use in their pastoral ministry with families.

Finally, we have pointed to some problems in the pastoral care of the nuclear family. The over idealizing of the nuclear family blinds us to one of its more important functions and, that is the mediation of love and work or the private and public life of the individual. Moreover, over idealizing the structure of the nuclear family limits us in our understanding of other types of families and family life. The nuclear family, like other family forms, is full of flux. It is dynamic and ambiguous, but such is God's creation for which we have been called to care.

NOTES

1. In our understanding of the household the nuclear family can also consist of persons who have no blood ties to the parental couple. Examples of this are the legal adoption of children and, of course, the special case of the reconstituted, or blended, family, which will be discussed in chapter 7.

2. Augustus Y. Napier with Carl A. Whitaker, *The Family Crucible* (New York: Harper, 1978).

3. *Theological dynamics* is a phrase associated with the work of Seward Hiltner; see *Theological Dynamics* (Nashville: Abingdon Press, 1972), pp. 13-14 and 182-201.

4. As another example of dynamic categories for describing the family, see Herbert Anderson, *The Family and Pastoral Care* (Philadelphia: Fortress Press, 1984).

5. For example, Robert Beavers, *Successful Marriage* (New York: W. W. Norton, 1985), pp. 147-52.

6. John Calvin, *Institutes of the Christian Religion*, Book I, xiv, 20, edited by John T. McNeill, trans. Ford Lewis Battles (Philadelphia: Westminster Press, 1960).

7. Paul Tillich, *Systematic Theology*, vol. III (Chicago: The University of Chicago Press, 1963), pp. 308-9.

8. Kenneth Kaye, "Toward a Developmental Psychology of the Family." In *The Handbook of Family Psychology and Therapy*, edited by Luciano L'Abate (Homewood, Ill.: The Dorsey Press, 1985).

9. William Johnson Everett, *Blessed Be the Bond* (Philadelphia: Fortress Press, 1985), p. 47.

10. Bernard Haring, *Marriage in the Modern World* (Westminster, Md.: Newman Press, 1965).
11. Everett, *Blessed Be the Bond*, p. 51.
12. Tillich, *Systematic Theology*, vol. I, p. 177.
13. Gustaf Wingren, *Luther on Vocation* (Edinburgh: Oliver and Boyd, 1958), p. 43.
14. James W. Fowler, *To See the Kingdom: The Theological Vision of H. Richard Niebuhr* (Nashville: Abingdon, 1974), pp. 164 ff.
15. John H. Elliot, *A Home for the Homeless* (Philadelphia: Fortress Press, 1981), pp. 167 ff.
16. Brian H. Childs, "The Possible Connection Between 'Private Speech' and Prayer." *Pastoral Psychology*, vol. 32, 1 (Fall 1983), 24-32.
17. Ibid., p. 32.
18. Herbert Anderson, *The Family and Pastoral Care* (Philadelphia: Fortress Press, 1984), p. 48.
19. Ibid.
20. For a more detailed look at psycho-social perspectives on the family, see: Luciano L'Abate, *Handbook of Family Psychology and Therapy* (Homewood, Ill.: Dorsey Press, 1985); Alan S. Gurman and David P. Knisker, eds., *The Handbook of Family Therapy* (New York: Bruner/Mazel, 1981). For a synthesis of object relations theory with family systems theory, see Samuel Slipp, *Objects Relations: A Dynamic Bridge Between Individual and Family Treatment* (New York: Aronson, 1984). For a general introduction to family systems theory and the various schools of family therapy, see Michael Nichols, *Family Therapy: Concepts and Methods* (New York: Gardner Press, 1984).
21. Salvadore Minuchin, *Families and Family Therapy* (Cambridge, Mass.: Harvard University Press, 1974).
22. Murray Bowen, "Family Therapy and Family Group Therapy." In H. Kaplan and B. Saaddock, eds., *Comprehensive Group Psychotherapy*, (Baltimore: Williams and Wilkins, 1971).
23. L. C. Wynne, I. Ryckoff, J. Day, and S. I. Hirsch, "Pseudo-mutuality in the Family Relationships of Schizophrenics," *Psychiatry*, vol. 21, (1958), 205-20.
24. Helm Stierlin, Ingeborg Rucker-Embden, Norbert Wetzel, and Michael Wirsching, *The First Interview with the Family* (New York: Brunner/Mazel, 1980), p. 16.
25. Ibid., p. 17.
26. Victor G. Cicirelli, "Sibling Relationships Through the Life Cycle" in L'Abate, *The Handbook of Family Psychology and Therapy*, p. 184.
27. Ivan Boszormenyi-Nagy and Barbara R. Krasner, *Between Give and Take* (New York: Bruner/Mazel, 1986), p. 191.
28. Stierlin, *The First Interview with the Family*, p. 23.
29. Nathan W. Ackerman, *The Psychodynamics of Family Life* (New York: Basic Books, 1958), pp. 68-69.
30. Nichols, *Family Therapy*, p. 585.
31. Lynn Hoffman, *Foundations of Family Therapy* (New York: Basic Books, 1981), p. 157.

32. For a fascinating theoretical discussion of stability and change from the theoretical father of the family therapy movement, see Gregory Bateson's essay, "Every Schoolboy Knows. . . " In *Mind and Nature: A Necessary Unity* (New York: Bantam Books, 1980), pp. 25-71.

33. Hoffman, *Foundations of Family Therapy*, p. 341.

34. For a typical family counseling request, see John Patton, *Pastoral Counseling: A Ministry of the Church* (Nashville: Abingdon Press, 1983), pp. 83-84.

35. Monica McGoldrick and Randy Gerson, *The Genogram in Family Assessment* (New York: W. W. Norton, 1985) is a particularly useful book for pastors.

36. Norman L. Paul and Betty B. Paul, "Death and Changes in Sexual Behavior," in Walsh, ed., *Normal Family Processes* (New York: Guilford Press, 1982), pp. 229-50.

37. Harry J. Aponte and John M. Van Deusen, "Structural Family Therapy," in Gurman and Kniskern, *The Handbook of Family Therapy*, p. 330.

38. Christopher Lasch, *Haven in a Heartless World: The Family Besieged* (New York: Basic Books, 1977).

39. Virginia Goldner, "Warning: Family Therapy May Be Hazardous to Your Health," *The Family Therapy Networker* (November-December 1985), vol. 9, no. 6, 19-23.

CHAPTER SIX

CARING THROUGH SEPARATION AND LOSS

But those who marry will have pain and grief in this bodily life, and my aim is to spare you. (I Cor. 7:28b NEB)

Although Paul's concern in the Corinthian correspondence—pointing out how sexuality can complicate religious commitment—is a different one from ours today. His words are an accurate prediction of the pain and grief involved in relationships and the loss of them.

During her third session with the pastoral counselor, Sara began to talk about her ambivalent feelings concerning her former husband. He was such a good father to their three children, she said, and he so wanted to be friendly with her. He even wanted to be close, and Sara was having difficulty with this. It reminded her of all the years of wanting closeness with Mark and not having it and then those final years of the marriage, with their anger and pain. Sara wanted now only to be able to direct her energy, and her desire for intimacy in other directions. Having Mark around now, after it was all over, seemed to make that reinvestment of herself with others all the more difficult.

Sara: I told him that whenever I think of the future I still think of him, too.

Pastor: You still have fantasies of having a life with him.

Sara: No . . . of course, he always will be our children's father and he is such a good one at that. It's that I spent so many years thinking about the future with him. We had plans and goals. After a few years into the marriage, we bought a small piece of property on the Jersey shore. We had always planned to build a boat and sail around the world, living aboard and being self-sufficient, sleeping under the stars. When I think into the future, I think of what that would have been like. In fact, he is building the boat now. It will be finished next year.

Pastor: It is difficult to know you will not go on the voyage.

Sara: No. He can go. He can even take somebody else along with him, another woman. I knew years before our actual divorce that they were just dreams. We were not going to make it. But I still care for him—especially the "him" in those dreams—just as I care for, and he cares for, our children.

After fifteen years of marriage to Mark, Sara found herself divorced, the custodial parent of three children, and a working parent. In part, because of the trauma of being a combat veteran of the Vietnam war, Mark had frozen Sara and the children out. He had been moody and on several occasions had disappeared for days. He also had had an affair with another woman. Counseling did not help, or perhaps it came too late. They divorced after a couple of years of real pain. Now, after the divorce, Mark was so much more available than before, but it was too late. Mark lived alone and because he was a college professor had a certain amount of flexibility with respect to his time. He chose to spend much of it with his children and in helping out around the house that the children and Sara lived in.

Sara could not tell him to stop his playing house with *her* house, which was no longer his or theirs. She may be bitter; yet, she does not seem to be. She is sustained now by true caring for her children, and she is grateful that Mark is able to share in that caring in many remarkable ways. She also cares for Mark and herself in a somewhat romantic way through the dream of the voyage on the home-made boat. Mark could even have the trip with another woman, for at least the dream could in some way come true.

At the same time, Sara felt that her caring, with the exception of that for her children, was superficial and abstract. She was fearful of human closeness and intimacy, and this was the problem that brought her to counseling—the way she related to those who cared for her. She seemed unable to make the final step toward true intimacy. As she put it one time to her counselor, "I have a hard time sharing care with people other than my children. They can share it with me, but I just can't seem to give it back, except in superficial ways." She could not risk direct communication, intimacy, even physical touch; yet, she still wanted all of that badly.

DIVORCE AS A FAILURE IN GENERATIONAL CARE

James Emerson has used the concept "fullness of time" to express how everything that has happened in the past can be caught up in one moment.

> Time is an experience of relationship, not of the memory. And this is exactly what everyone has in personal experience. A man who is about to get married is not just the result of an experience that happened five minutes before the wedding march. He is the result of all the experiences of his life bearing in on him at one moment.[1]

The "fullness of time" points to the moment of decision, emphasized by the existentialists, who are more concerned with the decision making than the content of the decision itself. In the case of marriage and divorce, the decision to do either is bounded by the "fullness of time," in which all that one is and may become confronts the self.

Because human life is relational, the greatest threat to that life is loss of relationship. Anxiety about relationship is a part of the very structure of human life, motivating us to move toward and away from one another. In his Gifford lectures, philosopher John Macmurray has spoken of "the rhythm of withdrawal and return" in human life and has described the ultimate threat to human existence as "isolation from the Other by the act of the Other."[2]

In discussing the process of separation and divorce, issues that were discussed in earlier chapters reappear, if not in focus, in the background. In chapter 1 we articulated our view of generational care. Human beings are created by God to be in relationship first with God and then with all of creation. The importance of relationality among humans is underscored in the creation story by the man's not being created to be alone but to be in communion with woman. Sexual relationality is highlighted by excitement and intensity and often results in the responsibility for long-term caring in the raising of children. The very fact of reproduction implies some long-term consideration for the care of children and their support from absolute dependency to maturity.

In discussing the divorce process, we also are involved in

dealing with the polarity of life, which Paul Tillich has identified as individualization and participation that, in the context of a marriage relationship, is expressed in the question, "How can I be deeply and personally involved in this relationship without losing the most cherished dimensions of myself?" Divorce also involves the way one separates from one's family of origin. Disappointments with one's spouse often originated in the relationship to the prior generation. The question of how one maintains sufficient separateness in the marriage relationship itself is a part of the divorcing process. Divorce represents a failure to achieve separation in any way other than physical. What commitment means is an inescapable issue in divorce. On the most primitive level, it involves the fear of having made a great mistake, of having "married Leah" and of being trapped with her for the rest of one's life. At another level, the question of commitment's meaning involves identifying the several commitments made in the process of marrying and being married and deciding how best to honor them.

If we understand divorce as a failure in generational care, we can best understand how it takes place by looking at how the two considering divorce are related to their respective families of origin. As we have suggested in our chapter on marriage, divorce is first considered because of a person's inadequate differentiation from his or her family of origin. When the excitement of the marriage wears off, the person begins to experience a new enmeshment in relationship, which inhibits his or her individuality. He or she cannot believe that one can really be separate in an intimate relationship. This is why the pastoral counseling of couples, as we have described it, is more concerned with helping couples experience their individuality in the presence of their spouses than in suggesting ways in which they might be closer. Thanks to the marvelous gift of sexuality, couples can usually devise interesting ways to get close to each other if they can deal with the anxiety of losing themselves in the other.

John Barnett has emphasized the powerful effect of spouses' having to give up their idealized images of their marital partners, and, using the biblical image in a very specialized way, describes this process as "the Fall." There are, he says, three courses of action

> available to married couples in the throes of the Fall. First is the choice of getting rid of the real person intruding into the marriage

and holding on to the fantasied ideal of a marital partner. Second, there can be a shoring up of roles and development of apathy in regard to marital growth. Third a couple can actively engage in the turmoil of establishing real people in a real marriage. So the choices are Divorce, Robotization, and Creative Turmoil.[3]

A real marriage relationship, as Barnett describes it, is "creative turmoil," and those who cannot tolerate the kind of realism about themselves and their marital partner resort to the other alternatives. Divorce can be a way of externalizing and simplifying the issue of living in a real, intimate relationship by concluding that "if only I hadn't married Leah, everything would be all right." What he calls "robotization" involves maintaining rigid marital roles and behaviors in order to stabilize the marriage and avoid divorce. In a variety of ways, couples deny their feelings and their individuality in order to maintain the security of relationship, or, to use his symbol, they become robots rather than real persons. Marriage is learning to deal with the reality of oneself and one's partner and with all the relational anxiety that involves.

Boszormenyi-Nagy and Krasner have described the same issue in a somewhat different way. They note how current "real" interactions between people are guided by subjective and unconscious agendas, as in: "Why aren't you acting as I wish my father would have acted? Haven't I extended you the privilege of getting closer to me than my father ever was?" In other words, "I want you to behave in ways that can address my earlier inner needs, without consideration of what you want or need to do."[4] The problem is that people are not only attempting to relate to some image but are also relating to a *real* human being who is independent of the other's internalized history. The potential for confusion and outright exploitation in a marital relationship is very great.

In spite of this struggle to face the reality of intimate relationship, Barnett concludes that the "painful intensity" of creative turmoil can diminish as the couple experience a real loss of innocence, take personal responsibility, become less dependent and discover that personal responsibility does not depend on their spouse. In our terms, they have sufficiently separated from the prior generation not to mix those relationships and the dependency and loyalty involved in them with the peer relationship of marriage. Or they have found ways to "parent" a member of the generation that follows them so that their marriage relationship does not have to be turned into one of parent and child.

Although the most common *reasons* given for divorce involve the challenges to marriage and the family discussed earlier—the conflict between love and work and the competition for intimacy between friends and one's spouse—the more fundamental reasons are the fear of losing self and the confusion of generations in the marriage. The former is a real issue, but is in fact an expression of the fundamental human struggle to be related intimately and personally to others without losing touch with who one is. That may be acted out in an affair with a sexual partner or with one's best friend. It may be seen clearly in the consistent choice of career over family relationships or in the denial of one's public vocation in order to retreat to the home as an alleged haven from anxiety. In either case, the struggle to care for one's generations may been seen underneath the more obvious manifestations of behavior.

Without any extensive analysis of Sara's story, one can see in what has been presented thus far her struggles with realism about her marriage relationship, with her needs to care and be cared for, and in the responsibilities she feels for her generations. Having touched on some of the reasons for the decision to separate and divorce—interpreted in the context of care for one's generations—we move to an examination of the separation and divorce process, how it might most usefully be understood, and how it is experienced.

DIVORCE AS LOSS OF RELATIONSHIP

Although the most profound relational loss, death, is the prototype of all other human losses, we have chosen not to discuss its effect on care in the family for two reasons. First, there is already extensive literature on death in the family and the pastoral care of the bereaved. Second is the fact that divorce is the most significant loss of relationship which, to a great degree, involves the intentional moving away from relationship. One can often see intentionality in death, but it most often seems to come as a result of circumstance. Divorce, on the other hand, involves a choice to withdraw from one's most significant adult relationship.

Melanie Klein, among the psychoanalytic theorists, has most

powerfully described the experience and fear of loss. Anxiety, as she presents it, is "infantile mourning." The presence of the mother increases the child's trust in his or her own powers and in whatever benevolence there may be in the world. "The non-appearance of his mother or the lack of her love can leave him at the mercy of his depressive and persecutory fears. Depressive anxieties are stirred at every step of development.... The depressive feelings are reactivated by every loss, and every step in development implies some loss."[5]

John Bowlby's massive trilogy *Attachment and Loss* deals with the fundamental nature of human relationality under the apparently more scientific rubric of "attachment." Relating human attachment behavior to that of the higher primates, Bowlby sees it as necessary for biological survival and continuous throughout life. It is distinct from feeding behavior and sexual behavior and of at least equal significance in human life. Human dependence on caretakers changes, but the need for attachment remains. Attachment behavior, he says, plays "a vital role" in human life "from the cradle to the grave."[6]

In studying children separated from their mothers, Bowlby observed a three-stage reaction process. The infant: (1) protests acutely; (2) falls into deep despair; and (3) finally gives up and becomes superficially adjusted to the separation, but detached. Infants who are repeatedly left and disappointed will do whatever they can to adapt to what appears to be their abandonment and chronically unmet needs. Self-negation begins when the natural response to chronic frustration becomes too much to bear.[7]

Resonating with Melanie Klein, but with a very different language, Bowlby affirms the power of separation anxiety as a natural and inevitable response to the absence of an attachment figure. His own view is a variation of Freud's "signal theory," in which anxiety is essentially a warning of danger—in this case, the leaving of the parenting one—and an announcement of a frustrated attachment, which is distressing in itself and not just a signal of something more dangerous.[8] With respect to the loss itself, Bowlby identifies five characteristics of the loss that affect the type of grief taking place: (1) the identity and role of the person lost; (2) the age and sex of the person bereaved; (3) the causes and circumstances of the loss; (4) the social and psychological circumstances affecting the bereaved about the time of and after the loss; and (5) the personality of the bereaved, with special reference to his or her capacities for making love relationships and for responding to stressful situations. Persons most likely to have what Bowlby calls "disordered mourning" are those "whose attachments are insecure and anxious . . . those disposed toward compulsive care giving," and those who, "whilst protesting emotional self-sufficiency, show plainly that it is precariously based."[9]

Separation and divorce are human situations that affect personal identity just as does marriage. It is impossible to understand one process without understanding the other. Marriage alters the person's sense of identity from that of a single person to that of a married person. The loss of that identity in separation and divorce alters that identity once again. Identity and attachment to a loved object are closely related. Peter S. Weiss has developed a theoretical line of thought that attempts to connect the vital roles of attachment in early and later childhood and in marriage to the notions of self-image and self-identity. Using Bowlby's attachment theory, Weiss details the power of identity with the marriage that affects the functioning of the separated partners long after the relationship has ended.

Attachment has a natural history that begins just after birth, when the child attains comfort and security from a primary attachment figure, usually the mother. In addition to the primary attachment figure, there are secondary figures (fathers, siblings, and even inanimate objects, such as toys and blankets). Growth through adolescence is a process of giving up the primary and secondary attachments with the development of attachment energy toward peers and especially members of the opposite sex (or objects of sexual desire of the same sex, in the case of homosexuality).

Adult identity is a combination of self-identity and a partnership with someone compatible with that self-identity. "The prospective figure will have to make sense as a life partner, given the person the individual is and wants to be. Indeed, the attachment choice may help to crystallize a particular identity."[10] Finding and deciding on the attachment choice in marriage is a precarious task, and the person making that choice has but limited flexibility in making it. Much depends on the luck of "good enough parenting." All persons make use of "self-objects," or the internalized images of persons, the mother and father being the primary and most important.[11] These self-objects play the role of maintaining basic continuity of the notion of the self over time. Attachment figures are selected, then, in a way that complements in some fashion the internalized others.

Most young adults have more than one strong attachment figure of a romantic nature before they settle down with one at a time, if they settle in disorientation and self-doubt. Finally, most people settle down with one person and feel assured of a permanent attachment figure. The attachment that develops during courting and the early years of marriage is part of the nomic function of marriage as described by Berger (cf. chapter 4).

The attachment that develops during marriage, like the attachment of early childhood, seems to persist even when the attachment figure no longer is present.

> The [estranged] spouses resemble battered children in their feelings: They may be angry, even furious, with one another; they may hate one another for past injuries and fear one another's next outburst of rage; after a quarrel they may find consolation in fantasies of confrontation and revenge in which they imagine themselves saying, "You can just take your things and get out of here" or "Don't try to find me because I'm not coming back." But when they actually consider leaving their marriage they become almost paralyzed with fear. (*Marital Separation*, p. 44)

By the fourth counseling session, it became clear that Sara's approach/avoidance experience with intimacy had as much to do with her relationship with her father and mother as it did with the once unavailable and brooding veteran and now hail fellow and responsible father to her children. Early on, Sara found that caring too much for somebody could lead to significant pain and an insult to self-esteem.

Her family of origin on both her mother's and father's side were old New Jersey families, dating themselves from before the Revolution. These were not rich people and landed gentry, but rather hard working farmers whose ancestors were probably more like indentured servants than aristocracy. Sara's father was always an enigma. Her mother described him as being very loyal but never living up to his considerable potential. Sara remembers her mother's saying that everybody in the community wanted to hear what Edgar had to say; it was just that he never said anything at all.

Sara also remembered her father's squatting on the ground with her brothers and sisters, talking of things that were important to children. They talked of dogs and cats they had on the farm and how each child could have his or her own garden. That all changed drastically one day. When Sara was about seven years old, her father went away from their isolated farm and did not return for some nine months. He never said good-bye, and no one would tell her where he had gone. He was never talked about. When he did return, he was withdrawn and did not have the energy he once had. There was no more talk about puppies and gardens. Sara later learned after his death and just a year before she and Mark were divorced that her father had been committed to a state hospital and had had psycho-surgery—a frontal lobotomy, a procedure fairly common in the early 1950s for everything from depression to attacks of rage. Her father lived in quiet slow motion for the rest of his days. He was productive but never up to his potential, including the quality of his loving. Sara's mother was never able to take up the slack. The family was too alone and isolated, and there was no help.

Sarah was well acquainted with grief and loss prior to her marriage and subsequent divorce. In her divorce, she not only lost a person, her husband, Mark, but also the corporate identity they had developed together. Couples develop a corporate identity at the same time that each partner is also developing a new self-identity. This self-identity is compromised when the marriage breaks up. This is apparent in Sara's comment to the pastor about Mark: "I told him that whenever I think of the future I think of him, too." She had no illusions of ever being married to him again. In fact, starting over again with Mark was not something that she even desired. At the same time, a large part of her self-concept, her self-identity, was tied up in being Mark's wife and the mother of their three children. There was even some evidence that her continued identification with her former marriage had deprived her of feeling free enough to develop other relationships. This fear of new relationships, in combination with her rather traumatic relationship with her father, caused Sara to seek pastoral counseling.

THE EXPERIENCE OF SEPARATION AND DIVORCE

While marriage and divorce statistics are fairly easy to come by, they are often difficult to interpret. It is commonly argued that the high divorce rate is a sign of an unstable society that has given up on the religious norms that so many hold to be valuable. According to G. P. Murdock, however, most societies since the beginning of recorded time have developed ways for marriages to be dissolved. In addition, only sixteen societies have a lower divorce rate than the United States and twenty-four of them have higher rates. It appears, according to Murdock, that the American divorce rate is well within the limits that a society can tolerate with safety.[12] Nevertheless because divorced persons have apparently failed in the commitments to family life, which stabilize society, divorce is commonly viewed by the church and by many other persons and institutions simply as pathology to be prevented or denied. Thus the divorced have been in some way cut off from consideration when Christian family life was discussed or celebrated in the church.

As we have suggested earlier, this view of divorce as separating persons from Christian family living is inconsistent with our norm for the family—generational caring. Persons who care responsibly for their generations can express Christian family living whatever the form of their household. Depending on the relational circumstances, both marriage and divorce can destroy or reduce the human capacity for caring. The structures and commitments involved in marriage are designed to facilitate care, but sometimes they do not. Under such circumstances, divorce may contribute to generational care more than it limits or destroys it. In our understanding of Christian family living, it is more important to maintain and actualize the function of caring than to maintain the structure of marriage.

As with any other painful life experience, there are with divorce a wide range of feelings, all of which therapists, pastors, and friends of the divorcing couple may expect to see. Sometimes the impact of the loss of a marriage has been compared to that of the loss of a limb. Sara's continued participation in the fantasy of the world cruise seems to be somewhat like a phantom limb phenomenon. "It is many times of going places together, eating meals together, consulting each other on parenting issues and household management, being a couple, sharing a home, an automobile, a bedroom, that makes a marriage part of who we are."

Florence Kaslow, in reviewing some of the literature on divorces of persons married more than twenty years, notes that divorce was rated higher than any other major life event in terms of causing stress. One might expect the stress of persons divorced after shorter relationships to be somewhat less, but there are other significant variables, such as parenting responsibilities, which would prevent a simple relationship between degree of stress and length of marriage.[13]

More important for the pastor or other concerned persons responding to that stress are the ways that it is manifested. Again, following Kaslow, affectively it may be manifested by feelings of disillusionment, dissatisfaction with life, and alienation from others. There are often feelings of dread with regard to the future, pain, and anguish with an accompanying sense of complete personal inadequacy. Also frequent are feelings of detachment, anger and self-pity, confusion, and intense loneliness. Behaviorally there may be a physical and emotional withdrawal, pretending that everything is all right and attempts to win back the other's affection at all costs. More dramatically the person's emotionality may be expressed in ways that he or she or the concerned others have never experienced before—screaming, threatening, suicide attempts, physical illness. These and other manifestations of pain and stress are what the pastor and others may meet in attempting to be helpful to the divorcing or divorced person.

However, the experience of divorce is not simply a grief process. It is more complicated because both the divorcing person and all his or her family members can maintain fantasies that the loss or end of the relationship has not really taken place. Moreover, in addition to the loss there are the powerful feelings of personal failure and shame, which may be present in a loss such as death but are not as directly related to it. In spite of these and other complications, however, all that one knows about grief can be helpful in the care of persons experiencing divorce. Even though these feelings normally diminish gradually with the passage of time, as in the case of death and grief, they may reemerge at most any time, and, as with Sara, be stimulated by a continued relationship with the partner who has been lost.

Finally, in considering some of the phenomena associated with divorce, it is important to consider not just how the divorcing person experiences the particular situation, but also his or her attitude toward divorce itself. Along with the person's own attitude, the attitudes of family, friends, and the therapist or pastor who attempts to care for the divorcing or divorced person must also be considered. We have already touched on persons' attitudes of shame and personal failure, which often cause earlier shame experiences to become reactivated. Divorce is a failure in a life enterprise that one has publicly proclaimed as important; therefore, coming to terms with that experience without undue denial of it is a central feature of dealing with the divorce process. Persons who have rigid ideas of and attitudes about right and wrong and who have assumed meaningful life depends on avoiding sin and failure may have an extremely difficult time in self-acceptance and in maintaining relationships with friends who have divorced. The article on continued coital intimacy of divorced evangelicals, referred to in chapter 4, is a good example of rigid attitudes on behavior.

What seems most important in dealing with the destructive effects of one's attitudes and assumptions toward divorce on a caring relationship is the acknowledgment that they are inescapably there, just as the effects of one's culture and one's intellectual and emotional biases are there. For most pastors, this needs to be acknowledged openly with the persons to whom they attempt to minister, indicating how pastors' beliefs may affect the way they respond, but affirming at the same time, if that is honestly possible, that their primary concern is for the care of the persons involved in this particular pain.

Most important for pastors and others who would assist parishioners and friends in dealing with their divorce process is the pastors' clarifying their own attitudes toward it. Although understanding the pastor's function in relation to separation and divorce as "saving the marriage" is not as prevalent as it once was, it is still almost impossible to avoid getting caught up in that goal. The "success" criterion for the clergy's work with couples is still popularly understood as saving a marriage, and if a pastor genuinely values marriage he or she can probably never be immune from sometimes making use of this criterion. The major problem with being bound by this attitude is that the marriage becomes the primary patient, often to the exclusion of one or both of the partners in it. The pastor ends up caring for a structure rather than for persons or defending his church's concept of marriage against the intrusion of reality.

THE PROCESS OF SEPARATION AND DIVORCE

Our choice of approach to generational caring in family living has avoided theorizing in terms of stages, perferring to emphasize function and circumstances that may exist at almost any point in the life process. With respect to divorce, which is too often conceptualized as a one-time event, identification of a divorce process is important for adequate caring. There have been a number of useful conceptualizations of the divorce process in the literature. Kaslow has reviewed the advantages and disadvantages of several of these schemes, which identify from two to seven stages. Most important to us, however, is the recognition that divorce or divorcing is not something that simply happens or does not happen, but is a complex and traumatic process, even if the outcome may be demonstrated to be more satisfactory than the circumstances which seemed to precipitate it. (See Kaslow, pp. 662-96.)

Some of the descriptions of stages in the divorcing process identify it with the process of dying as conceptualized by Elisabeth Kübler-Ross and make adaptations of her familiar stages. None of the conceptualizations of the process seem fully satisfactory, including our own. Nevertheless, as we have reflected on the conceptualizations of the divorce process in relation to our experience as pastors, three things seem most important to be taken into account: (1) that the phenomena of the divorce process do not occur in an invariant sequence; (2) that what is going on affectively and cognitively needs to be distinguished from what is occurring behaviorally; and (3) that the needs of at least three generations, as well as those of the divorcing couple, be recognized. We describe some of the phenomena we have seen occurring at each stage, but resist naming the stages because of the danger that even our stages might be etched in someone's stone. Moreover, rather than using the term *stage*, following Turner and Strine,[14] we use the term *phase* because it seems less rigid.

The first phase in the divorce process does not occur at any one time but appears intermittently over a long or short period. It appears with the fear that "I might have married Leah," a feeling of being trapped, disappointment and disillusionment with the relationship, the discovery of how much this other person in the marriage is "not like me," and the affective consideration of divorce. In all three generations during this period, there is an increase in anxiety and an activation of the denial process as a means of dealing with the anxiety.

The second phase appears when the initial fear is conceptualized verbally or behaviorally by one or both members of the generation of the marriage—the marriage partners. This may have happened earlier in the generations of the couple's parents or children in response to the anxiety they felt: "Are you and Jim getting along all right?" or "Are you and Daddy going to get divorced?" In the first stage, this is denied. In the second, it is acknowledged in some way by one or both members of the couple, but usually not to members of the first or third generation. It may be announced by an affair, a direct question about one, by a statement that "we need to do something about our relationship" or broaching the subject of going to a marital therapist.

The third phase appears when something is actually done *directly* about the marriage itself. An affair, whether with an emotional or sexual partner or with one's work or other activity, is an indirect "doing something about it" and, in our categorization, a second stage. The doing something about it may be going to a therapist, some kind of overt physical separation, such as changing bedrooms or one partner's actually moving out, or, less obvious to the other generations, a restructuring of the couple's life and time together in a self-therapeutic behavioral therapy. During this phase, there is increased anxiety in the other generations, usually with some kind of behavioral manifestation, such as children having illnesses or school problems and needing more care. The families of origin are doing a variety of things to "try to help" or, if they are at a sufficient distance, still trying to maintain their denial. It is important to remember that in this and in all phases the movement is back and forth, toward and away from divorcing. In this phase, however, the third phase is a central feature of the process as one or both partners begin to think and talk about the advantages and disadvantages of divorce versus marriage.

The fourth phase in the divorce process begins when

something is actually done about divorce itself. The separation, in whatever form, is at this stage not identified as a therapeutic exercise designed to help the marriage or, temporarily, one of the marriage partners, but is acknowledged to be "because we can't get along any more." In this phase, the children and the families of origin are officially told about the divorce, specific plans are made, and lawyers or mediators are consulted. Helping persons who are involved in this stage inevitably must deal with the practical problems and decisions being considered as much as or more than the so-called broader life issues of the individual or couple themselves. Who will actually file for the divorce and when? What will be the arrangements about finances and children? Questions such as these are addressed to pastors, therapists, and friends as well as to lawyers.

The fifth phase involves the actual legal divorce and the immediate adjustments to it. It is particularly important to recognize the necessary length of this stage. Kaslow has commented that the "healthier" divorced persons "who recuperate and live productive and fulfilling lives seem to need approximately two years from the time the separation first occurs until the psychic divorce is complete."[15] We refer to her comment not because we feel that her two years' time should be normative, but to emphasize that a significant period of time is needed by every person involved in a divorce. The central feature of this phase for all generations is facing the reality of the marriage's death and learning to go on with one's life in the light of that fact. The most common phenomenon that, as pastoral counselors, we have seen among divorced couples is the ways they maintain the marriage—often some of the worst parts—even though they are divorced. Sara is somewhat unusual in being able to hang on to some of the best of Mark in divorce, but she pays for it by being unable to get on with her life.

One can see Sara's expression of care for the generations through her separation and divorce. Early on, as Mark became more and more withdrawn and less physically present, she had primary responsibility for the welfare of their three children. After the divorce she was the custodial parent, even though Mark took more and more responsibility for the children. Through the demise of the marriage, Sara also expressed care for her parents with an interplay of her care for herself and for her internalized objects.

Sara: I found Mark to be the best of all that I wanted. He had some of the qualities my father had. Mark liked to make things, and he was a dreamer. The big difference was that he made many of his dreams come true. The boat is a good example.

Pastor: Your father did not have the chance to make his dreams come true.

Sara: No. I hoped that he and Mark could have made some of them come true together. But he ended up leaving, too. There was so much silent pain.

Pastor: You had hopes for both of them.

Sara: Yes. Hopes.

Pastor: How about your mother?

Sara: My feelings have changed about her about a dozen times over my forty years. I don't remember her ever hugging me. She never really allowed me to confide in her. We lived so alone. She worked so hard, keeping things going. When my father came back he could not farm anymore, and he got a job as a clerk in a co-op station. He didn't make much, so Mother had to make up the rest and make the house run. I see now that she had to keep things balanced. She had a hard life. She loves her grandkids, and they love her, though they do get on her nerves sometimes. She has really supported me over these past few years.

Pastor: You are ambivalent about your mother.

Sara: You bet. She has been hard to figure out, but she has always been there, too. I want her to live the rest of her life with some ease as best she can.

Sara's relationship with her parents had had a dominant effect on her. She remembers the care that her father gave to her when she was young, and she was understandably confused when the intensity of that care disappeared. She cared for her father in return. During her growing up years, she was her father's favorite. She would sit with him while he read his poetry and his Bible. In many ways her current complaint of her inability to develop close relationships with others since her divorce may have much to do with her care for her father.

First, Sara found herself in a split loyalty conflict with her mother and father. Her loyalty to her father seemed at points in her life to be to risk betraying her loyalty to her mother, who in her memory was never warm but who did keep the family going. This loyalty conflict further became complicated after her father's hospitalization. His seeming distance and lack of concern confused Sara and made her yearn for the closeness of days gone by, further limiting her contact with her mother on an emotional plane. Even in her adulthood she attempted to maintain her loyalty in her choice of a mate. Mark was felt to be the man who could recreate her moments with the dreaming and loving father.

When Mark went into a depression and finally left the marriage, the loyalty conflict further became complicated. To whom should Sara be loyal now? Her identity as daughter and wife was made ambiguous, and she found herself unable to direct her emotional desires in any direction. Of course, her mother cared for her, mostly in terms of physical needs if not always her emotional ones. Her mother's caring was an anxious one. She was never sure when the next emotional catastrophe would occur, so she withheld emotion and instead at least maintained order in her life. More than anyone, with the possible exception of Sara as an adult, she did what she could to keep things together and yet was always being confronted with a new problem.

One very important aspect of Sara's counseling was her reevaluation of her mother's genuine loyalty to her own children and Sara's reclaiming her mother as an important source of her own identity. A reevaluation of her mother as a finite and good enough mother allowed for further explorations in relationships with others. Sara's own inability to establish emotional relationships with others in many ways mirrored her own mother's fear of emotional entanglement. As we have discussed in chapter 4, it is more difficult for women to separate, "harder for her or her mother to know where one ends and the other begins."

Lucy Rose Fischer has argued that the "caring orientation of adult daughters and their mothers—the centrality of mother in both of their lives—means that their lives are linked from generation to generation." The labor of mothering, she says,

> lasts for only a small proportion of their years, especially in families with few children. But their commitment to and involvement with their children stretches over the length of their lives. The birth of grandchildren . . . revives their mothering responsibilities. They also may provide "mothering" care to their own mothers and, in their turn, when they are very old, they may find themselves "mothered" by their daughters. The family roles of women provide a meeting ground for the interweaving of generations.[16]

Sara's second source of identity came from Mark. He was the dashing dreamer she remembered her father had once been. For fifteen years of marriage, she nurtured Mark and tried to console him after his tour of duty in Vietnam. His sullenness and depression, what probably was post traumatic stress syndrome, went on too long, and the marriage lost its reciprocity. Mark went elsewhere to try to rejuvenate himself. Sara stayed at home and, much like her mother, kept order in the house. Her third source of identity is through the caring for her three children, a task now shared with Mark. They are the heirs of what she and Mark developed together and are central to what they, as individuals, will become.

THE PASTORAL CARE OF THE SEPARATED AND DIVORCED

Sara's express reason for asking for pastoral counseling underscores one of the central questions of the pastoral care of the separated and divorced: "How can I risk caring again for someone of my own generation when caring has caused me such pain?"

Sara: There is a man I'm seeing some now. He is truly infatuated with me. I like him, and he is a good and kind man. I think that I do love him, but I just can't say it.

Pastor: There seems too much at stake for you.

Sara: I don't know. You see, it's just not as obvious that I've been burned. You see, I have a girlfriend who told me how much I mean to her. She was really sincere and would do anything for me and the kids. She even still likes Mark. She is what anybody would want as a best friend. I just cannot let myself give back to her. I want to; I really do. I guess that is why I am here to see you now. It's time.

Sara recognizes, as some do not, that all care is of a piece, and when the caring process is disrupted at one point, it tends to be disturbed at others. She is having difficulty not only in getting close to another man, but even in getting close to a woman friend who reaches out to her as well. The process of reconnection in other relationships is the one perhaps most benefited by counseling and psychotherapy.

The care of the whole process of separation and divorce, however, involves a number of different features. There are four types of care that are appropriate for most persons who are experiencing the process of separation and divorce.[17] They are overlapping and not mutually exclusive, but they are identifiable as (1) crisis intervention, (2) support and guidance, (3) examination of one's marriage and family relationships, and (4) grief work. All are familiar, to some degree at least, to most pastors.

1. Crisis intervention. The ability to understand the dynamics of crisis situations and manage them is essential for any pastoral care giver. In divorce, when self-identity is compromised or temporarily lost, the world of the separated or divorced person becomes chaotic, and his or her ability to deal with mounting stress and problem solving becomes diminished. Perhaps the initial function of the pastor or specialized pastoral counselor is in calming the chaos by his or her presence as one who is not as disturbed by the situation as in the counselee. Beginning to hear the story and putting the chaos into the context of the person's whole life story is one way to convey that life will probably go on in spite of all that has happened.

Quite often during the process of the initial separation there will be a crisis involving a child. A child will become symptomatic, particularly when the tension and anger is high between the parents. A child may become delinquent, become school phobic, or even become physically ill. This additional crisis experience with the child will often bring the warring parents together to deal with the issues at hand. More often than not, however, it is just a temporary reunion, for as the crisis passes, the old marital dissatisfactions resurface. However one theorizes about the crisis experience or delineates methods for dealing with it, it is most important not to underestimate the power of the pastor's presence.[18] We have been related to many people in pastoral care and counseling who have reported satisfaction from being with us in their crisis, but with whom we have no idea what we did to be helpful.

2. *Support and guidance.* Obviously related to the phenomenon of the pastor's presence as intervenor in the crisis of separation and divorce is the type of pastoral counseling that offers support and guidance. In this type of pastoral care, the pastor needs to be more direct and active in the caring process than is the case in much pastoral work. Even after the initial crisis has passed, persons facing separation and divorce often feel paralyzed and incapable of doing what they need to do in their present situation. The appropriate pastoral response is direct focus on what the separated or divorcing person needs to do, sometimes offering information and encouraging seeking more competent specialized advice as needed. Most persons, in our experience, are not emotionally capable of handling their own divorce and the necessary arrangements related to it. Competent legal counsel and/or the services of a divorce mediator are usually needed to be sure that the divorcing person takes appropriate care of herself or himself and those for whom he or she must care in the future.

Such issues as advising each party to be clear about legal rights and responsibilities, not making any sudden or drastic job and career changes, not making any sudden or drastic moves, not even entering too quickly into other relationships—all these issues are part of the guidance aspect of the pastoral care of the separating and the divorcing. Another issue that is emotionally important is deciding who will take the first legal step toward the divorce. It has seemed important in our experience that the partner who is resistant to divorcing not be forced by some indirect means into initiating the divorce action. It is important both theologically and psychologically for persons to make their own decisions and to be responsible for them. The pastor's guidance counseling can facilitate the process of care for oneself and one's generations by facilitating decision making.

Another time when pastoral guidance is important is in the post-divorce time of adjustment to a new style of life. We noted earlier Kaslow's normative statement about the length of a normal divorce process. What divorced persons tend not to recognize is the extent to which they are functionally still married long after the divorce. The story of Sara, which has appeared at various points in this chapter, illustrates some of the ways in which this "still married" condition is expressed. Some of the specific ways it appears is in the necessary ways that divorced couples are forced to interact—for example, in relation to the children and support money. If the wife was usually late when going somewhere with her husband during the marriage, she will likely be late in coming home to receive the children when they return from a visit to their father's. If the husband picked a fight over the way that his wife took care of the children in the marriage, he is likely to continue this even after the divorce. Each divorced person we see in counseling provides a new example of how marriage is unconsciously continued in divorce.

The pastor may help the counselee or parishioner deal with divorce by pointing it out with a calm, non-blaming interpretation, such as: "It looks like you've found another way to stay married. Do you really want to do this?" The "divorced-married" person will typically say that he or she does not, but will then proceed to say how whatever the continued marital act was really has to be done. The pastor's gentle argument or questioning about this will eventually make some impact, but the effects of the divorced person's marital relationship are long-term and exceedingly deceptive.

The pastor supports directly. She or he also facilitates the giving and receiving of support within the family system. As we have discussed above, the self-identity developed in marriage is devastated in separation and divorce. There is no doubt that the pastor's encouraging Sara to explore her caring and being cared for was a major element in the counseling process. Turner and Strine emphasize the generational aspect of support in commenting on the "need for grandparental support," support from one's own parents. It is typical, they say,

> for grandparents to perceive divorce as a reflection on their own parenting skills ("Where did I go wrong in raising my child?"). Hence, they are often understandably not able to accept or support the demise of their offspring's marriage. If grandparents are willing to be involved in the offsprings' therapeutic process, then

> family therapy with the extended family system may effectively deal with their hurt and disappointment. ("Separation and Divorce," p. 494)

If, as is more usual, the generation before is not able or willing to become involved therapeutically, the pastor's supportive response involves interpretation of the family problem within the context of the broader family's history. Middle and older aged adults who divorce need the support of the generation that comes after them, their adult children. Turner and Strine note that these children often become outraged at having their emotional security, their intact family, stripped away from them when they are going through important individual and marital development.

3. Examination of marriage and family relationships. Our approach of generational care gives us some further issues that can be dealt with in the counseling of the separated and the divorced. Divorce affects more than just the marital couple. Many separated or divorced persons have difficulty in telling their parents of the impending end of a marriage. Sara and Mark had been separated for over two months before Sara told her parents. She said that she remembered thinking: "They had so many of their own problems, and I just did not want to add to them. I waited until I could see them face to face and not on the phone so they could see me and know that I was not going to blow up or go crazy." Because care is a generational issue centering on loyalty, it is essential that an individual's own agenda with the generation before be explored and confronted. Often parents will want the grown child to come home and live with them again, especially if the child is a woman. This regression to prior powerful attachments (from spouse to parents) should be avoided except under the most dire economic circumstances. Developing a new identity, and not regression to an old one, is what heals.[19]

Dealing with older primary and secondary attachments in terms of the adult attachment to a spouse is essential. In Sara's case, one can see that the old psychodynamic adage can be invoked: women marry men like their fathers, and men marry women like their mothers. Sara married a man who could give her both her mother and her father. She found a man who dreamed and made some of his dreams come true, or so it seemed. She also found a man who, in contrast to her mother's emotional distance, promised to give her passion. Dealing with and grieving for the loss of idealized expectations of parents may be just as important in the grief work of separation and divorce as is the grief work dealing with the loss of the spouse and in certain circumstances the loss of the custodial care of children.

In addition to helping the counselee obtain the insight necessary to understand old identities, it is important to support them in maintaining current ones. If there are children involved, it is important to facilitate the custodial relationship and responsibility. For the custodial parent, this means walking a tightrope of being an adequate parent and still being in relationship with the non-custodial parent. At times children can be involved in the counseling. It often makes sense, from a systemic family therapy point of view, to include both the custodial and the non-custodial parent in counseling sessions dealing with the management of children. But this may not always be the case.

> Since both fathers and mothers play a vital role in the life of the children, the work must be with fathers and mothers together, having them close ranks and reach agreements without utilizing the children. The problem with this approach is that it too often misses the main consideration, which is that one adult in the family must now recover leverage where two adults had it. A more economic focus is on strengthening the custodial parent as executive, as enforcer of child care rules, while proceeding to intensify negotiations between the parents.[20]

Having both the custodial and the non-custodial parent in the session seems to encourage fantasies that all will return to "normal" for both children and parents. This may well be a mistake that the counselor will want to avoid. It also seems to halt the process of developing a new identity of caring parent, albeit a single one. The issue of blended or remarried families and the pastoral care of these families is the subject of another chapter.

Joint custody of children has been experimented with for a number of years and there are indications that such arrangements are increasing. It appears to be an ideal way for couples who have long-term commitments to live in the same area to deal at the same time with their responsibilities to care and also with their fear of loss and loneliness. Bryan E. Robinson and Robert L. Barret have surveyed the research on joint custody and noted that there is significant disagreement "over the value of joint custody in which children have not only two homes, but also two sets of clothes, toys, and even in some cases two sets of friends."[21] Although the Robinson and Barret review is generally positive about the value of joint custody, it still appears to us that it is most likely to lose its effectiveness logistically. Circumstances outside the family affect the commitment to common location; parents move, and the trauma of children leaving familiar neighborhoods and schools often seem to outweigh the benefits of alternating relationships with biological, but no longer married, parents.

Other problems in joint custody stem from the compromising of the ideal of household continuity. When so much has been made of that ideal, the trauma that occurs should it break down after one to ten years can be greater than the original compromise, which granted primary custody to one parent. Younger children need constant custodial attention, which seems to be offered most consistently in one household. From this secure base, other households, such as the father's house or the homes of grandparents, can be seen as good places to visit and the primary household the place to which to return. With two primary households, the possibility of confusion of authority and loyalty may facilitate care less than the benefits of regular involvement of the biological parents provide it. The jury, so to speak, is still out, but our concern with the denial of loss involved in joint custody still seems to be an important one.

4. Grief work. Much of the pastoral care and counseling of the separated and the divorced is grief work. The psychological theory of attachment and loss, which we presented earlier, is relevant to all that we say here. The terrific losses that one must endure in the breakup of a marriage must be worked through. There are usually significant economic and social losses that are not easy to leave behind, as well as losses of identity, for which one must grieve in order for future attachments to take place. Grief work involves the decathexing of psychic energy toward the former loved one, thereby allowing for the directing of that affiliative energy toward other potential loves. Human beings were not meant to be alone.

It seems unnecessary here to present another discussion of the grief process. This has been done quite effectively elsewhere.[22] We simply want to assert here, following a central thrust of psychoanalytic theory, that separation and loss are built into the human experience from the very beginning of life until its end. Human living may accurately be characterized as a process of making attachments, developing relationships, and then losing all or part of them. Sometimes the loss involves unrealistic hopes and images of the other. At other times, real and permanent loss must be coped with. However one understands the Christian message of resurrection and hope, it offers no escape from the realness of death and loss. It comes only after the death and loss have taken place. As Frederick Buechner puts it in the title of one of his sermons, "All's Lost—All's Found."[23]

A THEOLOGY OF SEPARATION AND DIVORCE?

We see the implications of generational care for a "theology of divorce," centered around the question of whether marriage is a structure that, like the church, is to be preserved to the end of time or a functional, committed relationship between a man and a woman of the same generation. The church's theology of marriage has traditionally focused more on preserving the structure of marriage than affirming the relationship of the persons involved in it. In contrast to this concern for preserving human structures is the attitude of Jesus as recorded in the Synoptic Gospels: "The Sabbath was made for man, not man for the Sabbath;" (Mark 2:27a RSV). We see marriage as a comparable human structure designed to facilitate human care for the earth and all that is in it, not something to be primarily a focus of care itself.

Although we believe that this point of view is not in conflict with the Christian tradition and is, in fact, expressive of it, we also believe that it is related to our experience as marriage and family therapists. When the helping person attempts to preserve an existing structure, rather than examining what that structure means in the family members' frustrated attempts to care for one another, the caring of the couple, as well as that of the pastor or therapist, tends to deteriorate.

A theology of divorce that is something other than the negation of marriage is based on the finitude of human beings and the limitedness of all human structures, even those the church has chosen to bless. Further basis for a theology of divorce may be found in the fact of separation and loss, which has been the theoretical focus of this chapter. The fact of separation and loss is built into the very fabric of human life and culture and seems to exist apart from human frailty and sin as well as being a result of it. The words of the prophet, which have been used to describe the Christ as "a man of sorrows and acquainted with grief," are in some ways normative for all human beings.

There seems to be some hesitancy of the part of many pastoral caregivers to allow the full process of grief and healing in the case of divorce. This hesitancy may stem from the conviction that since divorce is a sign of our sin, leaving it behind through successful grief work and, perhaps, remarrying, is to turn our backs on our essential recognition of our sin and finitude. We agree with the tradition that divorce inevitably involves human sin. The tradition has erred, however, in the oversimplification of its view of the sin in divorce. Although the actual fact of the termination of a marriage may indeed be a sin, the most significant sin in divorce can only be seen in the relational facts of the particular marriage relationship and the responsibilities of each party in the marriage for them. The actual sin in the breakdown of the marriage may be considerably less for all the generations involved than the ongoing destructiveness of continuing the marriage relationship.

It is central to the Christian tradition to face and acknowledge death, including the death of relationships. Life involves what Judith Viorst has called *Necessary Losses*,[24] and divorce is one of the most significant. A theology of divorce requires an interpretation of divorce as one of the losses of life, which partially involves fallible human choice, but which also involves circumstances for which human beings have no responsibility. Thus it must also involve an affirmation of the relation of God with the world and all that is within it along with humankind's relationship with that same world. A great deal more needs to be said about a theology of divorce, but our immediate concerns lie elsewhere; it must wait for another book or other authors.

If caring is constitutive of what it means to be human and caring in the marital relationship is a major part of obtaining self-identity, then separation and divorce can be catastrophic. The sense of completeness that one obtains in the hope of marriage, the completeness that Genesis speaks of in the creation of both male and female, is torn asunder in divorce. Marriages can die; yet, life goes on for whatever time the former partners in that marriage have left to live, and if God does indeed call us to have dominion over creation, caring does not end with the demise of a marriage. Caring continues, just as do the generations.

NOTES

1. James G. Emerson Jr., *Divorce, the Church, and Remarriage* (Philadelphia: Westminster Press, 1961), p. 39.
2. John Macmurray, *Persons in Relation* (New York: Harper, 1961), p. 89.
3. John Barnett, "The Natural History of a Marriage." *Pilgrimage*, vol. 9, no. 1 (Spring, 1981) 12.
4. See Ivan Boszormenyi-Nagy and Barbara R. Krasner, *Between Give and Take*, p. 26.
5. Hanna Segal, *Klein* (Brighton: The Harvester Press, 1979), pp. 82, 135.
6. John Bowlby, *Attachment* (New York: Basic Books, 1969), p. 208.
7. Ibid., pp. 27-29.
8. See Bowlby, *Separation*, 1973, p. 377.
9. Bowlby, *Loss*, 1980, pp. 172, 212.
10. Peter S. Weiss, *Marital Separation* (New York: Basic Books, 1975), p. 42.
11. For a fuller discussion of this process, see Heinz Kohut, *The Analysis of the Self* (New York: International Universities Press, 1971).
12. G. P. Murdock, "Family Stability in Non-European Cultures." *The Annals* (1950), 197-99, 272.
13. See Florence W. Kaslow, "Divorce and Divorce Therapy." *Handbook of Family Therapy*, ed. Alan S. Gurman and David P. Kniskern (New York: Bruner/Mazel, 1981), p. 677.
14. See Nathan W. Turner and Sandra Strine, "Separation and Divorce: Clinical Implications for Parents and Children," *Contemporary Marriage: Special Issues in Couples Therapy*, ed. Daniel C. Goldberg (Homewood, Ill.: Dorsey Press, 1985).
15. Kaslow, "Divorce and Divorce Therapy," p. 675.
16. Lucy Rose Fischer, *Linked Lives: Adult Daughters and Their Mothers* (San Francisco: Harper, 1986), p. 201.
17. These categories are similar to ones outlined by Rice and Rice, *Living Through Divorce: A Developmental Approach to Divorce Therapy* (New York: Guilford Press, 1986).
18. For a detailed presentation of the crisis intervention process, see David Switzer, *The Minister as Crisis Counselor* (Nashville: Abingdon Press, 1974). For a more theologically based presentation, see Charles Gerkin, *Crisis Experience in Modern Life: Theory and Theology for Pastoral Care* (Nashville: Abingdon Press, 1979).
19. See Weiss, *Marital Separation*, p. 142.
20. Braulio Montalvo, "Interpersonal Arrangements in Disrupted

Families." *Normal Family Processes*, ed. Froma Walsh (New York: Guilford Press, 1982), p. 282.

21. Bryan E. Robinson and Robert L. Barret, *The Developing Father* (New York: Guilford Press, 1986), pp. 88-92.

22. See Kenneth R. Mitchell and Herbert Anderson, *All Our Losses, All Our Griefs* (Philadelphia: Westminster Press, 1983).

23. See Frederick Buechner, "All's Lost—All's Found." In *A Room Called Remember.* (San Francisco: Harper, 1984).

24. See Judith Viorst, *Necessary Losses* (New York: Simon & Schuster, 1986).

CHAPTER SEVEN

CARE IN THE BLENDED FAMILY

Do not neglect to show hospitality to strangers, for thereby some have entertained angels unawares.
(Hebrews 13:2 RSV)

The New Testament has a fascinating way of reversing the expected norm for human values and behavior. The symbol of the "incognito angel" in Hebrews is a troubling, but lovely, example of this. It resonates with the reversals in Jesus' parables, which suggest that those who belong at the family dinner table may not be those whom we expect. Throughout this book, we have emphasized a functional view of marriage and family life. Our preference for a functional view over a structural one has been based in part on the theological anthropology of human care for the generations. Generational care is relational, and one powerful medium for the exercise of generational care is through marriage and family. We have also considered generational care from outside kinship bonds and have argued that to define generational care solely on the basis of kinship is just as much a mistake as emphasizing the structure of marriage and family life. Generational care should be considered within the tension of the private and the public, the family and the rest of humanity.

Because humans as God's creatures are called to care for creation through their relationships one with another, we have stressed the natural quality of the marital and family function. Marriage, no matter what form it may take, has been central to virtually every culture known to history. The expansion of marriage to family with the coming of children is a natural expression of this reality. Caring for the generations, therefore, is an all inclusive notion and not an exclusive one. While persons, for whatever reason, may not be married and not living in two or more generational households, they nonetheless are members of a family and are called to be in relationship with their generations. This is true whether those with whom they are in relationship are kin or not. Not being married does not exempt one from being generational.

In the previous chapter, we pointed to some of the possible themes for a theology of separation and divorce. We affirmed that marriage was made for humanity, not humanity for marriage, and that the purpose of marriage is to facilitate human caring, instead of the preservation of the structure of marriage. Because human beings are both finite and sinful, many marriage relationships are destructive ones. While we agree with our tradition that divorce inevitably involves sin, we also believe that the tradition has erred in the oversimplification of defining the divorce as the primary sin. While divorce involves sin, the most profound expression of that sin is less likely to be found in the act of divorcing than in the breakdown of relationality and the responsibilities of vocation and covenant within the marriage.

Another emphasis of the previous chapter is the understanding of divorce as a dramatic example of the ubiquity of loss in our lives—loss of relationships, loss of identity, and loss of status. Loss and grief are central features of divorce. Our pastoral concern, then, is to facilitate grief work, and the result of "good grief" is the ability to redirect one's energy toward other relationships when the previous one has died. As painful and as sinful as divorce can be, it also in some paradoxical way can underscore the value and importance of the marital relationship. As Heidegger has pointed out, brokenness can point to the functional value of wholeness rather than just to destruction. We may understand the function of relationship with more clarity when the relationship no longer works. While we do not believe this is the best or most desirable way to learn this, it does leave open the possibility for hope; what is, in all its pain and destructiveness, does not have to be.

REMARRIAGE

According to some studies, one-third of those people between the ages of twenty-nine and thirty-five who were married in 1979 will experience divorce. A total of 80 percent of these people will remarry, with 60 percent of those marriages involving one or more children from the previous marriage.[1] The whys and wherefores of these remarriages are undoubtedly various and complex. As pastoral caregivers, we are all aware of reasons for remarriage that are less than healthy and noble. Many people probably remarry solely as a hedge against loneliness. While on the one hand we have pointed out that humans were not meant to be alone, we also believe, on the other hand, that being in relationship depends greatly on a certain sense of individuation and self-identity in order for the relationship to be a healthy one. There are other reasons—some of them social, economic, and even just laziness—but the very fact of the high incidence of remarriage is indicative of the naturalness of marriage.

Samuel Johnson is reported to have said upon hearing of the remarriage of a certain man: "That is an example of hope in triumph over experience." It is not known whether this man was a widower or divorced from his wife. While there is a difference in the experience of both, one thing is constant, and that is the pain of the loss of an intense relationship. Johnson's comment points to the profound ability of humans to transcend the pain of our limits to enter into other relationships, even after the experience of loss and pain. The intensity of the marital relationship is so strong and desirable that it underscores its naturalness. People will reenter a marital relationship even in spite of the knowledge of its eventual end either through death or the potential of divorce. Human relationality is just that powerful.

Although James Emerson's book *Divorce, the Church, and Remarriage* is now somewhat dated in its psychological and sociological materials, it continues to be important for interpreting Christian remarriage. Emerson presents seven "facts" about remarriage and offers three conditions for Christian remarriage.[2] His first "fact" is one we have emphasized throughout this book, that separation and loss are significant and inevitable parts of life. Human relationships are limited by time and other circumstances of life, and thus the experience of loss is central to being human. To experience loss, including the loss of relationships, is part of being human.

Second, God's act of creation was the making of a unified whole. It was a universe that was perfectly formed. Human limitation and human limited freedom in the act of separation and divorce creates a split in God's creation. The split in the relationship between a man and a woman also effects a split in God's creation. "A split in one marriage is related, therefore, to the whole of creation's need for God's grace." Third, just as marriage is a given in life, so, too, regrettably, is the fact that marriages die. The fourth "fact" is that remarriage has been traditionally considered legitimate in the case of the death of a spouse. Even the most conservative circles of Christians allow for the remarriage of widows and widowers.

It follows, then, as a fifth "fact" that if marriages die as a result of the death of a spouse they can also die in the spirit. Remarriage after the spiritual death of a marriage should, therefore, be permissible. The sixth "fact" is that no decision to marry or to remarry is a decision based merely on historical time. It is a decision also based on the fullness of time as the time of reckoning and decision. Cause and effect alone cannot explain the decision to marry (or to divorce), but personal decision making is essential. Finally, divorce must never be approached unilaterally. It cannot occur in a vacuum, for there are many variables involved in such a painful decision. "The minister has to deal with the total picture of the man or the woman, and with personal problems, in the context of the corporate experience." This final "fact" is also a principle that most family therapists follow. No action occurs alone but influences other actions within the system even as it is influenced by them.

In the light of this argument, Emerson outlines conditions for Christian remarriage, which he understands, just as first marriage, as having the aim of a genuine "new creation." Remarriage must involve a desire for wholeness, and for this to occur the previous marriage must be totally over or dead. The total acceptance of the spiritual death of the previous marriage is essential.

The second condition for Christian remarriage is the necessity of individual decision making and an awareness of the responsibility involved in those decisions. The man and woman involved must decide that they are ready for remarriage and affirm that readiness publicly to the church and to the state (see *Divorce, the Church, and Remarriage*, pp. 164-68). The public nature of marriage is more important to recognize in remarriage than in first marriage because it affirms that in spite of previous sin and failure of committed relationship, the remarrying person believed that he or she is prepared to make a commitment again.

The third condition for Christian remarriage is that it be, as

Emerson puts it in traditional language, "in the Lord." It must be understood as a response to God's call to new creation in covenant. As we understand this call, it involves a belief that the marriage facilitates responding to God's call in both the private and the public domains of each individual's life. Marriage understood Christianly is a commitment within covenant. Christians who remarry may, because of having learned from their prior experience with marriage, have far more awareness of this responsibility than those who are marrying for the first time.

THE RIGHT NAME FOR THE NEW FAMILY

As noted earlier, some 60 percent of all remarriages involve one or more children from a previous marriage. Yet even with the existence of so many families of this type, our culture at the present time has an attitude of seeing them as somehow deprived. They are seen as results of bad marriages and destroyed homes. One term used for these kinds of families is the *stepfamily*. The term seems almost to imply a second-class status. The stepchild is a cast-off second class citizen of the family, and our culture is full of stories of the evil stepparent.[3] We do not believe that this pejorative connotation should be taken lightly in that we are not talking just about fairy tales or a conceptually limited cultural attitude. The term *stepfamily* has power; unfortunately, most of that power is negative.

Another phrase that has been used to describe this kind of family is *the reconstituted family*. We find this phrase to be as unacceptable as *stepfamily*, for it implies that a nuclear family has magically been reconstituted. Families can rarely be reconstituted. Reconstitution can only occur when divorced persons with children remarry themselves, thereby reuniting the original nuclear family in one household. A family with kin and non-kin children and parents cannot reconstitute, for new traditions and new lines of relationships are created, even while old ties are maintained with biological parents, grandparents, aunts, and so on. These ties continue to be a powerful presence in the new family even when there is no custodial relationship with the absent biological kin. The fact of the matter is that in divorce, while a family's structure is compromised, very important elements of what it is to be a family continue. Traditions continue, bloodlines remain unaltered, and generational relationships continue, though with different patterns. At the same time, other family traditions and legacies come into play. To use the term *reconstituted* implies to us a romantic and unrealistic notion that a new idealized "nuclear" family is formed. This is not the case, for the result of remarriage with children involved does not yield a nuclear family but rather a family with multiple traditions and patterns of behavior. The family in this condition is not reconstituted but is a new, and in many ways, an even more complex constellation.

Another phrase used is *the remarried family*. Although this designation avoids some of the problems inherent in the other two terms, its weakness is that it seems to emphasize the role of those who do the remarrying more than the role and place of the children who are brought into the new household.[4] Children in such families have relationships outside the newly formed family unit. These relationships were prior to the remarriage of parents and so-called step-parents and have considerable force on the family style.

Although none of the terms and phrases that have been used to describe this kind of family structure seem adequate, we have chosen to adopt another of the commonly used phrases, *the blended family*. Blending suggests the bringing together of two or more generational kinship lines with different traditions, attitudes, and family systemic rules of behavior. The phrase has a more dynamic quality, involving the needs, desires, and responsibilities of two or more generations of kin and non-kin. Much is blended—personal histories, kin and non-kin relationships, genetic attributes, and roles and rules of behavior, to name a few. It is the task of this new family to make it a palatable blend. More often than not, this is a difficult task and, though the blend may have some bitter aftertaste, it is a blend nonetheless.

One further note should be made concerning the structure of the blended family. There are a variety of possible structures.

> A stepfamily may have a structure that includes a biological mother and a stepfather who had no children from a previous marriage (or the stepfather could have been single before marrying for the first time). This same stepfamily may include no children produced by the remarried adults and it may have full or part time custody of any, all, some or none of the children from the biological mother's

first marriage. The number of variables that could be altered conveys the many types of stepfamily structures that potentially exist. To generalize about *all* stepfamilies based on the wide structural variations may leave one open to making some false conclusions.[5]

Each structural variation has its own tasks to perform, and it would be a mistake to assume that all blended families are alike. There are nevertheless some important things to be seen in the blended family that go beyond its varied forms and the difficulties in naming it.

A SYMBOL FOR THE CARE OF OUR GENERATIONS

The previous discussion of remarriage, the criteria for Christian remarriage, and the problem of finding a proper name for the blended family underscore some of the ambiguity and difficulty of family living today. It is rather easy to long for a simpler, less complex time when divorce and remarriage were less frequent and—as we remember it—people did "what they ought to do." It is not necessary here to point out the fallacies in this kind of "good old days" thinking. We mention it because it is a common characteristic of all of us to avoid the complexity of the present by idealizing the past and remembering it as far better than it really was. Actually, the blended family, far from being simply a deviation from the way things ought it be, provides a new picture of the opportunities for Christian family care in our time.

Throughout this book, we have noted the critical principle that questions easy assumptions about the importance of family relationships. The Christian tradition is certainly *for* the family, but it also reminds us repeatedly that family living is not necessarily most important. Moreover, at the beginning of this chapter, we reflected briefly on the New Testament's way of reversing the expected and underscoring the unexpected. The stranger may actually be an angel. Don't be too sure that you know who and what is most important. Our perspective on the blended family is that it may in our time be the family structure that most clearly reveals how we may care for our generations. In the blending of families, there are tasks and issues that need to be confronted, which in many ways recapitulate the issues associated with other family forms.

The Esposito family came to the pastor when Sonya's former husband, Vern, asked to have Seth, his son by his marriage to Sonya, live with him for a year "in order to see what another part of the country is like." Vern first brought up this idea with Seth on an Easter vacation visit. Seth was excited about the idea. As one can imagine, Sonya and her husband, Jorge, were far less enthusiastic. Sonya's mother was terrified at the very idea and expressed fears that Vern might "kidnap" her grandson. Sonya's own guess was that Vern had finally learned how to be a father through the children of his second marriage. He felt guilty over abandoning Seth when he was so young and was bothered by Seth's calling him Vern instead of Dad. Jorge, who had legally adopted Seth, seemed confused and somewhat angry—with Vern certainly, but with Seth too. He didn't like how excited Seth was with the idea of living with his biological father.

The decision faced by Sonya and Jorge was not just an ethical one, simply understood as doing the right thing, although it surely involved doing what was best for Seth and for both families. Neither can it be viewed in developmental terms alone—that is, whether the Esposito family and Vern's family were at the "right" stage of their individual and corporate development to be able to manage the change healthily. It certainly involved the way Sonya and Jorge use parental authority and the way they understand and value the way they use it. But there are other issues that can usefully be taken into account if one looks at this family problem in terms of the norm of caring for your generations. Some of these considerations may not be immediately useful in reaching a conclusion about Seth's living with his father for a year, but some of the basic anthropological assumptions that the pastor carries can be used to help the Esposito family in making some kind of decision.

In this book, we have presented a number of relational contexts in which persons express the care of their generations and that are also, some of the time, contexts for pastoral care and counseling. Because we grow up in families we learn generational care through our relationships to the parental generation, to peers—most notably the siblings who are close to us in age—and to those to whom we are authoritative or parental, such as younger siblings and other younger relatives. In non-familial situations, such as school and work, we also have to deal with authorities, peers, and those who see us as seniors and authorities.

The contexts in which we have examined generational care are singleness, preparation for marriage, marriage without children, the nuclear family, separation and loss, and finally in this chapter the blended family. While no person lives in isolation from the care of her or his generations, each context also has its special tasks and its own perspective. The blended family, however, with all its complexity and cultural ambiguity, must deal with most of the tasks and issues of the other contexts. In forming the blended family, the family members have confronted the pain of loss, the trials of commitment, the ambiguity and anxiety of choosing a mate, the caring for a real future generation, and the development of family styles and legacies. To some extent the issues of caring in the blended family are a summation of all the previous contexts for care. By looking at the Esposito family in the light of the issues of individuality, preparation for marriage, commitment in marriage, the nuclear family, and separation and loss, we bring the care of your generations into focus for all sorts and conditions of family living.

THE ESPOSITOS' BLENDED FAMILY

Jorge and Sonya married when Sonya's son Seth was three years old. She had been married to Vern, Seth's father, for three years before their divorce. They had been very young when they married, and Sonya says that she got married to get out of the house, where her father was an abusive alcoholic. The marriage was rocky from the very beginning, and getting pregnant seemed to be an attempt to save a rapidly failing marriage. Seth was barely a year old when his father moved out. When Vern and Sonya divorced, Sonya moved back into her mother's home. Her father had died a year prior to this.

Jorge had never married before. He met Sonya when her mother contracted with the company Jorge worked for to do some major plumbing work at her house. Jorge and Sonya dated for nearly a year and then married. Eighteen months later, Sonya became pregnant and gave birth to John, the son she and Jorge share as biological parents. Seth visits his father, who had moved several states away and who had remarried and has two children with his wife. Seth visits for two months each summer and occasional holidays during the year.

Jorge was born in Puerto Rico, and his mother and two sisters still live there. His father died when Jorge was quite young, and his mother sent him to New York to live with her sister when he was fifteen. His mother wanted him to go to America to find a better life. After high school and a term in the Navy, he became a journeyman plumber highly regarded by his boss and co-workers. Jorge was Presbyterian, as his family in Puerto Rico was for two generations before him.

Although her family had never practiced their religion, Sonya grew up culturally Jewish. When she and Jorge married, it was in the Presbyterian church, where she was later baptized. She has one married older brother with whom she is friendly but not overly close. Though he lives not far from the Espositos, they only see each other four or five times a year. He, too, escaped from their alcoholic father in his own way. Sonya's mother still lives close by and spends quite a bit of time with the family. At times she is seen by Jorge as intrusive, but in general the relationship is a sound one for all of them. Seth was legally adopted by Jorge just after John's birth. Seth calls Jorge Dad and his biological father Vern.

ISSUES OF INDIVIDUALITY AND SINGLENESS

Jorge and Sonya did not meet and decide to marry as two self-contained individuals but as persons struggling with the relational issues of singleness—individualization and participation, separation and loss, loyalty and commitment. From early in her life, Sonya was enmeshed, as are many children of alcoholic parents, with her parents. Almost every moment of every day she dreaded her father's erratic outbursts. She also found herself as her mother's little mother. She listened to her mother's worries about her father and their shaky financial future. She was caught between her loyalty to her martyred mother and her loyalty to the hope of a loving father. Her brother, as Rubin's interpretation of gender differentiation explains,[6] had an easier time of staying away from the home than did Sonya. Whereas normal development involves empathy and the sense of being continuous with another, Sonya felt trapped in her parents' marriage. Her only way out seemed to be marriage, and then her only way to hold on to the marriage seemed to be getting pregnant. Because she was not able to maintain a mature commitment in her relationship with Vern, the marriage collapsed. She found herself again in the home with her mother, but this time she brought with her an infant son.

Sonya: I used to call Mom at least five times a day. If I didn't call, she would. Vern was at work and that is all I had to do. I remember asking her what Dad did last night. Did he go to work today? Did you measure how much he drank?

Pastor: It's like you never left home.

Sonya: I felt like I couldn't. Mom would get so upset. Before Seth was born, I would go home and sit with her, waiting for Dad to come staggering in . . . lurching about and yelling. I was afraid he would hit her.

Pastor: How did Vern take all of this?

Sonya: Well, it gave him all the time he wanted to be with the boys and go bowling. We really didn't have much. After Dad died and I became pregnant things really didn't change. I had to be with mother, and Vern kept on bowling. He was drinking a lot of beer.

In Sonya's first marriage, she was involved in the conflict between her loyalty to her mother and, in some sense, her father and her ability to be committed to Vern in her marriage. In chapter 2, we contrasted commitment and loyalty, describing the former as involving conscious intention and choice and the latter as involving a relationship of kinship about which one has no choice. Although Sonya's commitment to Vern may be seen as an only partially conscious attempt to flee from her entrapment with her parents, it was also an attempt to make an adult effort at commitment and to develop more strength to deal responsibly with her life.

Jorge experienced separation and commitment in a different way. He came to the mainland of the United States years after the death of his father and at a time in his life that he could participate in the decision to "better himself." Though he moved in with his aunt, as a male, he was expected to have a sense of independence.

The expectations of him and the obvious challenge of moving to a new place made his transition easier than it might have been under other circumstances. He also had had some experience being on his own in the Navy and then living alone as he developed in his career as a plumber.

When Jorge and Sonya met and began courting, the issue of separation and commitment was again brought into sharp focus. For Sonya, the issue was to be able to make a commitment, not just escape, and to honor her mother in direct, adult ways, not just attempting to please her. For Jorge, the issue was being able to commit to an intimate relationship and to give up some of his individual freedom. In terms of Margaret Farley's work on personal commitment, they had to be able to discern what was essential to a commitment and what was accidental to it.[7] Of course, Jorge also had to deal with commitment to a child that was not his own, but that is an issue to be discussed later.

PREPARATION FOR MARRIAGE

The issues we identified in chapter 3 as most important in premarital pastoral care are: (1) the anxiety and ambiguity of making a marital choice, (2) caring for the prior generaton as it is experienced in the families of origin and in the church they have chosen for their marriage, (3) caring for their own generation through the development of a peer relationship with each other, and (4) care for the future generation in planning for the care of children. Sonya's decision to marry the first time turned out badly and Jorge's family had already cautioned him about marrying a woman who had been divorced. There were also the very real cultural and religious differences between them to be taken into account. Some of these differences and the anxiety the couple felt were evident fairly early in the premarital counseling.

Pastor: (to Jorge) Though Sonya didn't have any premarital counseling the first time, in a way she has been through this before. How is that for you?

Jorge: Uh . . . but what she went through before was different.

Pastor: Nothing at all the same.

Jorge:	No. He was not a member of the church. He was a Baptist, wasn't he, Sonya? (she nods yes) Uh . . . well . . . he was, I mean his family were from England . . . Anglo.
Pastor:	Sorta like a "Bridgette loves Bernie" but not quite.
Jorge:	Who?
Pastor:	I'm sorry. You know the story of how a Catholic girl falls in love with a Jewish boy and neither of their families think it is a good idea for them to marry.
Jorge:	Sure, this is America, but Lord knows. . . . I mean.
Pastor:	Always a little open ended.
Jorge:	Yes.
Sonya:	Hey, you're not alone, hombre! I'm a one time loser. I really don't mean that but I know there are no sure things either.
Pastor:	You want to get married. So let's talk about where you have come from.

The pastor was operating with an assumption about premarital counseling, that it inevitably involves anxiety about the marital choice and the fact that the issues affecting that choice are ambiguous. His concern, therefore, was to reduce the anxiety insofar as possible by focusing his inquiry on the respective families of origin. He discussed family relational styles, myths, and traditions in both Jorge's and Sonya's families of origin and through these discussions led the couple toward an awareness of their own marriage expectations. In the case of a blended family, the premarital counseling must also take into consideration an understanding of the relational style of the prior marriage.

As with most premarital counseling, the pastor was able to address these issues through the kind of structured interview process described in chapter 3. We have found the genogram to be of particular helpfulness in this process. In the case of a blended family, the genogram, including the relationships that are in place from the previous marriage, is most helpful in identifying issues of step-parenting as it applies to the continued, though non-custodial, parenting of the absent biological parent. The biological givenness of Seth's father and his father's own nuclear and extended family need to be taken into account. These relationships, though they may not be as active as once before, can and will affect the functioning of the new blended family. The issue of Seth's father's wanting him to spend a year with him and his new wife is an example of the kind of issue that can be discussed fairly comfortably when it emerges through the genogram.

Finally, the pastor needed to investigate Jorge's and Sonya's attitudes toward the future generation. Even though the family-to-be already included a child, the issue of further children was important whether Jorge was to adopt Seth or not. In Jorge and Sonya's case, the question was whether there was any feeling that having a child together was essential for them to feel that they were creating something together and thus were really married to each other. They both felt that this was important as a sign of their commitment to each other, but there was anxiety about it as well. The question that needed to be addressed was their motivation for having another child. Did the new marriage need the validation of having a child in common? If so, what did that say about the security of the marriage commitment? Is that a reason in and of itself to bring another child into the world? The issue ultimately is a moral and ethical one that cannot be taken lightly.

Jorge:	At first I was happy to have a ready made one. . . . I mean family.
Pastor:	At first.
Sonya:	We have talked about it. Jorge feels . . . well . . . .
Jorge:	I can say it. I don't know if I can be a real father to Seth. I am not his real father, and I want to be one. Is that wrong?
Pastor:	Maybe the real issue is: Can you and Sonya care for more than one child in the house?

The questions involved in preparing for a blended family are the same as those involved in preparing for any family, but the urgency in addressing them is greater and the answers to them seem more important to the concerned couple. Although it was not the case with Sonya and Jorge, the premarital interview for the family about to be blended may include more than the couple. Particularly if the children are school age and above, they can helpfully be included in at least one premarital interview.

MARRIAGE

Jorge and Sonya married in the church, and soon afterward Sonya was baptized. Developing and maintaining intimacy was important and difficult for Jorge and Sonya at first. The greatest problem for them both was the closeness that Sonya already had with Seth. Sonya's mother used to say that Seth's devotion to Sonya was just like Sonya's devotion to her. In reality it was a different kind. While an attachment to a mother was what both relationships had in common, one was at the expense of individuation, while the other was a relationship that preceded the process of individuation. Following Lillian Rubin's theory, we can see that Sonya and Seth's relationship was between a primary caregiver and a nearly totally dependent child. The mother is the one "with whom we make our first attachment, she with whom we form a symbiotic bond . . . it is a woman who is the object of our most profound attachment, a woman who becomes our first loved other."[8] In the Espositos' blended family, Sonya and Jorge's relationship did not have historical or emotional priority. Seth and Sonya had a relationship based on mutual identity that predated Jorge's coming on the scene. Usually in marriage the husband and wife have a time together, an exclusive time together, without the needs and demands of other primary relationships that children bring. In most blended families, one or more children get there first, and this can cause genuine turmoil.

Jorge:	The honeymoon didn't last long.
Pastor:	From Niagara Falls to "familyhood" in one week.
Sonya:	I know that it's a bad scene. I have asked Mother to take Seth so we could go out to dinner.
Jorge:	Yeah. We set aside quiet times when Seth goes to sleep, but by then we are tired. It's like we just didn't have enough time before . . . well Seth was here before I was.
Pastor:	How are you handling the other things? You know, like the checkbook, talking about another child, how Seth and Vern will be together.
Jorge:	That works well, those things. We are on the same beam on most of that stuff.

Sonya:	We are buying a camper. We've talked about some trips, and Jorge is going to customize it.
Pastor:	Sonya, how does your mother fit into all of this?
Sonya:	She's been around a lot less. We have been too busy, and I told her so.
Pastor:	Seems you are together more than you say you are.

Intimacy is more than just the intense I-thou experience described by Martin Buber. As our chapter 4 points out, it is also the mutual dealing with daily tasks, problem solving, and the development of mutuality. It is also caring for and being cared for by those dependent on us. For Jorge, his development of a close relationship with Seth gave him an arena for the testing of intimacy. They were lucky because there could have easily developed an antagonistic relationship between the two males in competition for Sonya's attention. Sonya had a great deal to do with this in her sensitivity for Jorge's needs as well as her sensitivity to her mother's doting on Seth. Her mother's encouraging an exclusive relationship between herself and Sonya was a reenacting of the relationship that she had enjoyed with her daughter when her husband was still alive. After his death, when Sonya and Seth moved in, this relationship continued and even was intensified. But the couple also needed to tend to the daily tasks that families must attend to. With the help of the pastor, both the close emotional relationships and some of the daily tasks of family living were addressed. Dealing with these issues nourished Jorge and Sonya's intimacy as they developed a mutually satisfying order for dealing with family tasks in the home. Mutuality and intimacy can be facilitated through developing an appropriate balance between the family's private and public life. This is done more often than not by a mutual plan for bringing order and intentionality into the family's life patterns.

THE NUCLEAR FAMILY

Blended or not, the Esposito family must confront all the tasks and issues that any nuclear family must face. There are issues of authority and of negotiated and renegotiated family covenant as the children grow and change. The family must also continue to work out the tension of its private life and its public vocation, the tension between family caring for its own generations and for the generations outside its kinship circle. In addition, the family finds itself challenged to develop an ideology and a sense of values that guide its life together.

While the blended family has these tasks to confront, it must confront them through renegotiation rather than negotiating them for the first time. Some of the members have dealt with these issues previously in another family, and they remember these prior agreements. On the other hand, it has been pointed out that blended families come together with few *shared* memories.[9] Jorge, Sonya, and Seth did not have any shared memories of an earlier life together. Jorge did not participate in the decision to have a first child. That decision was made before he came on the scene. He was not present at the birth nor did he participate in the first and important year of Seth's life, in which there could have been a mutual learning of each other's personalities. Jorge's authority had to be learned and earned, for it did not reside in biological necessity. For this reason various members of the blended family operate more in the realm of conscious covenant rather than in the realm of the assumed covenant of biological relationship and authority. As Robinson and Barret have pointed out, one of the greatest mistakes that members of a blended family can make is to assume that a blended family is no different from a biological one. A blended family is very different because its members are living in two previously existing primary families. Robinson and Barret use the work of John and Emily Visher in identifying what they see as the major differences. "Biological families have family trees, but stepfamilies have family forests." The blended family is not an imitation of a biological family. It is a blending of different families. Members of a blended family cannot be expected to instantly love one another and have clear-cut rules of living. This takes time. "Biological fathers have the luxury of time to negotiate each successive problem. Stepfathers, in contrast, instantly encounter all these problems at once and must face them collectively and immediately."[10]

In a very real sense time has a primary affect on the blended family because there is less time. The ability of the family to have a notion of itself, a sense of continuity, is couched in time. The nonbiological parent and the biological parent have little time to make family traditions and to create family identities. Anxiety and ambiguity about the situation are commonplace. Parental authority, while yearned for by the nonbiological parent, is not given by the act of marriage. Negotiation and renegotiation—the making of covenants—is primary, accompanied at the same time by an awareness of the varied history and understanding of those making them.

SEPARATION AND LOSS

Dealing with separation and loss is one of the most important issues to be addressed by the blended family. Remarriage can be psychologically and theologically appropriate when the divorced party is reconciled to the death of the first marriage—that is, when complete mourning has occurred. An important part of mourning the loss of a marital relationship is mourning the loss of an identity that was developed as a married person. As has been pointed out earlier, marriage is a *nomic* event. It creates for the married person a way of understanding the self and the world in terms of the marital relationship. How one deals with family and non-family is part of this understanding. In the loss of a marriage, this understanding is torn asunder.

In order for Jorge and Sonya's marriage to take place in a healthy way, Sonya's mourning of her first marriage with Vern had to take place. She had to develop, possibly for the first time, her own sense of individuality and to be able to reconcile that with taking the risk of marrying again. Marital relationality involves the risk of loss. Because of the limits of time and human fallibility, there is a risk that relationship can never fully and adequately be expressed. Those who remarry have lost their naïveté and are more clearly aware of this than they might wish.

Sonya returned home after her divorce. While it could be argued that she never left home, she nonetheless returned home after living with Vern for some years and after having a child. It was in her home that she had the task of renegotiating her relationship with her mother, developing a relationship with her infant son, and learning to mourn her marriage in order to be able to have relationships again with those outside the family. She had to discover her individuality and her boundaries with family members in order to make another commitment to someone outside the kinship circle.

Just as important as it is for Sonya to mourn successfully her ending of a marriage with Vern, it was just as important for Jorge to acknowledge and accept that end. The crisis that brought the family to the pastor in the first place only underscores this important point. Jorge needed to be secure in his peer relationship of commitment with Sonya even though he was not the biological parent of Seth. Vern had rights of kinship to know Seth and to parent him. Any dramatic insecurity in Jorge's relationship with Sonya would compromise his ability to help in deciding what was best for his adopted son.

Just as it was important for Jorge to understand the death of Sonya's first marriage, so also it was important for Sonya's mother to accept the death of that relationship. She was an important and influential member of the family system. In fact, she had expressed her fears that Vern could even possibly have designs of "kidnapping" her grandson. Not only were there issues of her ability to mourn the death of the first marriage, but also there were questions of what role she should play in the life of the family that was now blended. Sonya had begun to make some movement in restricting her mother's role in the family life. This undoubtedly would be a continuing issue.

THE PASTORAL CARE OF THE BLENDED FAMILY

Because the blended family is viewed with such ambivalence in our culture it is not surprising that there has been so little written thus far that considers the issues peculiar to the pastoral care of such families. Douglas Slaughter, a pastoral counselor, who at the time of this writing was completing a Ph.D. in pastoral theology at the University of Denver, argues that step-children have special problems in relationship with the church when they spend weekends with a non-custodial parent only to return to the custodial parent's church and find that they missed the first part of a two-part Sunday school project. This experience is symbolic of the problem, and the church has not yet found ways to deal with this new family phenomenon. "Have you ever heard," asks Slaughter, "a pastoral prayer that lifted up the concerns, joys, and hopes of the stepmother or stepfather, to say nothing of the stepchildren or stepgrandparents? On the other hand, it is not hard to find many examples of ritual and liturgy that celebrate motherhood or fatherhood."[11]

The pastor who wishes to be available to blended families needs to have certain operating principles in mind. First, as we have emphasized in this book, he or she needs to avoid certain notions of what an ideal family is like. The danger in having an idealized notion of the nuclear family is that it creates the inclination to try to mold blended families into that ideal structure. While blended families are a type of nuclear family, they are a very special type with some of the critical differences in structure we have noted above.

Visher and Visher summarize the structure of the blended family in the following way:

1) All stepfamily members have experienced important losses.
2) All members come with past family histories.
3) Parent-child bonds predate the new couple relationship.
4) There is a biological parent elsewhere, either living or deceased.
5) Children often are members of two households.
6) No legal relationship exists between stepparent and stepchild.[12]

Each of these structural characteristics requires certain tasks. The first characteristic requires that each family member be able to mourn the loss of prior relationships. In the blended family, children not only lose regular daily contact with a biological parent, but often biological grandparents also become less accessible. The custodial parent has lost his or her previous identity as someone else's spouse as well as a set of parents-in-law. Children and parents need to have the sensitivity of caring pastors in identifying these feelings of loss and anger. The new step-parent, too, needs support, for it is often the case that he or she will see this mourning as a rejection of his or her presence in the new family, when in fact successfully completed mourning is a process that will make true entry into the family possible.

The second and third characteristics can often be dealt with as one. The process of bonding in a blended family is a process of developing the tension of authority and covenant in a new way—that is, in ways different from those of the first family. As has been pointed out earlier, the blended family does not become created with family traditions *de novo;* the traditions and relationships have to be developed and negotiated. "With understanding and creativity, stepfamilies can immediately begin to join together round shared activities, special rituals developed for this particular household and arrived at by input from all members."[13]

The fourth and fifth characteristics can also be collapsed together. Children in blended families have the special task of maintaining old alliances, while at the same time developing new ones. According to Messinger, blended families must have fairly permeable boundaries, particularly if children share much time between custodial and non-custodial households. As Visher and Visher have pointed out, sharing parents and sharing children is a most difficult task, and those families that are able to adjust to this process are the ones that are best able to integrate the new blended family unit.[14]

The last characteristic is one of the most difficult to deal with, even in the case of legal adoption. In contrast to the situation of natural children, who follow a natural sequence with their parents from dependence and nurturance to limit setting and negotiation, step-parents have the difficult task of finding themselves in the role of authority without a history of primary nurturance. According to Stern, it takes from one and one-half to two years for step-fathers to have a friendly relationship with step-children and to achieve equal disciplinary status with their wives, the natural parent of the children. The primary role the pastor can play here is to allow the parents, in private, to negotiate step-parent roles before attempting to include the children. This is especially important in the early years of the marriage, when the marital relationship and style are somewhat tenuous.[15]

From our point of view, the most important role the pastor can play with the blended family is in supporting the parental couple. The unity and the commitment between the parents is by far the most effective way to sustain family integration that is healthy and lasting. A parental couple secure in their commitment to each other allow the one who is the nonbiological parent to take the risk of developing closeness with his or her nonbiological child.

The Esposito family came to the pastor, involved in the crisis of deciding whether Seth should spend a year with his biological father, Vern. The pastor decided to address the problem by seeing Jorge and Sonya alone for three sessions. The purpose of these sessions was to clarify their parental expectations and their style of parental authority. In addition, it was important to take into consideration what role Seth could play in making the decision. Seth was eight at the time, and at that age it could be expected that he should have something to say about the decision, but not be responsible for it. As important as that input was, however, it was secondary to the strength of his relationship with Jorge, for Jorge, who had legally adopted him, was his primary male caretaker. Subsequent sessions included ones with the three of them and one with just Jorge and Seth. The final decision was to wait one year and then reconsider the offer.

Finally, the pastor can use the institutional authority and power of the church to minister to blended families. As Andrew Cherlin has observed, "The difficulties of couples in remarriages after divorce stem from a lack of institutionalized guidelines for solving many common problems of their remarried life."[16] We believe that a revised norm for Christian family living, like caring for your generations, could move the church away from its grief over the idealized family that might have been toward an inclusive view of the family as many different combinations of human beings who care for those before and after them.

SUMMARY

In this chapter, we have described the nature and roles of the blended family. We have underscored the unique problems that confront that family, while at the same time, we have seen the blended family as a compelling and natural form of relatedness among human beings. We have also seen that the blended family, while being a unique context for generational caring, is also an important symbol for the relatedness that is found in other contexts for family living. Those tasks and issues that are to be found in the other contexts seem in many ways to be recapitulated in the process of constructing and integrating members into the blended family.

Although the blended family is a more and more common occurrence in our society, the church, reflecting the rest of culture, has not developed any particular means of recognizing and caring for this type of family. It is our experience that the blended family context offers an amalgam of tasks and issues that each of the other contexts holds to be unique to it. The blended family stands in many ways as a dramatic example of the triumph of hope over experience and, while it has its own special experience, it also recapitulates the experiences of other contexts. The blended family stands as an example that we cannot idealize what a marriage or a family should be. Christian family living can take many shapes and structural forms. The tasks and issues of generational care are essentially the same whatever the form of the family in which the carer lives or to which he or she ministers.

NOTES

1. O. V. Baker, J. M. Druckman, and J. E. Flagle, *Helping Youth and Families of Separation, Divorce, and Remarriage* (Palo Alto: Calif.: American Institutes for Research, 1980).
2. James G. Emerson, *Divorce, the Church, and Remarriage* (Philadelphia: Westminster, 1961), pp. 163-79.
3. See John S. Visher and Emily B. Visher, "Stepfamilies and Stepparenting," in *Normal Family Processes*, Froma Walsh, ed. (New York: Guilford, 1982), pp. 331-53.
4. See Clifford J. Sager, Hollis Steer Brown, Helen Crohn, Tamara Engel, Evelyn Rodstein, and Libby Walker, *Treating the Remarried Family* (New York: Brunner/Mazel, 1983).
5. Douglas W. Slaughter, "The Psychological and Relational Dynamics of the Stepfamily." Ph.D. dissertation in progress (Denver, Colo.: University of Denver), pp. 58-59.
6. See Lillian Rubin, *Intimate Strangers*.
7. See Margaret Farley, *Personal Commitments*, p. 90.
8. Rubin, *Intimate Strangers*, p. 49.
9. See Visher and Visher, "Stepfamilies and Stepparenting," p. 344.
10. Bryan E. Robinson and Robert L. Barret, *The Developing Father* (New York: Guilford, 1986), pp. 117-19.
11. Douglas W. Slaughter, "What Can the Church Offer the Stepfamily?" *Stepfamily Bulletin* (Summer 1984), 2-4.
12. Visher and Visher, "Stepfamilies and Stepparenting," p. 344.
13. L. Messinger, "Remarriage Between Divorced People with Children from a Previous Marriage: A Proposal for Preparation for Remarriage," *Journal of Marriage and Family Counseling* (1976) 2, 193-200.
14. See Visher and Visher, "Stepfamilies and Stepparenting," p. 345.
15. See P. N. Stern, "Stepfather Families: Integration Around Child Discipline." *Issues in Mental Health Nursing* (1978), I, 50-56.
16. Andrew J. Cherlin, "Remarriage as an Incomplete Institution," *American Journal of Sociology*, 84 (November 1978) 642.

CHAPTER EIGHT

PERSONAL AND PASTORAL CARING FOR OUR GENERATIONS

> *If a man does not know how to control his own family, how can he look after a congregation of God's people? (I Timothy 3:5 NEB)*

Whether Christian pastors are regular readers of first Timothy, the shaming words from the third chapter are probably somewhere in their awareness. And, as the number of woman pastors increases, those same words—heard as "If a woman can't *care* for her own family, how can she care for a *family* of God's people?"—may be even more painfully experienced. We are intentional in our use of the term *shame* because of its relational nature. To be shamed involves exposure and vulnerability to another; in the case of a pastor, those "others" are those to whom he or she seeks to minister.

A woman pastor, early in her ministry as an associate in a parish, shared with her counselor a dream in which she was in the chancel assisting in the celebration of the holy communion. She looked out at the congregation and saw the communicants kneeling for prayer, but instead of looking down at the prayer book or having their eyes closed, everyone had his or her eyes open, looking straight at the pastor. What she remembered most was how big those eyes seemed. Shame involves exposure to eyes like that and, whether it should be or not, the family living of the pastor is subject to the big eyes of the congregation.

THE SEARCH FOR THE IDEAL FAMILY

In many ways, this is as it should be. The minister is seen, inescapably, as *parson* or representative person, one who has heard and responded to a call to live and to serve others in the light of the Christian faith. The claim of that faith certainly includes the conviction that faith will make a difference in one's life, including one's family life. The problem has come, however, at the point of how much difference it should make and in what form that difference should be expressed. The church through the centuries has struggled with the question of how the minister's holiness should be expressed, and the "faithful" have ambivalently demanded some kind of ideal type of life and alternately raged or sighed with relief when someone discovered that the minister had failed to live up to it.

The ideal for family life has been expressed in a variety of forms, sometimes as virginity and celibacy, other times as the minister's spouse and four perfectly behaved children sitting quietly at worship in the second pew. The latter picture is in keeping with one of the Christian marriage rituals, which suggests that if you do really keep your marriage vows "your home will be a haven of blessing and a place of peace." In fact, because the pastor has been a special case of the church's expectations of all who received its blessing on their marriage, her or his home is expected to be a visible haven. However the ideal is expressed, it has been our experience in the pastoral care of pastors that the clergy seem to have special expectations for family living placed on them, most obviously in their avoidance of divorce and in their having children who do not embarrass the pastor or the congregation with their unruly behavior.

Because what was "Christian" in family living has so long been identified with form rather than function, with preserving structures rather than developing relationships, the response of clergy families to this pressure has often been an attempt to make things look good and a denial of the way their family relationships really were. The "eyes" looking at the pastor may be bigger, but there are eyes on anyone who intentionally tries to live his or her understanding of Christian faith and to express care for others in some way in accordance with that faith. There is, in fact, pressure within virtually every family to maintain its boundaries and to present an official image to those outside, whatever the relational realities within. What can be seen by those outside the family is simply who lives together in the household and the family's public behavior when they are with others. What cannot be seen by those who do not know a family quite well is the actual quality of caring that takes place in the family members' relationships with one another. This means that with significant pressure to maintain the structure of an intact family it is quite easy to exert more emotional energy in the direction of making things look good outside than in experiencing and practicing caring within.

Any counselor who has worked with clergy families or with those for whom the church's picture of the ideal family has been strongly influential is familiar with the degree of denial of anything wrong and the constant fear of embarrassment and shame that can be present. Indeed, the family member who does something illegal or antisocial in order to shame the family and, in effect, remove some of the pressure for putting up a good front, is quite common. This kind of behavior can often be understood as a move from the shame of being seen to the shamelessness of not caring at all in order to remove the pressure of making things look good. Indeed, "the eyes have it"—that is, the eyes of the congregation or some other group looking on or the imagination that they are looking on can become the major influence on family life. The therapeutic issue, then, for the whole family or the various members of it when they move out of that household is the discovery of realism in personal relationships or, sometimes, what personal relationships really are. Many persons in families, who have been in bondage to what they thought a family ought to be, have lost the ability to distinguish between a personal and a formal, or structural, relationship.

The other common result of bondage to a picture of the ideal family is a pervasive sense of failure to live up to it. "What's wrong with us or with me that we can't be like the such-and-such family? Their marriage seems perfect; their children do well in school and are popular with other children. It's not fair that we're not like that." Some of the most powerful family experiences are a parent's disappointment with a child and a child's with a parent. These are usually experiences that are denied or avoided and which, because of that, become more powerful and influential in the family's and the individual's life. Actually, getting caught in the generalization that "I have a bad child (parent)," or even "I have a good child (parent)" can insulate either the child or the parent from getting to know what the other is really like.

There are a number of ways that one might interpret these expectations of the family, theologically as well as psychologically. One that seems useful to us is understanding it as an over-identification of healing and salvation. In contrast to this, we reject any view that identifies salvation and health. Salvation is possible in spite of the fact that perfect health is impossible, or, to express this another way, the family can be cared for but cannot be cured. Many Christians, however, have expected those who were saved to be healed, and this has included an ideal family life, or at least one that looked good to the observer. One that did not look so good seemed to raise questions about the efficacy of the faith and thus was threatening to the believer. The church could separate family life from priesthood in an effort to avoid the threat, but that "solution" involved the loss of the kind of minister who struggles with the same things in life as did his or her parishioners.

Whatever interpretation one makes of why the picture of the ideal family has been so strong an influence among persons who sought to be Christian, the painful experiences of shame and denial that have come at least partially because of such a view argue strongly for a Christian norm for the family that is functional and specific, one that can be realized in particular acts of caring, whatever the structural circumstances of the family. When the norm lies in the function of care rather than the structure of the family, the blended family can be as expressive of Christian family living as the intact, nuclear family.

"CONTROLLING" THE FAMILY

Our discussion thus far suggests that what we referred to earlier as First Timothy's "shaming" comment about "controlling the family" needs not only to be reacted to but also to be examined in more detail. The word *proistami* in First Timothy, which is often translated and understood as "control," has had two meanings in both biblical and other historical documents. The first is to exert political authority or to lead; the second meaning is to assist, to help, or to care. The word occurs eight times in the New Testament. In most cases, *proistami* seems to mean "to lead," but the context shows in each case that one must also take into account the second meaning, "to care for." Caring was understood to be the obligation of leading members of the infant church. Romans 12:8, for example, describes the gifts of God as having been given for the primary task of caring for others. The emphasis is on pastoral care and not the exercise of the political power of authority.

First Timothy 3:12, for example, describes good deacons as

"those who care well for their own houses (families and servants). The author certainly has in view the authority of the head of the household but his attention is primarily directed, not to the exercise of power, but to the discretion and care to be shown therein."[1] The issue of control is not a structural one of who is in charge and how that power of authority is carried out in a political sense. It is, instead, a functional issue. *Proistami,* or "control," is *caring* for the generations, not just *ordering* them.

The way the phrase *pastoral care* has been understood by the church is consistent with this biblical interpretation. There have been two primary meanings. *Pastoral,* which is sometimes very close in meaning to *parental,* involves leadership and oversight. It consistently has an administrative dimension. The *care-full* pastor is one who exerts the authority of one's person and one's office (or role and function) on behalf of the overall unit of care over which he or she has responsibility and control. Using the biblical image of the good shepherd, one finds that pastoral care involves responsibility for all the sheep, the one and the ninety and nine. Thus it involves the tender, personal care of all members of the family or of the congregation—sometimes seeking and caring for the one at the expense of the ninety and nine.

Although they are not identical, this view of care is consistent with the two understandings of care we presented in the first chapter. Tender, personal care is essentially the same as care for the other as presented in Mayeroff and Noddings. The care of self, on the other hand, is related both to care as oversight and care as personal. The existential meanings of care suggest "worry about" and "responsibility for" oneself and for others. We have been created as relational and, therefore, have a sense of—a care of—ourselves in relation to others and care for the other to whom we are related. We have been told, paradoxically, in the Sermon on the Mount to "have no care for anything," which suggests the folly of "over-care" or an exaggerated sense of the importance of our caring. That picture of the possibilities of the kingdom, however, seems to us in the context discussed here not to negate but to underscore the importance of care and to offer a promise that some of its burdens can be relieved—to some degree in this world and, finally, in the next. Caring is essential to humanity, but it does not have to be the anxious and uncertain experience we tend to make it.

The care of self in the one caring represents two things: the limits of my caring and the necessity of offering myself in the caring process. Because of my care of self, I cannot simply give up myself for the other. In doing so, I would destroy our relationship because there would not be two selves, only one. But how is this view of care related to the central Christian conviction about the sacrifice of the Christ for us or to Jesus' teaching that one must lose one's life in order to save it? A detailed theological discussion of the implications of these theological themes for care would take us too far beyond the concerns in this chapter. Perhaps it is enough here to offer the interpretation that Jesus' caring loss of his life on the cross did not, by God's grace, involve the final loss of himself. The meaning of that act may be seen in the affirmation that in spite of the loss of his life, relationship to the Christ continues to be possible. Sacrifice in Christian caring involves loss, but it does not mean the final loss of oneself for another. This formulation expresses both the limits of the one caring because of the care of self and the possibilities of care because of the necessity of giving the self in the process of caring.

Touching on another dimension of what the "control" of one's family, suggested in First Timothy, may mean today, we suggest that it means authority of the kind discussed in chapter 5 in relation to the concept of covenant. Care involves the expression of the responsibility given to us by God in his covenant of faithfulness to his people. Care for the earth, including care for one's family, involves the taking of authority and carrying it out responsibly, much as the ordination service in a number of Christian communion uses, along with the laying on of hands, the powerful words: "Take thou authority. . . . " There is a principle of authority within the family, whatever its particular form, which, when taken and expressed in care for the family, can still order what the *Book of Common Prayer* calls our "wills and unruly affections."

Important to our thesis, however, is the understanding of authority as an expression of care for persons who themselves also have authority and freedom to respond to God's call. We do not understand *proistami* in First Timothy as a demand for conformity. Generally speaking—and we recognize that there is risk to speaking generally about the Bible and the Christian tradition—the biblical witness is considerably more realistic than it is idealistic. Thus it speaks of the redemption of what is more than it exhorts about what ought to be.

THE CRITICAL PRINCIPLE

Although we have presented the family as important and representative of a significant dimension of our care for the earth, we do not see it as ultimately important. Tillich's protestant principle reminds us to be critical of the family, along with all other human structures. The most powerful biblical symbol supporting this critique of the family is Jesus' question in Matthew 12: "Who are my mother and brothers?" Although our interpretation here is more imaginatively than exegetically based, it does not take much stretch of the imagination to see those who were skeptical of or threatened by Jesus as attempting to divert him from his calling by saying, in effect, "Hey Jesus, take care of your mother and work out your differences with your brothers!" Jesus' response is not a clear-cut choice of religious duty over family obligation. It is an expression of the tension of human living in covenant with God. One's mission in the world is conditioned by one's family responsibilities, sometimes yielding to them and sometimes neglecting them. Likewise, one's caring for the generations of the family is continually challenged by responsibilities to a larger community. Family caring alone cannot be an adequate expression of the demands of faith for any of its members.

We have addressed this conflict and these tensions in terms of the relationship of work, family, and friendship. The powerful little drama played out in Matthew 12 points to the importance of these relationships. The family is one of the areas of life and relationship in which one works out her or his destiny, using the reformed tradition's language, as a "child of the covenant." The reality with which we deal, however, is that most children and families of the covenant do not work out in the way that the prior, or even the present, generation anticipates or hopes. Carrying out the covenant is usually not done "decently and in order" or, as another marvelous prayer book phrase expresses it, "in all Godly quietness."[2] It is carried out in family living, as in all human endeavors, imperfectly, ambiguously, and, sometimes, quite disappointingly to us.

The critical principle applied to the family, which we have identified with Tillich's protestant principle, applies not only to forms of the family that tend to become idealized but to the function of care itself. We believe that this critical principle has been evident in each chapter as we have attempted to make a constructive statement about how care might be expressed in various forms of family living. With respect to our thesis about the care of your generations, for example, care is expressed constructively through relationship, but relationship is limited and, in effect, *criticized* by time, human finitude, and the fact of loss. Human caring, though normative, is also fully expressive of human limitation and sin in relationship.

Looking back at some of the specific issues in generational care we have discussed, one can see the critical principle running through all of them. Tillich's polarity of individualization and participation is one example of how the principle is expressed dialectically. Overdevelopment of individualization is criticized and corrected by participation and vice versa. Specifically, for the individual, the task of separation from one's family of origin without simply cutting oneself off from it must be accomplished successfully if one is to live as a mature human being in adult life.

The critical principle appears in the relationship between commitment and loyalty. To whom one chooses to be committed is a major determining factor of adult life. We have distinguished commitment from loyalty, the concept with which it is most often confused. Commitment in family care involves an ongoing choice to care for a peer of the same generation, most commonly seen in marriage. Spouses may become more like each other, but they do not become kin. In generational care, a commitment is not simply made; it is continually remade. It is ongoing in that the choice of the other is continually repeated over a long period of time. It is not the same thing as loyalty, which involves dependent relationships like those between members of different generations. Commitment is not more important than loyalty, but it is different. The critical principle symbolized in "Who are my mother and brothers?" insists that commitment not be maintained by turning it into loyalty, but by a decision about how best to fulfill one's vocation at the particular time.

The chapter on caring in the preparation for marriage focuses on the anxiety about marrying "the right person," and then critically questions the assumption that if one can avoid marrying Leah, everything will be all right. It also emphasizes the importance of discerning the theological assumptions that persons bring into a marriage and, using Everett's four symbols for marriage, identifies the concept of marriage as a shared vocation as the most nearly adequate symbol for the marriage commitment. This view has particular value in addressing the tension between love and work, which is so evident in modern Western marriages. It can affirm that both man and woman have a calling at home and in the public sphere of work outside the home. Although each has an individual vocation, there is also a common vocation—sharing their individual callings in a way that creates an intimacy they share on equal terms. An important part of this is the decision about how to care for the generation that comes after them, through children of their own or younger persons whom they know in the public sphere.

In the chapter on marriage, the critical principle could be seen more in practice than in theory. In the pastoral counseling of Al and Ann, their "communication problem" was dealt with not by focusing on communication *per se* but on the couple's care for the generations before and after them. The marriage relationship is important, but even for a childless couple it cannot be focused on to the exclusion of care for the other generations. The critical principle appeared in the dialectical relationship between Al and Ann's everyday struggles and the Christian anthropological view of them as persons caring for their generations.

In chapter 5, the critical principle appears in the theological and psychological dynamics, describing the energy within the family structure and its relationships. Three dynamic pairs of concepts are related primarily in terms of the family's push to maintain its center and to avoid being fragmented by the concerns of its individual members. In the move toward and away from the family center, one can see operating the principle that is critical of all family structures. Tillich's concept of the "history-bearing, centered group" expresses it well. The family has a common history and a center of loyalty, but must share itself openly with individuals and groups outside itself in order to maintain its health and strength. It must maintain this open relationship with those outside it without losing its center or identity as a particular relational structure. It does this through a covenantal authority, which claims and names it, as in the naming of the generations of Adam or Noah. This authority within the family provides an ordering of the family dynamics of outward and inward movement, but because it is an authority given by God in covenant with the human family, it is conditioned and not absolute. It is criticized or held accountable for any turning away from those outside it by the love of God for all his children.

Another point that should be reaffirmed here is our understanding of the covenant as the theological symbol most nearly adequate for describing the family and vocation as the symbol most appropriate for marriage. We understand covenant to be the larger, or more inclusive, symbol, which describes God's relationship of care for the family and the family's care for one another. It involves the family members' loyalty to God and to one another. Within that covenant, however, the marriage relationship cannot be most effectively described by the covenant symbol. Marriage is a relationship of peers who have decided to share their calling to care for the earth. To suggest they covenant with each other inevitably suggests that one is above the other. Marriage, therefore, is more appropriately understood as a vocation within covenant, rather than a covenant itself. It involves an ongoing, or repeated, commitment to share one's call with the other in order to broaden and enrich their care of the earth and of each other. The principle of authority, which grows out of covenant and is expressed through vocation, is a shared authority of peers. We touch on this point again in the final section on learning to care.

When the family is understood as having a normative form, divorce can be understood only as the breaking of that form and, therefore, in itself sin. If, however, the family is understood functionally, as taking place within many forms, not simply preserving one, divorce can be understood—as we understand it—as loss, and care in separation and divorce as a form of grief work. Divorce is a loss, incurred more by the choice of one or both of the marriage partners than by circumstance. Thus in contrast to death, which is a loss more by circumstance than by choice, it may involve more shame and guilt on the part of those divorcing. This analysis is not to minimize or to deny the sin in divorce and the kind of pain and brokenness that results from it. It does, however, view sin as less involved in the fact of the divorce than in the failures of care, which are a part of the separation and divorce process. This is the focus of the "theology of divorce," which we point to but do not develop.

We see the blended family less as an anomoly or failure than as a new norm or constructive challenge for the care of our generations. Although the phrase *blended family* is an inadequate one insofar as it suggests that the blending of family commitments and loyalties can easily take place, it seems to be better than most of the alternative terms or phrases. The blended family represents an open challenge to care. This challenge may be present in the intact nuclear family, but it is often denied by the fact that its members are kin to one another or have not made previous commitments to intimacy. The blended family has within it the "stranger" to which the New Testament refers and who may be the "angel" of which we were unaware. Thus it is both a critique of our usual expectations of the Christian family and an example of an unusual opportunity. In the light of this understanding of the care of our generations and the critical principle operative even in that care, we turn to the care of the families of others, represented by the concept of pastoral care.

CARING FOR THE FAMILIES OF OTHERS

In his address on the theology of pastoral care, given to a group of clinical pastoral educators over forty years ago, Paul Tillich emphasized some things that continue to be important to all who care. He first addressed the problem with the phrase *pastoral care*, which, he says, seems to make the one cared for into an object. No one, says Tillich, "wants to become an object and, therefore, he resists such situations like pastoral care." He then wonders if this feeling and resistance is "a necessary concomitant of pastoral care? Perhaps it cannot be removed completely, but it can be reduced to a great extent." (Noddings addressed this same problem many years later in her careful distinctions between the one-caring and the cared-for.) The problem of objectification, according to Tillich, can be reduced to a great extent, however, because

> care, including pastoral care, is something universally human. It is going on always in every moment of human existence. The second more important reason is that care is essentially mutual: he who

gives care also receives care. In most acts of taking care of someone, it is possible for the person who is the object of care also to become a subject.[3]

The mutuality of care prevents the destructive objectification of the other. We "are taken care of if we take care of others. It is one act and not two, and only because it is one act is real care possible."

Although the pastoral carer's role places some limits on the way mutuality is expressed—in care that expresses the church's reaching out, the roles of the one-caring and the cared-for are not fully mutual—caring always involves some degree of mutuality. One cannot care in a fully objective manner. Caring requires one's personal involvement and affects one subjectively. The clergy's more clearly defined role, as compared to that of the laity, structures this more formally, but the care of laity and clergy are ultimately the same in their mutuality and genuine involvement of the person.

Applied to the care of the family, one of the important implications of Tillich's view of the mutuality of care is that one cannot attempt to care for others in their family struggles without in some way involving one's own feelings and experiences as a family member. James Framo's paper, "My Families, My Family," written some years ago, remains one of the most powerful examples of this. We believe that experiences something like this are appropriate and necessary for anyone who would care for the families of others. "In the living presence of a mother, father, brother and sisters," says Framo,

> the constellation in which most of us grew, one finds oneself transported back to old thoughts, longings, disharmonies, and joys in a way which can be more moving and reintegrative than one's own personal therapy or analysis. And each family we treat contains part of our own.[4]

What happens in pastoral care and counseling is not unlike Framo's acknowledgment:

> with my surface calm, official and important, hiding behind my degrees and the trapping of my profession, evaluating the dynamics of the family before me, figuring out strategy, avoiding

the traps, I communicate to the family only a small portion of the emotional connections I make with them, the places where we touch, protecting the private part of myself which few can reach. ("My Families, My Family")

He then proceeds to share some of the things he has heard and that have been said to him in family therapy (in quotation marks) and give his own, unvoiced response to what was said (in parentheses). We quote only a few of them to illustrate how involved our own family struggles are in our efforts to respond to the families of others.

> Son to father: "How can I respect you when you let Mom walk all over you? What do you expect me to do?" (Dad to me: "What am I going to do about the way your Mother treats me?" M, verbalized: "Gee, Dad, I don't know." Me angry, unverbalized: "She's your wife, not mine."). . . .
>
> Son to father: "Dad, who were you to me? What did we mean to each other?" (A twinge of envy here. This son was accomplishing something with his Dad which I could no longer do because mine had died at just the point when it became possible. . . .)
>
> Wife responding to husband: "I don't think my husband is all that interested in sex. He'll wait until late at night to approach me and then he does it with the delicacy of a Sherman tank. Or he'll pick a fight with me during the day to make sure nothing will happen that night. . . . The sad part is that we'll lie there all night unable to sleep or touch each other and then we don't talk to each other the next day." (Mutual avoidance of intimacy, one of the basic problems in marriage. Does everybody have that problem?) . . .
>
> Parent to me: "Oh, doctor, you know so much about families. You must have a perfect family life." ("How false I feel when I do not dispute the idealization. Should I mention my own particular Furies and hang-ups?") . . .
>
> Family member to me: "What do you want from me? What is it that I'm expected to give you? (If you are not getting gratification from your own family you are likely to want more from the family you are treating, in an irrational way. You are more likely to feel helpless and useless and you feed on them.) . . .
>
> Family member to me: Sometimes I wonder how many of the things you expect of our family you've been able to accomplish yourself. (Touché. Sometimes true. Settling the old family

conflicts and improving the new family is a never ending process.) . . .

Family member to me: "There's something I resent in you, doctor. I keep getting the feeling that you have some kind of ideal family image you expect us to live up to and that somehow we should be like your family." (My God can it be true?)

Any minister or therapist who has attempted to respond to family pain has felt some of these things, and one can see clearly something of the inevitable involvement of the family of the helping person in the process of help. Usually, as Framo illustrates, this is not in words but in feelings. Nevertheless, our ability to use these feelings without imposing our problems on others strongly affects whether we can help others in the care of their generations.

CULTIVATING THE PROFESSIONAL DIMENSION OF CARE

Framo's article deals with the involvement of the personal dimension of care in the professional. Tillich does this in recognizing the universality of the caring function, but he also gives an important insight into our development of the professional dimension of care in ourselves. Because care is a universally human function, it cannot be monopolized or controlled by any profession, including the ministry. The difference between those who offer care professionally and all other human beings is not that the professionals exercise this function and others do not; the difference is that professionals consciously exercise care, reflect upon it, and learn from it, whereas others express their care "indirectly, casually, and mostly unconsciously."

To apply this distinction to the difference between clergy and laity in the church, particularly with respect to the function of care, Tillich places the difference at the point of intentionality. Clergy are called to care and intend to care. Most others are caring without conscious intention. Moreover, as professionals, the clergy have a greater responsibility to learn from their experience and to embody or integrate what they have learned. Tillich's view of care here seems consistent with the interpretation of the *have dominion* over the earth of the first chapter of

Genesis as care in the sense of mastery or disciplined knowledge—professionalism viewed as empathetic involvement rather than detachment.

We emphasize Tillich's point because it underscores our own, that with respect to care what we say about pastors has some relevance for everyone, certainly for Christians concerned with caring for their generations. At the same time, it makes an appropriate differentiation between pastors and others. We go only slightly beyond Tillich when we say that the primary difference between pastors and all others concerned with caring is that pastors have a greater accountability for their caring and a greater responsibility to deepen their ministry by reflecting upon it and learning from it.

Some of the importance of this distinction and relationship may be seen in practical theology's current retreat from the so-called "clergy paradigm,"[5]—theological education's acceptance of Schleiermacher's identification of practical theology with the education of the clergy for practice. Theologians critical of this paradigm, who have gotten interested in practice from a theoretical point of view, have been rightly concerned with the separation of practical education from theology and the separation of education for the profession of ministry from the practical expression of faith by non-clergy Christians. Although this is an admirable concern, it seems important to us not to move too quickly beyond the clergy paradigm without taking with us some of its more important contributions.

In considering the care of their generations by both clergy and laity, what has been learned from within the clergy paradigm, or professional education from ministry, seems particularly important to us. Although the relation between the dethronement of theology as the queen of the sciences and the professionalization of ministry does not need to be discussed here, the continuing importance of the professionalization of ministry rests in the notion of accountability for one's actions and the development of professional standards for the nature of those actions. The minister is understood as accountable to ecclesiastical authority not primarily as a conduit for the church's pronouncements, but as one who interprets how her or his ministry is an appropriate expression of God's calling to ministry. The minister is also accountable to his or her peers in ministry, and sometimes to those specializing in a particular type of ministry, for maintaining standards of good practice in the same way that other professionals are accountable to their peers. A third accountability of professionalism, understood in its most positive sense, is the accountability of the minister to himself or herself to advance in the profession, to become more competent and a better representation of what the profession and/or the specialization within the profession stand for.

In our judgment, this digression on ministerial accountability does not take us far afield from this book's central concern for family caring. The pastoral care field has developed standards of practice that need to be attended to by those who would go beyond the clergy paradigm because these standards are informative and facilitative for both clergy and laity. How do we learn to care for our generations? Although, as Tillich points out, care is a universally human function, if one accepts that some are more effective in their caring than are others, it is reasonable to assume that some dimensions of caring can be learned or improved upon. What we present here are some of the things that have been learned in the pastoral education for caring that are relevant for both clergy and laity. We assume that the primary difference between committed laity and clergy rests primarily in the greater degree of accountability that the clergy have for their caring—to the church, to their peers, and to themselves.

One learns to care by being cared for in a family structure by a mothering person. The mother-child relationship is the paradigm for what Noddings calls "natural care." One learns to develop that caring beyond what is "natural" by personally experiencing the three relationships to which we have referred before and which replicate normative family experiencing. They are relationships: (1) with those who have authority over, but who also provide care; (2) with those who are our peers in caring and with whom care is reciprocal; and (3) with those for whom we have been given the responsibility to care and who look to us or the role we fill for care.

Because care is personal—that is, of the person—it is never simply doing something for another. It always involves some giving or sharing of oneself in the act of caring. Not only what I do, but also what I am—my person—is involved in caring. Those to whom I am accountable for my care are responsible for asking how both what I am and what I do are involved in the care I give.

And I am responsible to myself to ask how I am becoming a better carer in the process of care. Because one cannot care without also receiving care, my ability to care is best developed when all three basic relationships are a part of my experience—that is, when I am cared for by one who does not need much of my care in return, when I care reciprocally with a peer, and when I have an opportunity to give care without much attention to my own needs. These are some of the things that have been learned in the pastoral education of clergy and which have direct relevance for the practice of a caring ministry by laity. It seems important to us for the education of all who are concerned about their caring.

AWARENESS OF OURSELVES AND OF OUR GENERATIONS THROUGH THE CARE OF THE ELDERLY

We come to the end of this book, aware of the many issues in family caring left untouched. One of the most important of these is the care of their generations by elderly persons and our care of them. We have dealt with the care of the previous generation in several sections of the book, but we are still left without having addressed the problem and contribution to the caring for our generations offered by aging family members.

Because we have avoided a stage theory of family caring, approaching issues in the care and caring of the elderly as a stage in life has not been possible. The problem we face now may be due to the limits of the organizing principle of this book or of our failure to use it adequately. Our original thought had been to consider some of the concerns of persons who are elderly and alone in the chapter on individuality, pointing out the common issues of being a single person whatever age and family circumstance he or she may be living with. Although this seemed to be a logical approach, in the writing it did not work out because of our need to deal extensively with the processes of separation, commitment, and loyalty. We also considered addressing the topic in the chapter on separation and loss, for certainly one of the major tasks an elderly person faces is the repeated loss of persons and things that have had the most meaning in her or his life. This, too, would have been a logical placement, but again, we found ourselves saying so much about divorce that no room seemed to be left for dealing with separation and loss that was more by circumstance than by choice. We considered going back and adding to those chapters, but that did not work out very well. We decided, therefore, simply to acknowledge our problem to the reader, touch on it here, and hope that it can be dealt with by us or by someone else in another book.

Too often, persons think of aging parents or others of the parental generation primarily in terms of their limitations, ignoring the story they have to tell in spite of those limitations. Those who wish to develop the quality of their care would do well to seek and to reflect upon their times of being with the older members of the previous generations. In the simple pastoral event that follows, a young theological student—who could have been any caring person—follows his awareness of an elderly woman's aloneness to stumble into awkward questions about her family and her caring for them. That, fortunately, was enough.

Hope was a woman in her eighties whom the student chaplain had avoided because, as he put it, "She appeared to be in a semi-comatose condition and never seemed to notice my presence," and perhaps also because he had noted that her religious affiliation was Jewish, and he was not sure what to do with that. This is anxiety and care of oneself getting in the way of care for the other. As he entered the room and greeted the patient, he was further surprised that she greeted him in return. As he puts it in his notes, "I am amazed that she can talk. She is practically wasted away, curled up, looking out the window."

Chaplain:	(awkwardly, perhaps hoping that she will say no) Would you like to talk?
Patient:	Yes. . . . I can talk about anything.
Chaplain:	Did you have a family?
Patient:	Yes.
Chaplain:	Did you take care of them?
Patient:	Yes. . . . I did.
Chaplain:	(I follow her gaze out to the hillside facing us and see the fall colors on the leaves and the green of the pine trees, which break up the sunlight streaming into the room. I realize that this view is the only contact she has left with the outside world. No wonder she is always facing the window! I turn back to her, and as if in answer to my silent wonder, she continues:)

Patient:	My husband is out on a boat. I packed lunch for him in the morning. My son is twelve or thirteen. He's with him in the boat.
Chaplain:	Are they out fishing, or are they on the boat just for the fun of it?
Patient:	For the fun of it . . . But they came back with a mess of fish.
Chaplain:	Did you have to clean the fish?
Patient:	(scowling) Oh, no! I made *them* clean the fish.
Chaplain:	(laughing) You made them clean their own fish, huh?
Patient:	Yes. . . . Those were happy days. . . . And they're not over yet.
Chaplain:	(I am amazed that she has such a positive attitude and that she is actually able to enjoy herself and look forward to her future, trapped on this bed with only the view from her window. I am moved.)
Chaplain:	(Not quite knowing what to do with his amazement, the student chaplain asks:) Would you like to pray?
Patient:	Yes.
Chaplain:	What would you like to pray about?
Patient:	About a God . . . who is nearby. My God is not the real God.
Chaplain:	He's not the *real* God?
Patient:	No. He's very close. He's there when you need him.
Chaplain:	It's great to have a God who's always close to you, isn't it? (I muse from my own longing as much as from my experience.)
Patient:	Yes. You don't have to go off looking for him to find him; he's always *right there.*
Chaplain:	(I am smitten with guilt that I have not come to visit her until now. She has a sense of God's presence in spite of the chaplain's absence. I pray and express thanks for past blessings, happy memories and a sense of God's presence. I ask for a continued

	sense of his presence and for the ability to continue to enjoy the good experiences we have had.)
Patient:	(interrupts) That's enough. . . . That's good. . .
Chaplain:	Would you like to say the Lord's Prayer?
Patient:	Yes.

The visit concludes as they pray together.

This is the kind of pastoral event that raises theological questions about the nature of ministry, the nature of God, the meaning of human and divine care, and, practically, about the appropriateness of praying the Lord's Prayer with non-Christians. We can only touch on its meaning here. Although we can only speculate what Hope means by "the real God" in contrast to "the God who is near," the human yearning for a real God who is near seems clearly evident. Perhaps most important for our concerns is that the woman becomes aware of the God who is near as she remembers her own love and caring for her family, caring that is sometimes expressed in "I made *them* clean the fish." Perhaps it is not reaching too far to suggest that persons become aware of God's nearness and care for them as they become aware of their caring for their generations. Although we cannot know what was in the patient's mind, for us the images of Genesis are not far away—the God who walks in the garden and who blesses us as he gives us something to do, a task which through the sharing of memories may last until the end of life.

NOTES

1. Bo Reicke, "Proistami." *Theological Dictionary of the New Testament.* Gerhard Kittel, ed. Geoffrey W. Bromiley, trans. (Grand Rapids, Mich.: William B. Eerdmans, 1965), V, pp. 700-703.

2. *The Book of Common Prayer,* according to the use of the Protestant Episcopal Church in the United States of America (New York: The Church Pension Fund, 1928), p. 195.

3. Paul Tillich, "The Theology of Pastoral Care." *Pastoral Psychology,* vol. 10, no. 97 (October, 1959) 21-26.

4. James L. Framo, "My Families, My Family." *Voices,* vol. 4, no. 3 (Fall, 1968) 18-27.

5. See Edward Farley, "Theology and Practice Outside the Clerical Paradigm," in *Practical Theology,* Don S. Browning, ed. (San Francisco: Harper, 1983), pp. 21-41; and Dennis P. McCann and Charles R. Strain, *Polity and Praxis* (Minneapolis: Winston, 1985).

INDEX

Accountability, ministerial, 42, 96, 213, 217, 227-28
Ackerman, Nathan, 143
Affair, in room, 119-20
Anderson, Herbert, 80, 138, 187n.
Anthropology, Christian, 14, 104-5
Anxiety, 28, 29, 36, 230
　church's over marriage, 73
　Freud, 165
　over marital choice, 77
　separation, 165
Aponte, Harry J., 158n.
Authority, 42, 205, 131, 218
　of the family, 132

Baker, O. V., 211n.
Barnett, John, 102, 162
Barret, Robert L., 182, 205
Barth, Karl, 33, 35
Bateson, Gregory, 157n.
Bateson, Mary Catherine, 91
Beavers, Robert, 29, 116
Berger, Peter, 85, 120, 167
Blended family, 194-211
　as model for care, 197, 223
　structure of, 208
　See also Family
Boszormenyi-Nagy, Ivan, 62, 64, 66-70, 107, 142, 163
Bowlby, John, 165-66
Brueggemann, Walter, 90

Bowen, Murray, 50, 80, 140, 148
Browning, Don, 32, 232n.
Buber, Martin, 31, 107, 204
Buechner, Frederick, 184
Bultmann, Rudolph, 27

Care
　and the future, 89
　biblical views, 24, 27, 39
　contemporary views, 28-32
　definition of, 19
　of self, 218
　See also Blended family
Calvin, John, 131
Centered group, 132
Centripetal/centrifugal tension, 130-31
Cherlin, Andrew, 210
Childs, Brian H., 137
Church,
　and divorce, 184-86
　and ideal family, 214
　and marriage, 81-84, 100
　and premarital care, 73-76
　and professional care, 226-29
Chodorow, Nancy, 59, 110
Cicirelli, Victor G., 157n.
Clergy paradigm, 41, 227-28
Clinical method, 16
Cloyes, Shirley A., 39, 86, 136
Commitment, 56-66, 220, 229
Communion, 83-84, 100, 101, 134-37

233

Covenant, 82-83, 100, 101, 133-34, 193, 204, 205, 208, 218, 219, 222
Creativity, 137-39
Crisis intervention, 178-79

Davies, P. E., 43n.
Delegation, 142-45
Dependence, 139-42
Differentiation of self, 49-56
Dinnerstein, Dorothy, 59
Divorce
  as failure, 161-64
  as loss of relationship, 164-68
  experience of, 169-72
  process of, 172-77
Dominion, 25, 226
Double bind, 120
Druckman, J. M., 211n.
Dunne, Harry, 87
Dynamics, family, 130-31

Elderly, 229-32
Elliot, John H., 39, 137
Emerson, James, 191-93
Enmeshment, 135
Everett, William Johnson, 44n., 82-84, 133, 135

Family
  authority, 132
  reconstituted, 193
  remarried, 194
  step family, 193
  See also Blended family; Nuclear family
Farley, Edward, 232n.
Farley, Margaret, 56-57, 64-66, 200
Feminism, 30, 154
Fischer, Lucy Rose, 176
Flagle, J. E., 211n.
Flexibility, 38, 66, 68, 134

Fowler, James, 137
Framo, James, 80, 224-26
Framework. *See* Farley, Margaret
Function versus form, 14, 100, 189

Genogram, 81, 148-49, 201
Genealogy, 27
Gerkin, Charles, 109, 186n.
Gerson, Randy, 157n.
Goldner, Virginia, 154
Grandparenting, 32
Guilt, 31-32, 36, 40, 222

Hahn, Celia Allison, 24, 39
Hall, C. Margaret, 80
Haring, Berhnard, 135
Haughton, Rosemary, 101
Heidegger, Martin, 29, 189
Heterostasis, 145-47
Hiltner, Seward, 17, 156n.
Hoffman, Lynn, 146
Homeostasis, 145-47
Humanity
  as relational, 33-34
  as temporal, 35-38

Idealization, of marriage and family, 38, 153, 198, 214, 216
Individual, 48
  in family work, 51
  See also Differentiation
Individualization, 49
Individuation, 139-42
Intimacy, 106, 110, 119, 202, 204

Joint custody, 182-83
Johnson, Samuel, 191

Kaslow, Florence, 170, 172, 174
Kaye, Kenneth, 156n.

Kinship and non-kinship, 39, 88
Klein, Melanie, 164
Kohlberg, Lawrence, 30
Kohut, Heinz, 26, 186n.
Kornhaber, Arthur, 32
Kramer, Jeannette R. 52-54, 81
   checklist, 53-54
Kübler-Ross, Elisabeth, 172

L'Bate, Luciano, 157n.
Lasch, Christopher, 158n.
Ledger, family, 68
Legal counsel, importance of, 179
Loss, chapter 6, 190, 206-7
Love and work, 39, 87, 124, 153-54, 221
Loyalty, 56, 66-71, 142-45, 220, 229
   conflict of (split loyalty), 220
Luther, Martin, 136

McCann, Dennis P., 232n.
McGoldrick, Monica, 157n.
Macmurray, John, 161
Marriage
   as communion, 83-84
   as covenant, 82-83
   as sacrament, 82
   as vocation, 83
   church blessing, 81-84, 100
   previous, 91, 99
   structure of counseling, 114-15
   views of, 100-102
Mayeroff, Milton, 30, 217
Menninger, Karl, 109
Messinger, L., 209
Mitchell, Kenneth, 80, 138, 187n.
Moltmann, Jurgen, 25
Mother-child relationship, 31-32

Montalvo, Braulio, 196n.
Murdock, G. P., 169

Napier, Augustus, 106
Nease, Theron S., 96n.
Nichols, Michael, 157n.
Niebuhr, H. Richard, 36, 137
Noddings, Nel, 30-32, 217, 228
Nuclear family, 127-56
   definition of, 127-28, 156

Osherson, Samuel, 51, 63

Pastoral theology, 14
   of divorce, 184-86
Pastoral theological method, 23-24
Patton, John, 67, 100, 114, 119, 157n.
Paul, Normon and Betty, 158n.
Peer (peership), 16, 42, 56, 76, 84-86, 120, 142, 163, 166, 200, 206, 220, 222, 227-28
Premarital (prenuptial) agreement, 91-93
Premarital care
   function, 73
   structure of, 76, 93-97
Protestant principle, 219

Reconstituted family. *See* Family
Remarriage, 122, 190-95
Remarried family. *See* Family
Rice and Rice, 186n.
Riecke, Bo., 232n.
Robinson, Bryan E., 182, 205
Rubin, Lillian, 59, 85, 108, 119, 198, 203

Sacrament (sacramental), 82, 133. *See also* Marriage
Sager, Clifford, 211n.
Schleiermacher, Frederick, 227
Schumacher, E. F., 86

Segal, Hanna, 186n.
Separation
　care of, 177-84
　process, 172-77
　theology of, 184-86
　See also Divorce
Sexuality, 21, 26, 37, 45, 61, 78, 100-101, 112, 160, 162, 166
Shame, 34, 215, 222
Singleness, 47, 198-200
Sittler, Joseph, 25
Slaughter, Douglas, 207
Slipp, Samuel, 157n.
Soelle, Dorothee, 39, 86, 136
Solicitude. *See* Anxiety
solidarity, 137-39
Stepfamily. *See* Family
Stern, P. N., 209
Stierlin, Helm, 141
Strain, Charles R., 232n.
Strine, Sandra, 172, 180
Sullivan, Harry Stack, 69
Switzer, David, 186n.
Tillich, Paul, 34, 49, 50, 131-33, 140, 162, 220, 223-24, 226-27

Temporality, 35-38, 57, 66
Tracking, 148-53
Trinity, 135
Turner, Nathan W., 172, 180
Ulrich, David, 87
Van Deusen, John M., 158n.
Visher, John and Emily, 205, 208
Viorst, Judith, 185
Vocation, 83, 101, 126, 133, 134-37, 164, 204

Washington, Booker T., 147
Weiss, Peter S., 166
Westermann, Claus, 25, 26, 33-34, 35
Whitaker, Carl, 106
Wingren, Gustaf, 156n.
Winnicott, D. W., 29, 88
Work, 86-88, 131
　See also Love and work
Wynne, Lyman and Adele, 106-8, 119, 140, 153

www.ingramcontent.com/pod-product-compliance
Lightning Source LLC
Chambersburg PA
CBHW070249230426
43664CB00014B/2463